T0357239

Sorrowful Mysteries

SORROWFUL MYSTERIES

*The Shepherd Children of Fatima
and the Fate of the Twentieth Century*

Stephen Harrigan

Alfred A. Knopf
New York
2025

THIS IS A BORZOI BOOK
PUBLISHED BY ALFRED A. KNOPF

Published in the United States by Alfred A. Knopf,
a division of Penguin Random House LLC, New York,
and distributed in Canada by Penguin Random House
Canada Limited, Toronto.

www.aaknopf.com

Knopf, Borzoi Books, and the colophon are
registered trademarks of Penguin Random House LLC.

Library of Congress Cataloging-in-Publication Data
Names: Harrigan, Stephen, [date] author.
Title: Sorrowful mysteries : the shepherd children of Fatima
and the fate of the twentieth century / Stephen Harrigan.
Description: New York : Alfred A. Knopf, 2025. |
Includes bibliographical references and index. |
Identifiers: LCCN 2024002657 | ISBN 9780593534281 (hardcover) |
ISBN 9780593467404 (trade paperback) | ISBN 9780593534298 (ebook)
Subjects: LCSH: Fatima, Our Lady of. | Mary, Blessed Virgin, Saint—
Apparitions and miracles. | Catholic Church.
Classification: LCC BT660.F3 H37 2025 |
DDC 232.91/7092530946945—dc23/eng/20241025
LC record available at https://lccn.loc.gov/2024002657

Jacket images: (center) Three shepherd children: Lúcia Dos Santos (left) with her
cousins, Francisco and Jacinta Marto, who witnessed the apparitions of the Virgin
Mary in Fatima, Portugal, 1917. Gamma-Keystone/Getty Images; (background)
Fatima, Portugal. Bettmann/Getty Images; (torn paper) fotograzia/Getty Images
Jacket design by Janet Hansen

Manufactured in the United States of America
First Edition

Once more,
after almost fifty years of marriage,
for Sue Ellen

Contents

PART THREE

Pilgrimage

Pastorinhos

The Specter of 1960

"Do not be afraid."

Those were the words that the Virgin Mary spoke to three shepherd children when, they claimed, she appeared to them near Fatima, Portugal, in 1917. I must have been in the second or third grade when I learned about Fatima, around the time of my first confession and first communion, but before Catholicism commandeered my imagination with its full splendor and terrorizing power.

As a young child, I was still innocently baffled by the notion of sin and the punishments of purgatory and hell. Even so, those words—"Do not be afraid"—had a palliative effect on me, as did the fact that they had been spoken by the most benign entity in the church's spiritual hierarchy.

We knew her by various names: the Virgin Mary, the Blessed Virgin Mary, the Blessed Mother, the Madonna, Queen of Heaven, Immaculate Mary. Sometimes just by Mary or Our Mother. Or by Our Lady, with all its subcategories: Our Lady of Perpetual Help, Our Lady of Sorrows, Our Lady of Victory, Our Lady Star of the Sea. And then there were the names given to her by the places where she had revealed herself. There was Our Lady of Fatima, the apparition that would mean the most to me, but also Our Lady of Guadalupe, Our Lady of Lourdes, Our Lady of the Snows.

It wasn't as confusing as it might seem. I understood that despite all the different names, she was the same being. She was Our Lady. She was the "intercessor" who was human enough, compassionate enough, to plead our case before the awesome and unforgiving God who was, through some impossibly complicated historical and spiritual alchemy, her own son.

She wasn't the boss of heaven, but she was its human face. I remember an illustration at the beginning of a Catholic grade-school civics book, a pyramidal schematic that represented the flow of American political power. At the bottom were the voters. Above them were the House of Representatives, the Senate, and the Supreme Court. One level higher, all by himself, was the President. But then, hovering above Dwight Eisenhower with unspecified celestial authority, was the Virgin Mary.

She was usually depicted wearing a blue cloak, her arms spread at her sides with her hands open, palms up, her feet crushing the head of a snake that represented the devil. She gazed downward with a look of serenity that was shot through with a profound sadness. "Is there one who would not weep," went the words of the Stabat Mater, a droning hymn we sang in school about Mary, "whelm'd in miseries so deep?"

Miseries aside, her expression and body language communicated a mother's protective calmness. Throughout the magical and fearful years of my childhood I thought that she might appear to me. I went to sleep at night half expecting that I would be awakened by her radiant presence in the corner of the bedroom I shared with my brother. She would instruct me, as she had instructed the children at Fatima, to pray for "the conversion of Russia." I didn't know what the conversion of Russia meant. I wouldn't know what communism—godless communism—was until I was older. But the message didn't matter. What mattered was that she might choose me, out of all the children in the world, to reveal herself to. For Catholic children in those days, being visited by the Virgin Mary was the closest thing to discovering you had a superpower.

Catholicism was a feverish religion that helped to inflame a child's already wild imaginings. Once, during recess in third grade,

I found a rusty railroad spike at the edge of the playground. I can still recall the intense certainty with which I concluded that it was one of the huge nails that had been driven through Christ's hands and feet on the cross, and that had now fallen from heaven as a miraculous sign to be delivered specifically to me in Abilene, Texas.

Not all the signs were so welcome. Before I was discovered to be nearsighted, I would sit in a pew at Mass and stare at a small tapestry to one side of the altar. I couldn't make out any of the details of the tapestry. I had no idea what it was supposed to be a picture of. It was just a blur. But Sunday after Sunday the blur steadily cohered into a menacing shape that I finally realized with horror must be the face of Satan. It was not just a depiction of Satan, but an apparition, because the eyes in the undefined face were always staring directly and accusingly at me.

I was too private a kid to reveal such incidents of shivering dread to my own mother. Even if that hadn't been the case, I wouldn't have had the language to explain a fear that was so inchoate and primordial. A supernatural terror could only be neutralized by a supernatural antidote. Whenever that sneering image of the devil appeared in my mind, I did my best to banish it by thinking hard about Our Lady, the woman in the blue cloak who appeared to her children on earth in a nimbus of cleansing light, speaking to them in a soothing voice, telling them not to be afraid.

She was the uncomplicated, motherly presence that I imaginatively clung to throughout so much of my childhood, someone who existed only to console, to reassure—never, ever to frighten.

That was what I understood, that was what I desperately believed.

But that was before the nuns told us about the Fatima Letter.

———

In Abilene, the nuns were the Sisters of Divine Providence. In Corpus Christi, where we moved when I was in the middle of fifth grade, in 1959, they were the Sisters of the Incarnate Word. Both orders wore old-world religious garb that allowed only an oval glimpse of the nuns' faces. Their hair and ears were not visible, and the shape of their heads was something you could only guess at. There was just that mild, pale, peering face, framed by a white coif and stiff white wimple that extended past the chin down to the breastbone. When they turned their heads, they reminded me of the swiveling faces of owls.

Except for that white border around the face, the Sisters of Divine Providence dressed entirely in black: a black tunic covered by a black, nearly floor-length apron; an oversized rosary that hung from their belts and whose thick black beads clacked together as the nuns paced back and forth in the classroom. The Incarnate Word Sisters had a more colorful wardrobe, with a white tunic and a bright maroon apron whose front displayed a sort of coat of arms, with the Latin words "Amor Meus" (My Love, meaning Jesus) and the image of Jesus's Sacred Heart, encircled by a crown of thorns.

Though I have no clear recollection of when I first learned about Fatima and the Fatima Letter, I'm pretty sure it must have been by way of the Sisters of Divine Providence in Abilene. Occasionally at lunchtime, they would show us old movies like *Black Beauty* or *Captains Courageous*. One of the movies they screened was an unblushingly reverent Hollywood production, a newer release from 1952 called *The Miracle of Our Lady of Fatima*. My memories of the movie are faint, but when I watched it recently online and saw the scene where the Virgin Mary appears to the three Portuguese children, I had a head-snapping flashback, so vivid that I could recall the big Texas map hanging on a paneled wall to the left of my cafeteria table and smell the corn dogs the sisters were serving for lunch.

It may have been this movie that helped set my mental template for what an appearance by the Virgin should look like. The three children—ten-year-old Lucia and her cousins Francisco (eight) and Jacinta (seven)—are tending sheep in a meadow when lightning begins to strike out of a clear sky. Then a fog descends and slowly swirls into the gauzy shape of a human figure on top of a stunted tree. The children run in fear but a voice calls them back. "Don't be afraid. I won't hurt you. Come here to me, won't you?"

They turn around and approach the still-hazy outline of Our

Lady, floating there above the tree. "You're not frightened now, are you?" she asks.

If it hadn't been for that voice—so soothing and welcoming—I might have reacted as I had when I saw another visitation movie, *The War of the Worlds*, in which three men who stepped forward to welcome the occupants of an alien vehicle were blasted into nothingness by a death ray. But this was no horror movie. The gauzily seen Virgin Mary was voiced by an actress named Virginia Gibson, who later would appear in productions like *Seven Brides for Seven Brothers* and *I Killed Wild Bill Hickok*, and who spoke in the same calming tones as Glinda the Good Witch from *The Wizard of Oz*.

"I am from heaven," the vision says when Lucia asks who she is. She then explains that she wants the children to come to this same spot a total of six times, from May to October on the thirteenth day of the month, and at the same hour. "Then I will tell you who I am and what I want."

Lucia then asks her if she and Jacinta and Francisco will go to heaven. The Lady answers that they will, although eight-year-old Francisco—who until now has not been able to see the apparition—will for some unexplained reason have to say a lot of Rosaries before he will be allowed into the kingdom of God.

Then the Virgin Mary says this:

"Do you wish to offer yourself to God? To endure all the suffering he may please to send you? To help atone for the sins by which he is offended? And to ask for the conversion of sinners?"

Without hesitation the children say they do. And in response they are told, "Then you will have much to suffer. But the grace of God will be your comfort. . . . Say the Rosary every day to obtain peace for the world. And to end the war."

I was probably the age of Francisco or Jacinta when I saw the movie. I don't remember if I had a reaction to the news that these three young believers would have to suffer a great deal in order for God not to have to suffer himself; that it was up to innocent children to relieve an otherwise all-powerful being of the burden of being offended—not by them, but by unnamed others.

But I was a long way from a time when I could even begin to ask questions like that—questions that would instigate a chain reaction of collapsing logic. And anyway, suffering was something that I already understood as not just a trial to be endured but a gift to be craved. All of us children had been encouraged to believe that martyrdom was a pinnacle of human achievement. I was so inured from such an early age to ghastly images of Jesus in agony upon the cross, of his followers being stoned or flayed alive, that they were no more troubling than Saturday-morning cartoons or the illustrations in a Little Golden Book. I'll never forget the gleeful tone of approval in the voice of one of the sisters as she told us fourth graders about the exemplary martyrdom of Saint Lawrence, who held on to his sense of humor even as he was being roasted over hot coals. "Turn me over," he wisecracked to his tormentors, "I'm done on this side."

The movie tracked the various apparitions of Mary in Fatima, the initial skepticism of priests and villagers, and the arrest of the three children by the anticlerical republican authorities. It concluded with the "Miracle of the Sun," in which the Virgin creates a spectacle for a crowd of tens of thousands of pilgrims by making the sun "dance" and appear to fall from the sky. A blind woman among the onlookers discovers she can see. A boy throws down his crutches and begins to walk unaided. An agnostic villager played by Gilbert Roland takes off his hat and says, "Only the fools say there is no God."

It was an inspirational movie that ended on a triumphant, if murky, note. Before the magic trick she performs in the sky, the apparition finally answers Lucia's initial question of who she is by saying she is the Lady of the Rosary. She says that World War I will end and that God will triumph, and that's about it. I was too young to question why she had spent the whole movie being so evasive and cryptic, only to finally reveal herself as who she obviously was from the beginning, and to make bland pronouncements that were no more specific than the prophecies from a Magic 8 Ball. But even now when I watch this creaky old movie I have a hard time placing common sense above the reflexive credulity implanted in me by a long childhood of Catholic indoctrination.

But the Lady of the Rosary did predict suffering, and in that she was starkly accurate. The movie didn't dramatize what happened to the two younger children after the Virgin withdrew from their earthly sight. There was no incentive for Hollywood to mention that they both perished in the influenza epidemic, Francisco in 1919, his sister Jacinta a year later, in 1920.

And the movie didn't mention anything about the Virgin's horror of communism or her pleas for the conversion of Russia. Those concerns were only voiced years later in a series of memoirs by Lucia, the surviving member of the trio, who lived into old age as a mystic nun.

Neither did *The Miracle of Our Lady of Fatima* reference what was for me the scariest element of the whole story, something that would plague me throughout childhood and perplex me well into my adult life. This was what the nuns in my school referred to as the Fatima Letter, though it is better known these days among believers as the Third Part of the Secret of Fatima.

The Fatima Letter, we were told, was a prophecy. As I dimly understood it, it had been written down by Lucia many years after the events of 1917 and was her faithful recollection of what the Virgin Mary had told her during the Fatima apparitions about the future fate of the world. Lucia—by then a Dorothean nun—had given the letter to her local bishop, who then gave it to Pope Pius XII, with instructions from its author that it not be opened until 1960.

Nineteen sixty! To a young boy in the mid-1950s, the end of the decade might as well have been as remote in time as the end of the millennium. But as the days and months and finally years crawled by, I began to understand that, yes, I would be alive on the day that the pope opened the letter and revealed what was to become of the world and, by crucial association, what was to become of me.

There was much to ponder, and much to dread, during some of the most intense years of the Cold War, when "duck and cover" drills were routine parts of classroom learning and when people were beginning to build fallout shelters in their backyards; and when among Catholics there were robust ethical questions about the application of the "double-effect principle"—for instance, whether you would be justified in shooting your neighbors if, fleeing radiation and hunger, they threatened to overwhelm your shelter and eat all your family's canned goods.

When we moved to Corpus Christi there was much to get

used to: a new school, a new order of nuns whose two-toned eccle-siastical garb of maroon and white seemed to suggest, but did not exactly deliver, a lighter attitude than the crow-black robes of the Sisters of Divine Providence. There was a new city as well, of course, one that was named for the body of Christ and not, like Abilene, in homage to a bygone cattle-drive terminus in Kansas. A city not on the Texas plains, but on the state's hard-used Gulf coastline, where the air was so sodden and humid I felt like a lizard in a terrarium.

But one thing was the same: the countdown to 1960 contin-ued. We were not given a precise day when the pope—now the rotund and reforming Pope John XXIII—would open the enve-lope containing the Fatima Letter. All we knew was that it would happen sometime in 1960.

The fifth-grade teacher at Saint Patrick's School was Sister Mary John Vianney. Sixth grade was Sister Aloysius. So it must have been Sister Martha in seventh grade who was in charge of our young souls when 1960 finally began and—nothing . . .

No one said a word about the Fatima Letter! Nothing in the newspaper, at least nothing that I saw; nothing in any of the secular magazines—*Time* and *Saturday Review* and *Life*—my parents sub-scribed to at home; and nothing even in the Catholic magazines, like *America* and *Commonweal,* that I sometimes paged through while eating potato chips on the living-room couch.

What had happened? Nineteen sixty had come, and no one said a word about the most important revelation that could ever occur in our lifetimes. What had Our Lady of the Rosary said to Lucia? What was the secret of the Fatima Letter? Would we sur-vive, or had the world not said enough rosaries to forestall a meteor strike or, more likely, a fiery rain of Soviet ICBMs?

Finally, someone in seventh grade—I like to think it was me, but I might not have had the nerve—asked Sister Martha if she knew what the Fatima Letter had said.

"Oh, that," she said in a curiously flat voice. "Well, the pope read it, decided that what it said was so terrible that nobody could ever know, and put it right back in the envelope and sealed it up again."

Her casual comment hit me like an apocalyptic revelation. It was a definitive confirmation of my worst fears that the world was soon to end. Russia would not be converted after all. The leader of the atheistic Soviet empire, Nikita Khrushchev, would not suddenly fall to his knees in the Kremlin and declare his devotion to God and his Blessed Mother. We were all doomed.

To be alive in 1960 was to live with the background awareness that nuclear war could start at any moment. A too-imaginative child like me, already reckoning at every moment with the supersaturated rituals of Catholicism and the prospect of eternal torture in hell, was especially vulnerable. But somehow I got past the disappointment of having my curiosity about the Fatima Letter squelched and my fears of what it might contain reignited. Along with the rest of the world, I moved on from 1960, got older, and then much older still—living now deep into a new century with its own preoccupations about what to worship and what to fear.

But I never forgot about the Fatima Letter and the grip it had once held on my vulnerable consciousness. And when, forty years later, in 2000, its contents—the Third Part of the Secret—were finally revealed to the world, I found Lucia's supposed prophecy to be a colossal anticlimax. It was short, a few hundred words of fever-dream imagery—flaming swords, holy martyrs, a ruined city, angels gathering up the blood of the slaughtered—that might have been outtakes from the Book of Revelation. What I didn't understand at the time was how deeply the Third Part of the Secret, and the story of Fatima, were entwined with so many of the upheavals of the previous century and the one that had just started—with war, with pandemics, with assassinations, with the blood feuds of religious certainty. It was also a story that put me back in touch with the foundations of my own character and personality, with the credulous boy who grew away from his faith but who, like millions of other Catholics imprinted with the harsh demands of God and the mercy of Mary, could never quite grow out of it.

My own childhood experiences were incalculably different from those of the three shepherd children of Fatima, but not so different that those children ever felt like strangers. Growing up, I said the same prayers, sang many of the same hymns, felt ready for the same miraculous occurrences that Lucia, Francisco, and Jacinta witnessed.

This book will be, I hope, a clear-headed (i.e., secular and objective) narrative of those occurrences and the reverberating, world-shaking events that followed. But I don't think I can keep it from being a work of memory as much as a work of history, given the upbringing of chronic anxiety and vaulting mystery that awakened my interest in Fatima in the first place, and that made the story of those Portuguese children seem so unaccountably familiar. So it's a personal chronicle, with an unsolved personal quest at the heart of it. I don't mean a quest for faith. That matter was settled for me a very long time ago, when I first gave myself permission to question what I had always been taught were unquestionable tenets of faith. But there's still some phantom need to belong to something I can no longer belong to, along with a nostalgia for someone I can no longer be—an innermost Catholic self that can be neither thoroughly expelled nor honestly embraced.

It was that sense of unfinished business that led me back to Fatima, to the story of a boy and a girl who didn't live long enough to be tempted to separate childhood fantasy from religious faith, and of another girl who lived to be ninety-seven and for whom belief in the literal existence of a Blessed Mother was the unflagging constant of her life.

Their story began over a century ago in a radically different kind of world. But for everyone who has ever believed—or tried to believe, or been forced to believe—in an enveloping reality beyond our own, it might not seem so strange.

2

Console Your God

"May is the month of Our Mother," we sang in the springtime as we paraded outside the main building of Saint Joseph's Catholic School in Abilene. "Those blessed and beautiful days . . ."

We followed behind the older kids who carried a statue of the Virgin Mary at the front of the procession. The sky was as blue as her cloak, and the scent of massed flowers in semiarid West Texas hit my unprepared olfactory system with the force of an epiphany.

Blessed and beautiful days: I was ten years old and the words of the song were like a promise already fulfilled. I don't remember being happy very often in the vicinity of religious rituals, but the smell of the flowers that day, the perfect blue of the sky, and the aura of protection cast by that swaying, impassive statue all drew me into a swoon of deep contentment.

The month of May is named for the Greek goddess Maia, the most motherly of the Pleiades, the seven daughters of Atlas, who was secretly impregnated by Zeus and gave birth to the god Hermes. Maia's story—pregnant by one god, mother of another—is congruent enough to the Virgin Mary's to make it unsurprising that May eventually evolved into a month of commemoration for a nurturing goddess, this time a Christian one. Processions like the one I experienced on that long-ago day in the 1950s—an event that ended with a crown of flowers being placed upon the statue of Mary—were familiar to Catholics all over the world, and had been for centuries.

For Lucia Santos, the Portuguese village girl whose visions inflamed the imagination of millions, the month of Our Mother would certainly have carried rapturous possibilities. She, too, was at the impressionable age of ten when she reported seeing the Virgin Mary in May of 1917, and her family was steeped in old-world Catholic lore, ritual, and symbolism.

Lucia was the youngest of seven children. "Their parents," wrote a Portuguese Jesuit named Luiz Gonzaga da Fonseca, "were not among those who fear to give new life. They considered every new cradle a gift from heaven." Photographs of Lucia from the time of the apparitions depict a heavy-featured, grim-looking girl. ("Not a pretty child," in the opinion of Father John de Marchi, an Italian priest who knew and interviewed her later in life. "A physiognomist might have put her down as gross, even perverse.") But that unkind physical description is at odds with the light-hearted childhood portrait Lucia herself sometimes strains to present in the series of six brief memoirs she began writing in 1935, a year or so after taking her perpetual vows and living as a Dorothean sister in a convent in Pontevedra, Spain. She was directed by a Portuguese bishop to tell the story of her life, and she did so at first grudgingly, "in spite of the repugnance I feel." By that time in her life—she was twenty-eight—she was well practiced in humility and reluctant to write about her "miserable self." But the memoirs, though awkwardly composed—Lucia had been illiterate until she was finally sent away at fourteen to a school in Porto—are moving and revealing. In their vivid depiction of family life in an isolated rural community, they are like a rougher, more spontaneous Portuguese version of Laura Ingalls Wilder's *Little House* books.

"My father was of a kind nature," she wrote, "kindly and joyful . . . he loved to please everyone and to see everyone happy." Lucia herself seems to have been happiest when she was with her father, sitting with him on the stone seats near the threshing floor, listening as he pointed up to the stars and told her how they were lamps lit by angels and set in the windows of heaven. The brightest light in the sky—the moon—was the lamp of Our Lady. The sun, rising above the hillsides, was the lamp that God himself placed there, and thunderstorms were expressions of his anger at the sins of men.

"That is how the days, months and years were spent in this humble home," she wrote, "in quiet peace and joy, smiling at the future of the young people as they blossomed with the sweet-scented smell of the freshest rosebuds that bloomed every day in the climbing roses that decorated the walls of our house."

The Santos family lived in Aljustrel, a hamlet of a few stone houses with red-tiled roofs about eighty miles north of Lisbon, in rugged pastoral country at the northeastern flank of the Serra de Aire, a mountain range that is part of the network of rearing massifs and plateaus that define the landscape of much of central Portugal. Aljustrel was barely a mile away from the slightly larger village of Fatima, the center of a parish comprised of scattered townships with an aggregate population of several thousand people, most of whom were farming families. Fatima was the name of the daughter of the prophet Muhammad and is a primary female figure in the Islamic tradition. But the town and the parish were supposedly named after a Muslim girl who had been kidnapped by a Christian knight in 1158, when much of Portugal was still—as Father Fonseca tells us—"under the Mohammedan yoke." Whether Fatima willingly converted to Catholicism, or was forced into it, depends on your religion and which version of the legend you care to credit. In either case she appears to have given her name to the village of Fatima and the surrounding parish.

Lucia's family was relatively prosperous for the time and place in which they lived. They owned land around Aljustrel and Fatima, where Lucia's father, Antonio, trapped foxes, hares, and other small game whose hides he cured and sold. His modest businesses centered on a flock of white Merino sheep whose numbers fluctuated, depending upon the season, between about twenty and sixty animals. The sheep were penned up at night and grazed during the daytime on land owned by the family.

The house in Aljustrel where Lucia and the other Santos children grew up had belonged originally to the family of their mother, Maria Rosa. She and Antonio had moved in with her parents after they were married, and she nursed them, as well as an aunt and uncle from her extended family, until they died. For Lucia's mother, taking care of people seems to have been an instinctive drive that was amplified by the demands of her Catholic faith.

"Maria Rosa Ferreira," one author, M. Fernando Silva, declares, "personified the valiant woman of Sacred Scripture." In a parish where 92 percent of the female population was illiterate, she was an enthusiastic reader (particularly of lives of the saints), and was a skilled, if unschooled, nurse. Maria Rosa was intelligent, organized, tirelessly open-handed and compassionate, especially to people in need, but Lucia's memoirs leave you with the impression that her mother was also stern and unyielding. "She was always very serious," Lucia writes, "and everybody knew that what she said was like Scripture and must be obeyed without more ado. I never knew anyone to say a disrespectful word in her presence, or show her any lack of consideration. It was the general opinion among them, that my mother was worth more than all her daughters put together."

Lucia was an imaginative child who grew up in a household that demanded strict adherence to dogma but also made room for off-the-books flights of religious fantasy, like how the Virgin Mary and the angels lit up the sky at night, or how a white wicker basket in the Santos house had been the vehicle by which the newborn Lucia had arrived from heaven.

It's no mystery that such a child, from such a family, would tremble with religious fervor as her first communion approached. She was only six, much younger than normal to receive the sacrament, but she already knew her catechism and impressed the priest who examined her. Her sisters made her a white communion dress and she kept waking up the night before the ceremony in rapturous expectation. When the moment came and the priest placed the host on her tongue, "I felt an unalterable serenity and peace. I felt myself bathed in such a supernatural atmosphere that the presence of our dear Lord became as clearly perceptible to me as if I had seen and heard Him with my bodily senses."

The girl was too excited to eat afterward and discovered that she had "lost the taste and attraction for the things of the world." Now believing herself to be in direct communication with God, she asked him to make her a saint and to "keep my heart always pure, for You alone."

As she looked back upon this landmark event in the first volume of her memoirs, Sister Lucia made an uncharacteristic observation, one that is worth bearing in mind when considering the things she claimed to see and the events she set into motion a few years after that first childhood epiphany. "I don't know whether the facts I have related about my First Communion," she wrote, "were a reality or a little child's illusion."

In either case, Lucia had barely shaken off the wonder of her first communion when, in 1913, she walked right into another epiphany, one that she looked back upon as "A Mysterious Presage." She was seven by then, and had recently been judged old enough to be put in charge of the family's flock. Along with three other young shepherdesses, she drove her sheep up the eastern slope of a small rocky hill called the Cabeço. After lunch, as the sheep grazed, the children recited the Rosary. As they prayed, they saw an indistinct human form, "like a statue made of snow," hovering above the trees. It happened twice more, and each time the presence said nothing, just hung there in the air like a sentinel. Lucia reported the sighting to her mother, who scolded her for lying, and to her sisters, who made fun of her—"recalling that for some time after my First Communion I had been quite abstracted."

After three visits, this mute, vague figure didn't show itself again. But the next year a more defined form appeared: a beautiful young man, "whiter than snow, transparent as crystal," who drifted down from the tops of the olive trees onto the ground and announced that he was the Angel of Peace. This time Lucia was in the company of her cousins Francisco and Jacinta Marto. The cousins' mother, Olimpia, was the sister of Lucia's father, and the two families and their households were closely interwoven. The apparition of the angel occurred while the three children were shepherding their families' combined flocks near an olive grove at the top of a local hill.

In her memoirs, Lucia doesn't give an exact date for this new series of apparitions, but she was probably nine at the time. Francisco would have been eight, Jacinta six. Francisco comes across in Lucia's memoirs as a dreamy boy, calm and composed in a way that sometimes irritated his older cousin, who was energetic and agenda driven. "My own opinion," Lucia reflected much later in life about Francisco, "is that, if he had lived to manhood, his greatest defect would have been his attitude of 'never mind.'"

Like her cousin Lucia, Jacinta Marto was the youngest of seven children. Jacinta and Francisco's mother, Olimpia, recalled that her daughter's eyes were "light in colour." To Lucia they appeared brown, to others darker. To everyone they were strikingly vivid. "She was naturally good and the sweetest among our children," her father, Manuel, remembered. Lucia, in the way of exasperated and impatient older children, wrote that she sometimes found Jacinta "quite disagreeable," oversensitive and prone to pouting, but had fond memories of the girl who would "hold the little white lambs tightly in her arms, sitting with them on her lap, kissing them, and carrying them home at night on her shoulders so that they wouldn't get tired."

On his first appearance, Lucia wrote, the angel bowed down, touched his forehead to the ground, and intoned a prayer, which he demanded that the children repeat three times. "Pray thus," he told them. "The hearts of Jesus and Mary are attentive to your supplications."

The same entity came back again, appearing to the children at a well behind Lucia's house, and then—for a third and final time—when they were out again in the pastures. This time he produced a chalice full of blood and "a Sacred Host." He gave the host to Lucia and had Francisco and Jacinta drink the blood from the chalice. "Take and drink the Body and Blood of Jesus Christ, horribly outraged by ungrateful men! Make reparation for their crimes and console your God."

It's hard to believe that such young children, even a child as devout and yearning as Lucia, could have made sense of phrases like "attentive to your supplications" and "console your God." But Lucia didn't set them down in writing until 1937, after she had been a member of a religious order for over a decade and had developed a spiritual vocabulary that could be retroactively deployed in writing about otherworldly childhood experiences. She had a certain psychological power over her two younger cousins. She bossed

them around and appointed herself their "catechist," leading them
in religious instruction as they tended their flocks and then—it
seems—convincing them that an angel had come down from
heaven to land in the pasture in front of them. Children of that
age can believe anything—they can *see* anything if the desire of seeing it or the fear of seeing it is great enough. That's how as a little
boy I had convinced myself that one of the nails of Christ's cross
had fallen from heaven or that a church tapestry was the face of
Satan. It's easy to imagine myself standing in that field with Lucia
and agreeing with her that an angel had just landed in the pasture.

Lucia, already stung by the disapproval of her mother and the
scorn of her sisters after she had told them about her first mysterious visitor, warned Francisco and Jacinta not to say a word about
the angel. She may have sensed as well that another supernatural occurrence would be aggravating news in a family beset with
earthly worries.

Something had gone wrong in the Santos house. "Only later
did I come to understand," Lucia wrote, "how, even in the loveli-
est gardens the poisonous caterpillar appears." Her references to
exactly what happened are somewhat elliptical to begin with, and
in subsequent memoirs she said the hard times arrived later, during the troubles that began in 1917 after she claimed to have seen
the Virgin.

But her original recounting is the most direct and feels the
most honest. "My God, where has all the joy of our home gone?"
she quotes her mother as saying as she sat around the fire one
night, staring at the empty places at the dinner table. By that time,
the once-bustling household in Aljustrel was almost empty. Of the
family's six living children (one had died at birth), four—Lucia's
older sisters—had either married or been sent out to work as ser-
vants. "Our house was like a desert," Lucia remembered. Now
there were only her, her mother, her brother, and a father who,
Lucia wrote, "had fallen into bad company, and let his weakness
get the better of him."

She insisted in later writings that this "weakness" had to do
only with card playing, and not with alcohol, but the general understanding in the village seems to have been that Antonio Santos
had a serious drinking problem that had begun to undermine his

family's emotional and economic stability. (Lucia also referenced it, not so obliquely, in a 1922 letter to her brother, when she was at a boarding school in Porto. "When Mass finishes," she instructed him, "go home and don't stay in bars, because this is the downfall of so many men, as you well know, because you had this mirror to look into once.") There were other anxieties. In 1916, Portugal had been drawn into the First World War, and the family believed it was only a matter of time before Lucia's brother, Manuel, would be sent to the trenches. Then a new parish priest swept into their lives and condemned the "pagan custom" of dancing, which was part of the festas that had always given the lively Lucia such joy. Finally, her mother was not just beset with worry and worn out from work but severely ill with a heart problem and a dislocated vertebra.

Lucia withdrew into herself as the foundations of her family's life eroded. She spent a lot of time at the well behind her house, the site of the angel's second visitation, sobbing into the water. When Francisco and Jacinta came looking for her there and asked what was wrong, "my voice was choked with sobs and I couldn't say a word."

It would have been natural for such a forlorn child, one who had already convinced herself that she communicated directly with heavenly beings, to turn her imagination to the most comforting figure in the Catholic firmament. It was not just Lucia who was susceptible to reveries about the Mother of God; it was her country. "Portugal," writes M. Fernando Silva, "was born under Our Lady's mantle." He was referring to the 1646 oath made by King João IV, the country's sovereign after its break with Hapsburg Spain, that Portugal's patroness and spiritual queen was Our Lady of the Immaculate Conception, one of the many designations of the Virgin Mary. ("Immaculate conception," by the way, is often mistakenly thought to refer to Mary's feat of being miraculously impregnated by God and giving birth to Jesus while still a virgin. In fact, it's even more abstruse than that. It means that, unlike anyone else who ever lived with the exception of her son, her soul was conceived without the "stain" of Adam's original sin of disobedience to God.)

It's likely that Lucia, coming from such a devout family, was aware of other apparitions of the Virgin that had taken place in Portugal's deep past. In the twelfth century, a young shepherd—a *pastorinha,* like Lucia—had been saved from starvation after a mysterious lady appeared and told her to go home and check the bread box in her house, which turned out to be miraculously full. The fishing village of Nazaré, on the Portuguese coast not far from Fatima, was the site of a vibrant legend in which the Virgin, in 1182, saved the life of a knight named Fuas Roupinho as he galloped on his horse toward a steep cliff that he couldn't see ahead of him in the fog. There were similar occurrences all over Portugal throughout the centuries leading up to the Fatima apparitions—in Dornes, in Azambuja, in Quintela, on an island in the Azores, in Villa Franca do Campo, in São Vicente de Aljubarrota, and in a half dozen other places where local chapels had been built according to the Virgin's specifications and where local devotional cults had developed. There was even said to have been a previous apparition in the vicinity of Fatima itself, in 1758, where once again the Virgin revealed herself to a shepherd girl.

The Blessed Mother had appeared, time and again, to lonely people of pulsing faith who had fallen on hard times. How could it not occur to a disheartened dreamer like Lucia Santos, particularly in May, the month of Our Mother, that she might possibly be one of them?

3

The Cove of Peace

"The first thing I learned," Lucia remembered, "was the Hail Mary. While holding me in her arms, my mother taught it to my sister Carolina, the second youngest, and five years older than myself."

There's something very familiar to me, and I suspect to many others, about the notion of an infant first hearing the Hail Mary, the foundational prayer of the Catholic faith, at an age when she was still becoming aware of the sounds of the world. The Hail Mary is so deeply embedded in my own sense of self that it feels preconscious. I don't think of the prayer so much as a collection of words as a visual design, something like a concrete poem, with a top half and a bottom half.

The top half is:

Hail Mary, full of grace, the Lord is with thee. Blessed art thou amongst women and blessed is the fruit of thy womb, Jesus.

The bottom half is:

Holy Mary, mother of God, pray for us sinners, now and at the hour of our death. Amen.

How many thousands of times did I say those words while I was growing up, either out loud or in silent murmuring as I dutifully recited my prayers at night? For a Catholic of my generation, of my spiritual saturation level, the Hail Mary is verbal DNA, not just memorized but encoded. The "Hail Mary"/"Holy Mary" syllables that begin each half of the prayer create a subtle rhythmic stutter-step that gives it a hook like a pop song.

The prayer was originally stitched together from New Testament passages describing a scene depicted in holy cards and stained-glass windows throughout the Christian world: the Annunciation, when the angel Gabriel appeared to a young Mary and announced that she had been chosen to conceive and give birth to a son, "of the Most High," that she was to call Jesus. When she protested that she had no "knowledge of man," that she was still a virgin, the angel told her not to worry, that she would be made pregnant by the Holy Spirit—or, as this manifestation of God's tripartite nature used to be known when I was a kid, the Holy Ghost.

The Hail Mary is the essential building block of the rosary, the loop of beads that, as a young teenager, I carried in my pocket in a zippered case with my name embossed on it. Some form of knotted rope or beaded prayer-prompter had been used ever since the days of the early Christians, but it was in the twelfth century that the rosary morphed into a specific device to remember and venerate the Blessed Virgin.

A rosary is made up mostly of five "decades," five sets of ten beads, with a single bead in the spaces separating each set. As each bead passes through your fingers, you say a Hail Mary. When you get to the end of a decade, you come to a gap, where you say a Glory Be ("Glory be to the Father, and to the Son, and to the Holy Spirit [formerly Ghost], as it was in the beginning, is now, and ever shall be. Amen"), and then when you reach the single bead you say the Lord's Prayer—the Catholic version, without the "For thine is the kingdom, the power, and the glory" tagline.

But before the Lord's Prayer there are the Mysteries—Joyful, Sorrowful, and Glorious. (A fourth set of Mysteries—Luminous—was added in 2002.) Each category features five New Testament highlights from the life of Jesus or Mary. They're ticked off not as prayers but as announcements. For instance, "The First Sorrowful Mystery: the Agony of Our Lord in the Garden."

It's appropriate that the rosary is in the form of a loop, because the experience of praying it the way the nuns expected us to—on our knees, hitting every bead, saying every prayer, reflecting on every Mystery—has a mind-numbing circularity. The goal, it always seemed to me, was to put us in a trance state where we could be detached for a half hour or so from dangerous brain activity that might lead to unwholesome reveries or forbidden questions.

The temptation to speed-pray the Rosary was irresistible. Even now, many decades after making my escape from the Church, I can recite a Hail Mary with the velocity of one of those fast-talking announcers who list the side effects at the end of drug commercials.

The three *pastorinhos* of Fatima were deeply pious, but they were also children, and their parents' instructions to say the Rosary out in the fields every day after lunch severely tested their attention spans. "We worked out a fine way of getting through it quickly," Lucia wrote, describing a solution also discovered by generations of bored worshippers. "We simply passed the beads through our fingers, saying nothing but 'Hail Mary, Hail Mary . . .'" They did the same when they came to the singular beads representing the knotty Our Fathers. They just said the first two words and left it at that.

———

On May 13, 1917, Lucia, Francisco, and Jacinta were out in the fields with their sheep. They had blitzed through the Rosary after eating their lunch and were occupying themselves with building a little stone wall at the top of a slope. It was a Sunday, and the place where they had taken their flocks after they had gone to Mass was called the Cova da Iria, a field owned by Lucia's parents where maize and potatoes grew, along with wild olive trees and the native evergreens known in Portuguese as *azinheiras* and in English as "holm oaks." The word *cova* in Portuguese means "pit" or "hole," but in this case the translation is closer to "hollow," in reference to the broad basin shape of the pasture. The Cova da Iria was possibly named for Santa Iria, a martyred Portuguese maiden from the seventh century, whose name derives from the Greek Irene, the goddess of peace. That was one of the reasons the Cova da Iria would soon come to be known as the Cove of Peace.

The other reason had to do with what Lucia claimed happened that day as the children were building the wall. She said there was a "flash of lightning" in the sky, or at least something that looked like it. Thinking they were about to be caught in a thunderstorm, they began to herd the sheep down the slope toward the road. There was another flash of lightning, then "we beheld a lady all dressed in white. She was more brilliant than the sun . . . "

She was also aloft, levitating above the canopy of a young holm oak, only a few feet from where the three children were standing. In Lucia's telling, the interchange is roughly the same as it was in that movie I saw as a child. The Lady told them not to be afraid, Lucia asked her who she was, and she said she was from heaven.

"I have come to ask you to come here for six months in succession," the vision said in answer to Lucia's question about what she wanted from them, "on the thirteenth day, at this same hour. Later on, I will tell you who I am and what I want."

Lucia asked whether she and her cousins would go to heaven, and the Lady assured her that they would. But she made a point of saying that Francisco would have to say a lot of Rosaries to make it happen. She didn't mention why that should be the case, or why Francisco, alone among the three children, couldn't hear anything she was saying—he had to get all his information secondhand from Lucia. At first, according to later accounts, he couldn't see the apparition, either, and called out—in boyish frustration—"Throw a stone at it!"

But several months later, during a formal interrogation by a priest, Francisco gave a detailed description of the appearance of the mysterious lady. He said that she had moved quickly across the sky from the east and settled on the top of the tree, which he called a *carrasqueira*—the local name for an immature holm oak tree. She addressed herself only to Lucia and looked very grave. She wore a long dress with a long mantle, or veil, over it. Both were white, but the dress was trimmed in gold. She held a white rosary in her hands. She was "more beautiful than anyone I have ever seen."

During that first brief encounter in May, Lucia was anxious to ask the floating vision in gold-trimmed white about two young women from Aljustrel, friends of her eldest sister who had recently died. Were they in heaven? One of them was, but the other—whom Lucia remembered being about eighteen to twenty years old—was not, at least not yet. "She will be in purgatory until the end of the world."

I'm not sure what Lucia's understanding of purgatory was, but if it was anything like mine, this would have been a blood-freezing revelation. The Catechism of the Catholic Church, the book (seven hundred pages in the edition I have) that attempts to explain exactly what Catholics are supposed to believe, states that purgatory is a kind of waiting room, where people who are not condemned to hell but still have some work to do—to "undergo purification"—are kept before they're allowed to enter heaven. The catechism approvingly quotes the words of Saint Gregory the Great, who was the pope at the end of the sixth century, and who wrote of purgatory that "we must believe . . . there is a purifying fire."

Growing up, I was never encouraged to believe that fire, purifying or otherwise, was a metaphorical concept. I doubt that Lucia, Francisco, and Jacinta thought that way, either. Hell meant literal fire. So did purgatory, though in that case the poor souls who found themselves there had committed only venial (less serious) sins and could breathe a sigh of relief even as they were screaming in agony, knowing that at the end of their sentence—as potentially long, as we have seen, as the life of the world—they would finally be welcomed into heaven.

Lucia didn't report her reaction to the news of her friend's soul trapped in purgatory, but in her recounting of this event she seems eager for her own trials to begin.

"Are you willing to offer yourselves to God and bear all the sufferings He wills to send you," she says the Lady asked, "as an act of reparation for the sins by which He is offended, and of supplication for the conversion of sinners?" She said she was willing, and was informed that she and her cousins would have much to suffer, "but the grace of God will be your comfort."

"As she pronounced these last words . . . Our Lady opened her hands for the first time, communicating to us a light so intense that, as it streamed from her hands, its rays penetrated our hearts and the innermost depths of our souls . . ."

Lucia set down this account of the first appearance of the Virgin Mary in her fourth memoir, composed like the previous three at the request of her religious superiors. By the time she began writing it, in 1941, she was thirty-four and known as Sister Maria das Dores, or Sister Mary of the Sorrows. She was, she said, God's "poor and miserable instrument." She wrote in the attic of the convent, "lit by a single skylight, to which I withdraw whenever I can, in order to escape, as far as possible, from all human eyes." But her self-abnegation does not come across as self-loathing. You can detect pride and theatricality in her writing, qualities she must have had as a vision-prone little girl and as a bossy older cousin.

As in her second memoir, which she had written four years earlier and where she described the appearance of the angel, Lucia rendered the alleged dialogue between the Lady and the children in the ornate language of a nun who had spent decades in an echo chamber of theological reflection. What ten-year-old Lucia thought she heard and what she might have said in reply have been overwritten by her adult self. But her memoirs are still the primary source of the apparitions, the only fully rendered account from somebody who considered herself a firsthand witness.

Lucia, stung by the mockery she had experienced when word got out two years before that she had seen an angel, extracted a promise from Francisco and Jacinta not to mention this latest apparition. But Jacinta, who was only seven, couldn't keep it to herself and told her and Francisco's parents that same afternoon. They were indulgent, even receptive. "From the beginning of the world," their father, Manuel Marto, mused, "Our Lady has been appearing, at different times and in different ways . . . If there had not been such things the world would be even worse than it is."

But as word began to spread in Aljustrel and the neighboring villages of the Fatima parish, Maria Rosa—Lucia's rigid mother— grew annoyed and alarmed. She told her daughter "to consider well that she had never tolerated a single lie among her children, and much less would she allow a lie of this kind."

Maria Rosa Santos was devout, but she was also pragmatic, and Portugal in 1917 was a tricky place to be broadcasting stories about religious visitations. In February of 1908, King Carlos I had been assassinated in an open carriage in Lisbon, shot to death along with his elder son and heir, twenty-year-old Luis Filipe. His surviving son, Manuel, became king, but the monarchy that had been ruling Portugal for seven centuries was already limping toward modernist oblivion.

Eighteen years before the regicide, Portugal had lost much of its African territories to England, a humiliating global retrenchment for a country that had once led Europe into the Age of Discovery. By the time the king and the prince were assassinated, it had descended further into powerlessness, corruption, and political instability. The end of the monarchy came on October 5, 1910, when, after a flurry of hostilities, rebels took over the city hall in Lisbon and announced that Portugal was now a republic.

There was a new flag, a new national anthem, and—for this firmly secular, passionately anticlerical republican government—another new symbol. Our Lady of the Immaculate Conception, who had once been the "Advocate and Protector of the Kingdom of Portugal," was sidelined, replaced by another radiant female emblem named Maria, a version of the bare-breasted, barricade-storming icon of revolutionary France, Marianne.

In this "New Portugal" religious activity was severely curtailed, Christmas was renamed "Day of the Family," church property was nationalized, many priests were exiled, and those who were allowed to stay could not wear their clerical garb in public. The parish priests who had been the go-to authority figures in rural places like Fatima now served under the suspicious eyes of political administrators.

The new republic was tumultuous from the start, beset by foreign intervention, monarchist counterrevolutions, political violence, and an overall "heroic march to the sewer," as one disillusioned revolutionary termed it. The country's entry into the Great War was controversial and economically ruinous, leading to wheat shortages and bread rationing. On the day before Lucia, Francisco, and Jacinta claimed to see the Virgin Mary at the Cova da Iria, the bakeries were closed in Lisbon, which helped cause food riots and the deaths of two hundred or more people.

In this newly secular country, at a time when religious fervency could not just be thought of as superstition but be mistaken for sedition, it's no wonder that Maria Rosa had the impulse to check her daughter's runaway imagination. She tried to get her to admit that she had made the visit from the Virgin Mary up, and when Lucia wouldn't, she beat her with a broom handle. She took her to the parish priest, Father Ferreira, and instructed Lucia to get down on her knees before him and admit that she had lied. But once there, Lucia told substantially the same story. The priest, writes Father de Marchi, "was far from defending the children, and maintained an absolute reserve on the subject."

As the story of the apparitions grew, what Maria Rosa feared began to come to pass. The children—and their parents—were publicly mocked and taunted by the people of Aljustrel. The only comfort Lucia seems to have found was with her father, who, despite the drinking and gambling that had brought so much grief to the family, remained composed when it came to worrying about whether his daughter had or had not seen the Virgin Mary. He maintained, writes Lucia, "an attitude of faith and trust."

Not everyone doubted the children. Fifty or so people were intrigued enough by the story they had told to show up at the Cova da Iria the next month, on June 13, when the Virgin had promised she would make her next appearance. Among them were fourteen children who had made their first communion along with Lucia and who decided to skip a big festa, complete with music and fireworks, that was taking place in Fatima that day, on the Feast of Saint Anthony. "As usual," one of them remembered, "when Lucia proposed a thing no one contradicted her."

At the Cova da Iria, the little crowd watched as Lucia, Francisco, and Jacinta gathered in front of the holm oak. One of the witnesses described the tree as being "about a metre high. It was very well shaped with regular branches." Once more the children saw—or Lucia said they saw—a flash of lightning, and then the Lady arrived again at the top of the tree. None of the other people in the vicinity could see her, though one woman remembered "something like a tiny little voice, only we couldn't hear what it said. It was rather like the buzzing of a bee!"

The tiny little voice might have been Lucia's, once again asking the visitor from heaven what she wanted. The Lady repeated that she wanted the children to come to the Cova da Iria on the thirteenth of every month. She also said that she wanted Lucia to learn to read—something that the ambitious little girl who had learned the catechism by age seven might very well have wanted for herself.

Lucia says that she asked the Lady to take her and her cousins to heaven. The answer was disappointing, though probably flattering to Lucia's sense of being chosen. "I will take Jacinta and Francisco soon. But you are to stay here some time longer. Jesus wishes to make use of you to make me known and loved. He wants to establish in the world devotion to my Immaculate Heart . . . I will never forsake you. My Immaculate Heart will be your refuge . . ."

"Immaculate Heart" is one of those phrases Catholic children hear again and again. They see depictions of it in portraits of Mary, in which her hand often rests above a radiant red heart outside her body. Jesus also has an external heart, known as the Sacred Heart. In Catholic imagery, the hearts of both Mother and Son are frequently depicted as being on fire, bleeding or pierced by a sword representing unbearable sorrow, and by the crown of thorns placed upon Jesus's head before the crucifixion. When I was a kid, these images were not worthy of comment—they were as common as wallpaper patterns. We understood, from before we could understand much else, that both Jesus and Mary wanted you to see their innermost suffering selves. And if either had appeared to me, as I expected they would someday, the vision would have been incomplete without a flaming, beating heart with a sword stuck in it.

Lucia, too, would have had such images in her head, and it helps to explain what she reported seeing next. As she had in the first apparition, the Lady opened her hands and enveloped Lucia, Francisco, and Jacinta in a blast of celestial light. Within the light they saw "a heart encircled by thorns which pierced it. We understood that this was the Immaculate Heart of Mary, outraged by the sins of humanity, and seeking reparation."

Then she was gone. As the vision left the tree, Lucia turned to the crowd and cried out, "Look, there she goes! There she goes!"

The people gathered at the Cova da Iria could see nothing, nothing but three rapturous children and a stunted oak tree. But one of them later swore that she heard the Virgin Mary take off, back into heaven. "It sounded," she said, "rather like a rocket."

4

The Three-Part Secret

"Our Lady is coming!" Lucia cried on the afternoon of July 13, a month later, as she and her cousins said the Rosary once again in front of the oak tree. This time there was a huge crowd for the promised third apparition, two or three thousand people, so densely packed around the three shepherds that Francisco and Jacinta's father, Manuel Marto, had to elbow his way past bare-foot peasants, farmers in their Sunday suits and hobnailed boots, and upper-class curiosity seekers in fashionable city attire. When Marto finally reached the children, he thought that his niece Lucia had a "deathlike pallor" as she waited for the Virgin to once again appear on the tree. Like everyone else gathered at the Cova except for the three shepherd children, he didn't see the Lady, though he testified later that he saw a small cloud descend upon the oak and heard a sound "like a horse-fly in an empty water pot."

Manuel Marto required no further evidence that his children were telling the truth. "All this," he said, "was for me a great proof of the miracle." But his sister-in-law, Maria Rosa, still had what Lucia termed a "contemptuous attitude" toward her daughter's claims and was in the middle of a campaign to coerce her into recanting the previous apparitions and confess that they were lies.

In fact, Lucia had almost not come to the July 13 rendezvous with the mysterious lady. A few days before, Maria Rosa had marched her into another interrogation with Father Ferreira, instructing her to "let him do whatever he likes with you, just as long he forces you to admit that you have lied; and then I'll be satisfied."

When she entered the priest's study, Lucia was relieved to find that his questioning this time was gentle, but she was greatly alarmed by his conclusion.

"It doesn't seem to me like a revelation from heaven," he told her. And it very well could be, he continued, "a deceit of the devil."

This thought sent the little girl into a tailspin of doubt and fright. She had horrible dreams of the devil laughing at her in mockery as he dragged her down into hell. She couldn't face Francisco and Jacinta and kept to herself, searching out solitary places to sit down and weep. When she saw her cousins again, she told them to go without her to the July 13 meeting. "If the Lady asks for me, tell her I'm not going, because I'm afraid it may be the devil."

But when the day came, she went after all, "impelled by a strange force that I could hardly resist." The three children had to fight their own way through the dense crowds that were lined along the road to the Cova. When they got there, and knelt once again before the tree, they experienced another flash of light just before the vision appeared. There followed the now-familiar back-and-forth of Lucia asking the Lady what she wanted of them, the Lady telling them once again that she wanted them to say a Rosary and to come back here every month. Lucia asked her to perform a miracle, so that the crowds gathered in the Cova who could not see who or what the children were talking to could receive some sort of evidence that there was really somebody there.

"Continue to come here every month," the Lady said. "I will tell you who I am and what I want, and I will perform a miracle for all to see and believe."

It's important to emphasize once again that nobody could hear the words that were being said except—Lucia claimed—the two girls. And she did not give a written account of what she heard until years later. Francisco could by now see the vision, but he was still shut out of this exclusively female conversation. And none of the people pressing in and straining to see what the children were looking at and Lucia was speaking to saw anything but a stunted tree or heard anything other than a child's questioning voice.

Was there anything to see or hear in the first place? It's probably time for me to come straight out and say that I don't believe—can't believe—there was. Nothing was happening in front of all those people—or, rather, a lot was happening. A lonely, unhappy, commanding girl whose family was in crisis sought refuge in her own shimmering fantasies and willed into her sight what Catholic children of that time and place were primed to see—the most beautiful and reassuring figure available to their imaginations. I think the vision was authentic in the sense that Lucia really believed it was occurring. And her belief was infectious—not just to the two young cousins for whom she was a ringleader and role model but to the people of unquestioning faith who had gathered at the Cova to distract their minds from the war and the political upheavals that were tearing apart their country and their world.

This purported appearance of the Lady on July 13—the third of six apparition events between May 13 and October 13, 1917—would have ramifications deep into the future, galvanizing and puzzling the faithful and launching high-stakes theological thought wars. That was because, as Lucia put it, "This was the day on which Our Lady deigned to reveal to us the Secret."

The secret she referred to is the origin of the Fatima Letter that had so haunted my childhood: the handwritten prophecy that Lucia composed in 1944 and then sealed into an envelope, on the outside of which she made a notation that it should not be opened until 1960. This missive also became known as the Third Part of the Secret of Fatima. It was called that because, Lucia claimed, the Blessed Virgin revealed "a secret made up of three distinct parts" to the children at that July apparition.

William Thomas Walsh, a robustly Catholic historian who visited Portugal in the 1940s to interview Lucia in her convent and to research his influential book *Our Lady of Fatima*, writes that after the children said the Blessed Virgin had ascended back into the sky that day, "the crowd seemed to sense the apocalyptic solemnity and tenseness of a communication on which hangs, perhaps, the fate of the entire human race." They pelted the children with questions about the mysterious lady whom they themselves had neither seen nor heard.

"It's a secret," Lucia told one of these interrogators.

"Good or bad?"

"Good for some, for others bad."

"And you won't tell us?"

"No, sir. It's a secret and the Lady told us not to tell it."

Walsh wrote that Lucia would never disclose the "final secret . . . until the Queen of Heaven herself commands her to do so."

The children's insistence on withholding the secret inflamed the curiosity of the onlookers and increased the skepticism of both religious and secular officials, who found themselves having to deal with an eruption of unsanctioned devotion from people whose beliefs they could not control.

It would be a long time before Lucia would disclose any of the revelations that made up the secret. In 1941, the bishop of Leiria requested more details about the events she had already described in the two memoirs she had written up to that point. "This request," she wrote, "penetrated to the depths of my soul like a ray of light, giving me to know that the time has come to reveal the first two parts of the secret."

Part one, she said, was a "vision of hell."

She wrote that the Lady "showed us a great sea of fire which seemed to be under the earth. Plunged in this fire were demons and souls in human form, like transparent burning embers." The children heard "shrieks and groans of pain and despair, which horrified us and made us tremble with fear. The demons could be distinguished by their terrifying and repellent likeness to frightful and unknown animals, all black and transparent."

The second part of the secret was the prediction of the Lady that souls could be saved from hell if the world established "devotion to my Immaculate Heart." If this happened, Lucia said the vision told her, the First World War would end. If it didn't happen, there would be an even worse war during the papacy of Pope Pius XI. She also demanded "consecration of Russia to my Immaculate Heart . . . If my requests are heeded, Russia will be converted, and there will be peace; if not, she will spread her errors throughout the world, causing wars and persecutions of the Church. The good will be martyred; the Holy Father will have much to suffer; various nations will be annihilated."

The faithful followers of the message of Fatima are firm in their belief that the second part of the secret accurately predicted the end of World War I and the beginning of World War II during the pontificate of Pius XI—although in fact the pope died in February of 1939, seven months before Hitler's invasion of Poland. They also believed she foresaw the spread of Russian communism and, in the earlier June apparition, the deaths in childhood of Francisco and Jacinta. But, as mentioned earlier, Lucia didn't reveal any of these prophecies until 1941. Theologians straining to justify such discrepancies might call Lucia's revelations "post eventum," though ordinary people would call it predicting things that had already happened.

Lucia was a child of ten when she claimed to have learned these prophecies in 1917. It's not clear whether she and Francisco and Jacinta thought they were strictly enjoined from revealing them by the Lady herself or whether they just decided not to do so on their own. They were already annoyed by all the attention, and frightened by it, and Lucia comes close to admitting in her fourth memoir that after the second apparition the children had begun telling people that the things the Lady said were a secret as a way of deflecting harassing questions. "If they asked us why it was a secret, we shrugged our shoulders, lowered our heads and kept silent."

Lucia was in her thirties when she finally disclosed the first two parts of the secret in 1941, and it was not until three years later that she wrote the Fatima Letter—the Third Part of the Secret—and sealed it into the envelope that was not to be opened until 1960. Along with the rest of the world, I wouldn't know its mysterious contents until 2000. But as a boy I was already on unwelcome familiar terms with the first part of the secret, the one that would have been the most immediately terrifying to three young children: the vision of hell.

"Some people," Lucia wrote, "even the most devout, refuse to speak to children about hell, in case it would frighten them. Yet

God did not hesitate to show hell to three children, one of whom was only seven years old, knowing well that they would be horrified to the point of, I would almost dare to say, withering away with fear."

"Withering away with fear" pretty accurately describes the way I felt about hell as a child. Later in my Catholic education I heard hell described as a kind of lingering abstruse pain, an "absence from God," and not as a literal chamber of everlasting fire. But when it counted, when I was around the ages of the three children of Fatima and my imagination was at its most tender, the stakes were high when it came to eternal punishment.

I vividly remember one of the nuns who taught me in third or fourth grade reading from a book that featured reports from the damned souls trapped in hell. I was too young to be skeptical of these fictional first-person accounts—I just assumed that somehow, through some sort of supernatural samizdat network, these letters had been smuggled out so they could be read to horrified grade-school children in the above-ground world. "Oh, if I could just have a single drop of water on my tongue!" moaned one of the tormented sinners in the book as the flames kept him at a constant pitch of agony for all eternity.

Just so we could get the point of how never-ending the sufferings we might experience in hell would be, we were told to think about a giant golden ball, hard as steel. Every ten thousand years a dove would fly by and brush the ball with one of its wings. When, after an incalculably long time, the dove's wing had finally brushed the ball enough times to wear it down into nothing, that would be the moment when eternity began.

Even with that illustration, eternity could only be marveled at and feared, not grasped. But the point was clear: pain beyond anything we could conceive would last longer than any time span we could possibly imagine. My nightmares centered, naturally enough, upon fire. Sometimes, late at night, I would be awakened by a noise that was probably squirrels chasing each other around the outside of the house, but which my perplexed and frightened imagination concocted into the sound of doomed souls scrabbling about inside our walls, trying to claw their way out of hell.

The terror for Jacinta, the youngest of the three shepherds, was especially stark after the July apparition, when the children were supposedly shown a fiery vision of the underworld. But at least her fear for herself was blunted by the fact that she and Francisco had been told, in May, that they were soon to die and go to heaven. She doesn't appear to have been troubled, at least in Lucia's recounting, by the prediction that she would not survive childhood. She was too young to comprehend death but not too young to conjure up a childlike idea of paradise, and the fact that she believed she was going to heaven meant she would be immune from the tortures of hell.

But after the latest visitation Jacinta was aware that others might not have the same exit strategy. "Oh Hell! Hell!" Lucia reports her as saying with "shuddering" emotion. "How sorry I am for the souls who go to hell! And the people down there, burning alive, like wood in the fire!"

Even during World War I, Jacinta was tormented by horrid daydreams of the even more terrible war that the Lady had prophesied would come, and of the many sinful people who did not realize that after dying in that war they would be sent to hell, where their agonies would only begin.

But even though she knew she would not join those tormented souls, she had no idea of the earthly dread that the future would bring, beginning the next month with the kidnapping of the three young Fatima shepherds.

5

Offer It Up

Lucia's claims that she had seen the Blessed Virgin were rapidly making her an outcast in her own family. This was because much more was at stake than the indulging of a child's religious fantasies. The Cova da Iria, where the three apparitions had taken place, was the family's property and the source of its modest wealth—and it was now a muddy, barren, churned-up expanse. The maize, potatoes, cabbages, and other crops that Antonio Santos cultivated were gone. "Everything had been destroyed," Lucia wrote. The fields were trampled by pilgrims who had traveled there on foot or on donkeys, horses, or mules. As they prayed and waited for the Virgin to appear, they turned their animals loose to eat the grass that was meant for the Santos family's sheep—a flock that would soon have to be sold off.

The crowds were not confined to the Cova. They besieged Lucia's house in Aljustrel. There were believers demanding to talk to the children and question them about what they had seen, and irritated and inconvenienced neighbors who came to lecture Lucia's parents on how they would never have allowed their own children to create such a commotion.

Antonio escaped the crowds by disappearing during the day to a nearby tavern to play cards and drink wine with men his wife called "false friends." It was Lucia's duty to find her father at the end of the day and bring him home, where Maria Rosa would harangue him for leaving her alone with all the unwelcome visitors while he allowed himself to be carried off by the devil. "He has made life black for me here in the house. God help us!"

In Francisco and Jacinta's house there wasn't nearly as much tension, though it, too, was thronged by curiosity seekers and people begging for or demanding some sort of intercession with the Virgin Mary. Francisco and Jacinta's parents were more inclined to believe their children, and because their own land was not located at the Cova, their livelihood wasn't under as grave a threat. Lucia was envious, and wounded. Her mother was openly hostile and her father, with his fortunes sinking, seems no longer to have been quite as indulgent and understanding as she remembered him being a few years earlier, when he would sit with her on the threshing floor and point out the angels lighting the lamps in the night sky. "What hurt me most," she wrote, "was the indifference shown me by my parents."

The more Maria Rosa tried to get her daughter to admit that she had lied, the more she beat her with the broom handle, the more obdurate Lucia became—and the tighter she held on to the privileged information she believed she had received at the last apparition. The excitement and curiosity that had already been growing since word got out that the three children had seen the Virgin Mary was now inflamed by the idea that she had told them a secret they could not reveal.

People demanding answers pestered the other children, too, besieging all three. "What they wanted," Manuel Marto remembered, "was to get hold of the secret. They used to take Jacinta on her knees and worry her with questions. But she just answered as she wanted to! That secret . . . you couldn't get it out of her with a corkscrew!"

According to the timeline Lucia said she received from the Lady, a fourth apparition was due to take place on August 13. But that rendezvous ended up being derailed by the civil administrator of Vila Nova de Ourém (known today as simply Ourém), the municipality that included the parish of Fatima. The administrator was a blacksmith and former anticlerical newspaper columnist named Artur de Oliveira Santos. He shared a last name with Lucia but had no tolerance for her supposed visions or the threats to public order in his municipality that had erupted because of them.

On August 10, as anticipation was building for the next apparition, Santos issued a summons for the three shepherd children and their fathers to appear before him. Manuel Marto refused to take Francisco and Jacinta. Ourém was almost eight miles away, a long way for little children to walk or ride on a donkey, which was the only form of transportation the family had. But apparently no objections were raised in the Santos family. "Let her answer for herself," Lucia quotes her parents (she doesn't specify which one, but it sounds like her mother) as saying ". . . If she's lying, it's a good thing that she should be punished for it."

So the next day Lucia was taken to Ourém, riding on the donkey as her father and uncle walked. When they finally appeared before Santos, the administrator—according to Lucia—"was determined to force me to reveal the secret and to promise him never again to return to the Cova da Iria."

He got nowhere, although under his questioning Antonio Santos admitted that he didn't believe his daughter was credible. Back home in Fatima, he said, "we think it's all women's stories." Manuel Marto refused to concede. He told the administrator he believed his children, Francisco and Jacinta, were telling the truth. He also claimed that, in his frustration, Artur Santos repeatedly threatened Lucia and told her that if she didn't reveal the secret he would have her killed.

The administrator let the children go home, but he hadn't given up intimidating them. On the morning of August 13, the day of the scheduled apparition, he showed up in Aljustrel himself at the Marto house and ordered Lucia to be brought there so that he could interrogate her along with Francisco and Jacinta. He demanded that they reveal the secret and agree to stop visiting the Cova. After the children refused, he seemed to relent, and even offered to drive them to the site himself in his carriage, leaving the families with the impression that he wanted to see what would happen and that he might even be receptive if a miracle took place.

It was a ruse. Santos took them instead to Father Ferreira, the parish priest who had already questioned Lucia three times.

Perhaps under pressure from the secular administrator, perhaps alarmed by the ungovernable throngs traveling to the site of a series of miracles that were unsanctioned by the church and could lead to further repressions by the republican government, he now flatly accused her of spreading lies and warned her that she might go to hell.

Lucia, according to her uncle Manuel, was defiant. "If people who lie go to hell then I shall not go to hell, because I am not lying and I saw only what I say and what the Lady told me."

Santos, realizing that the priest's intervention was useless, hustled Lucia back out into his carriage, where Francisco and Jacinta were still waiting, and drove them to Ourém, against the flow of pilgrim traffic headed down the road for that day's promised apparition. "This isn't the way to the Cova," Lucia said, as she realized they had been abducted.

Santos apparently reasoned that by extracting the children from the scene, the apparition hysteria would die down on its own. That failed to happen. "If there were a lot of people in July," remembered Maria Carreira, a local woman who suffered from chronic illness and who had a handicapped son, "this month there were many, very many more." Like many of the thousands of people who were streaming to Fatima that day, Senhora Carreira was desperate for a healing miracle, and she and some other local people had thrown together a makeshift shrine in front of the holm oak where they believed the Lady would appear. There was a small table, and behind it a kind of archway. As one observer described it, the structure was made of "rough poles of pale wood that resembled a trapeze, that was surmounted by a small cross."

When word came that the children had been kidnapped, Senhora Carreira wrote, there was a clap of thunder, a flash of lightning, and then "we began to see a little cloud, very delicate, very white, which stopped for a few moments over the tree and then rose in the air and disappeared. As we looked around we noticed . . . our faces were reflecting all the colors of the rainbow, pink, red, blue . . . The trees seemed to be made not of leaves but of flowers; they seemed to be laden with flowers . . . The ground came out in colors and so did our clothes. The lanterns fixed to the arch looked like gold. Certainly Our Lady had come although she had not found the children there!"

The perceived atmospherics may have had a calming effect on many of the people gathered at the Cova, but there were others who set off for Fatima determined to confront Father Ferreira, who they thought had colluded with Santos in abducting the children. ("I deny this infamous and insidious calumny," the shaken priest declared in a letter to several newspapers.)

The threat to Father Ferreira evaporated, but in the meantime the children had missed their appointment with the Lady and were still in the administrator's custody in Ourém. He took them at first to his own house, where his wife treated them kindly and where they played with the Santos children. But the next day the administrator dispensed with his hospitality and began to grill them again. "It was the secret which Arthur Santos wanted at all costs to obtain," writes John de Marchi in his Fatima history, "and in his methods he followed in the footsteps of the great persecutors of the primitive Church."

At least that was the account that Lucia set forth in her memoirs, and presumably related to her family when she was reunited with them. After spending the night at the administrator's house, kept there against their will, the children were allegedly taken to the town hall, where Artur Santos and several others alternately bribed and threatened them to reveal the secret or to admit that they had made the whole story up. When they refused, Lucia wrote, they were thrown into prison, where "they told us they were coming soon to take us away to be fried alive."

Fatima chroniclers tend to go into lurid detail about the mock execution Santos supposedly staged to frighten the children into revealing the secret.

"In the presence of the children," de Marchi reports, "[Santos] gave orders for the preparation of boiling olive oil in which these insolent, these stubborn and stiff-necked peasants were to be fried alive. The first to be called was Jacinta . . . 'The oil is boiling. Tell the secret . . . it's your last chance.'"

In this rendition, a guard led Jacinta away, came back a short time later, and said, "She's well fried," then grabbed Francisco, took him away next, and returned for Lucia, who "recommended her soul to the Blessed Virgin and asked her not to desert her in the coming agony."

There may have been emotional agony, but nobody was fried in oil. Lucia was reunited with Francisco and Jacinta, and the next day the children were sent home to their parents.

Artur de Oliveira Santos vehemently denied these cruel mind games. "What is false," he wrote in 1924, "completely false, is that I threatened or intimidated the children, or kept them prisoners or unable to communicate with anyone, or that they suffered the slightest pressure or violence." He was still defending himself well into the 1950s, when he once again denied the charges to a priest named Joseph Pelletier, who had come to interview him. "By the man's face," Pelletier wrote, "which carried a two-day beard, his shabby suit, and neglected-looking house, for which he felt obliged to apologize, I gathered that he was not very prosperous."

Pelletier says that Santos was by that time a Christian, but that a short time later "he died a lonely and embittered man . . . without the Sacraments, without Christian burial."

However preposterous the frying-in-oil story might sound, it's true that the administrator did abduct the children so that they wouldn't appear at the Cova and he could, as he admitted, "stop the speculation about the so-called Miracle of Fatima." And no doubt it's true that the children were terrified at being taken away from their parents, held hostage in a stranger's house, and relentlessly interrogated and pressured to divulge the secret or admit that they were lying. But the mock executions Lucia and other writers describe strike me as the sort of martyrdom fantasies that the church has long specialized in implanting into vulnerable young minds. In her memoirs, Lucia wants us to believe that, in the moments before they thought they were about to be boiled alive, she and Francisco and Jacinta behaved just as brave Catholic children have always been expected to. They, like kids in my own generation, had been brought up to believe that renouncing your faith was the ultimate sin, and that undergoing earthly torture was a negligible price to pay for finally dying and being allowed to see the face of God in heaven.

"O my Jesus!" Lucia has Jacinta—a seven-year-old girl—proclaiming just before she is taken away to what she is promised will be an agonizing death, "This is for love of You, for the conversion of sinners, for the Holy Father, and in reparation for the sins committed against the Immaculate Heart of Mary!"

That was the sort of thing that the secular press in Portugal was only too eager to label as "Fanaticism in Action," the same religious nonsense the revolution had tried to extirpate but which still threatened to "surround and asphyxiate Portuguese society."

The fact that the children had not made it to the Cova for the fourth apparition ultimately did nothing to deter the crowds who had rendered the family's grazing lands unproductive and who now had stripped away the leaves and branches of the holm oak where the Virgin had appeared. Artur Santos had meant to short-circuit the frenzy by removing the visionaries from the vision, but in kidnapping the children he had only inflamed the Catholic faithful and raised the stakes for the next scheduled apparition in September.

Before that happened, however, there was another, more private, supernatural appearance. Several days after they came home, the children reported they saw the Lady again, only this time not at the Cova, but at another stretch of pastureland between Aljustrel and Fatima known as Valinhos. Once again, "we felt something supernatural approaching and enveloping us." Once again, the vision manifested herself on top of an oak tree. She told the children that, notwithstanding the interruption that had occurred when they were detained, she wanted to keep the schedule she had set and return to the Cova on September 13. Lucia asked her what they should do with the money that had been left by pilgrims at the makeshift altar. The Lady was curiously specific. She wanted the money distributed between two litters—one litter to be carried by Lucia and Jacinta and two other girls dressed in white, the other by Francisco and three other boys. She didn't say exactly where she wanted them to carry the litters, but they understood it was to be used to pay for a feast honoring Our Lady of the Rosary, and any leftover proceeds were to go to the construction of a chapel. Lucia, who like her cousins had been hounded by people demanding a miraculous intervention for sick family members, asked the Lady if she would answer their prayers. "Yes," Lucia heard her say, "I will cure some of them during the year."

———

After the events at the administrator's house and at Valinhos, Lucia reports, she and Francisco and Jacinta began to experiment with self-inflicted pain. They found a piece of coarse rope that had fallen off a cart in the road, cut it into thirds, and each of them tied it tightly around their waists, so tightly that "this instrument of penance often caused us terrible suffering." They also gave away their lunches to poorer children, and scratched their legs with nettles or squeezed them tight in their hands. "Look! Look!" Lucia quotes Jacinta as saying. "Here is something else with which we can mortify ourselves."

I don't believe Lucia's version of a seven-year-old girl's vocabulary, but I recognize the children's resolve to intentionally inflict pain upon themselves as a very Catholic thing to do. I understood from an early age that if you're in the right frame of mind, it should feel good to feel bad. Without some kind of brake—in the form of self-denial or mortification—pleasure was an ungovernable sleigh ride into depravity. "Offer it up!" was the brisk reply from my mother whenever I whined about having to get a shot or go to the dentist. It was short for "Offer it up to Jesus," a command that meant my suffering was inscrutably not in vain, that God would notice it with approval and add it to my account.

Mass on Fridays was compulsory in my grade school before the school day could begin, an ordeal made more unendurable by the rule that we couldn't rest our arms by setting our elbows on the back of the pews as we knelt. It wasn't so bad except when we had to say the Rosary, with its endless unabridged Hail Marys, and kneel there without fidgeting while the hard edge of the pew in front of us dug into the radial bones of our tender young forearms. Nuns patrolled the aisles to whack our wrists with their rulers if they noticed us using our elbows to give our arms a break, or if we committed the unholy offense of slouching back and half-sitting, half-kneeling. (I wouldn't learn until many years later that this position was known as the "Episcopal squat.") Keeping our posture straight and our elbows off the pews, the sisters told us, was the least we could do, since Jesus had hung in agony on the cross for three hours in order to—in some way I never quite understood and still don't—"redeem" us from sin. When we were a few years older, some of the more devout kids in school, those who would end up going to the junior seminary, would affect the wearing of scapulars. A scapular is a kind of necklace suspending two brown squares of wool. Kids wore them under their shirts, against their bare skin, and the idea was that the scratchy wool squares were to serve as a constant irritant, a reminder that to be comfortable was to be complacent. (At least that was our understanding at the time. When I looked up "scapulars" on the internet recently, I was directed to a website with an entrepreneurial bent that insisted, "A scapular isn't a penance . . . We use Australian merino wool that feels like a warm hug from your heavenly mother.")

———

Suffering was looked upon as a resource, even a gift—something to remind you of your impending mortality and bring you closer to God. Maybe that helps to explain the curiously flat and seemingly disinterested response the Lady gave to Lucia when she asked her if she would intervene with the sick people of Fatima, that she would cure only "some of them."

Chronic pain and debilitating diseases were a real-world step removed from the discomfort games played by Lucia and her cousins, and the children were frightened by the pleas of suffering adults desperate for a cure. "They all wanted to see and question us," Lucia remembered, "and recommend their petitions to us, so that we could transmit them to the most Holy Virgin . . . In the middle of all that crowd, we were like a ball in the hands of boys at play."

There were historical reasons for why all these people thought that the children could help them, just as there were precedents throughout Western Europe for the Virgin Mary appearing to very young people like Lucia at tumultuous and confusing times in their lives. In 1846, near a village in the French Alps called La

Salette, a fourteen-year-old girl and a ten-year-old boy, shepherds like Lucia who had troubled relationships with their own families, announced that they had encountered, near a dry mountain spring, a whirling light that manifested itself into a woman who stood up and walked toward them and said, "Come near, my children, don't be afraid! I am here to tell you great news."

But the news the vision gave them was frightening. "A great famine will come," she said. "Before the famine comes, the children under seven years of age will be seized by trembling and they will die in the hands of those who hold them . . . The walnuts will be worm-eaten and the grapes will rot."

Despite the apocalyptic warnings, the local inhabitants decided that the vision had been a peaceful presence—indeed the Virgin Mary herself. And after it rained and the dry spring began running again, people who drank the water or washed with it began to claim miraculous cures from blindness, lameness, and other afflictions.

Lucia Santos knew about the appearance of the Virgin at La Salette—her mother had read her a book about it—and she certainly would have been aware of the much more famous incident in France that had taken place twelve years later in the Pyrenees town of Lourdes, near the border of Spain about 650 miles northeast of Fatima. There, on a February day in 1858, a fourteen-year-old girl from an impoverished family named Bernadette Soubirous was gathering wood near a shallow cave known as the Grotte de Massabielle. This grotto was at the base of a limestone cliff, and just above it was a small declivity—"not unlike an ogival window of a cathedral," as Émile Zola described it in his 1894 novel *Lourdes.* That was where Bernadette said she saw a white shape that resolved into a human figure wearing a white dress with a blue sash. She originally believed the figure was a girl of her own age, though she soon described her as "the Mother of Angels." Bernadette said that the apparition requested her to return to the grotto every morning for fifteen days. As she did so, more and more curious and devout pilgrims followed her and watched as—just like Lucia—she carried on a private communication with the Lady.

On one of the visits, during one of these "ecstasies," Bernadette followed the instructions of the Mother of Angels and started digging with her hands in the back of the grotto until she discovered a sluggish spring opening and began to drink some of the muddy water. People began to fill bottles with the water, and soon there were miracles reported—the blind recovering their sight, the lame walking again. By the time of the Fatima apparitions, Lourdes's reputation as a holy site was well established, with a church built above the grotto (per the Virgin's request to Bernadette), its "miraculous" spring water sold all over the world, and tens of thousands of the hopeful and afflicted making the pilgrimage to the site every year.

Now, it seemed, there might be a Lourdes on Portuguese soil, a vibrant rebuke to the new secular republic, and a place where the suffering faithful might find relief.

"The priests have flocked to the place," fumed the editor of *O Mundo*, Portugal's most popular secular newspaper, "and—how odd!—they all find this young girl parroting the same things that Bernadette said at Lourdes." But his skeptical contempt went unnoticed by believers who, along with their priests, kept converging on Fatima.

"For the love of God, ask Our Lady to cure my son who is a cripple!" Lucia reported people calling to the children as they forced their way through the crowds toward the Cova on September 13, the date of the fifth apparition. "Yet another cried out: 'And to cure mine who is blind! . . . To cure mine who is deaf! . . . To convert a sinner! . . . To give me back my health as I have tuberculosis!'"

She wrote that the crowd showed her and Francisco and Jacinta "no human respect whatsoever." They climbed trees and stood on the top of the walls lining the road, shouting down to the children, begging or demanding that they provide some sort of intervention on their behalf with the Virgin, who was about to appear yet again.

When they finally reached the Cova, the children began to say the Rosary again and saw the customary light that heralded the arrival of the Lady. The thousands of people gathered in what used to be Antonio Santos's grazing land were primed to see something, even if they understood that the Virgin only appeared to the children. A priest from the nearby town of Leiria wrote that he—

and many others—saw a shimmering globelike object—"the means of transport—if one may so express it—which brought her from Heaven to the inhospitable waste of the Serra de Aire."

Lucia makes no mention of this phenomenon, just describes the Lady appearing once more on top of the holm oak. The conversation was brief. They were told by the apparition to continue praying the Rosary to "obtain the end of the war." She said that she would be back in October, and that she wouldn't be coming alone. With her would be Saint Joseph, the infant Jesus, and various other manifestations of Mary. She told Lucia to stop sleeping with the irritating rope around her waist—an instruction the child might have been glad to hear. Lucia asked her once again whether she was willing to perform any miraculous cures, and the Lady said, "Yes, I will cure some, but not others."

And then, just before disappearing, she raised the stakes even higher. She promised that at the last scheduled apparition on October 13, "I will perform a miracle so that all may believe."

6

The Spinning Sun

"It was three o'clock in the afternoon," recalled Father Manuel Nunes Formigão, "when I got off the train that had taken me from Torres Novas through Vila Nova de Ourém to the humble village, whose name is today uttered like a buoyant hope of heavenly blessings and grace pronounced by tens of thousands of lips, from one end of Portugal to the other."

Formigão was thirty-four in 1917, a professor of theology at a seminary in the city of Santarém, and an energetic leader in re-establishing the Catholic presence in Portugal that the revolution had tried to extirpate. When he arrived at Fatima, Formigão was already steeped in the culture of apparitions. As a young cleric, he had lived in Lourdes, where he claimed to have witnessed "astonishing cures that took place instantaneously" and had served as a nurse and stretcher bearer to the afflicted pilgrims who came there hoping for the same sort of miracle.

In time, he would become known as the "narrator, defender and bard" of the Fatima apparitions, the indispensable promulgator of the story of the Virgin Mary and the shepherd children, which he wrote about repeatedly—under the pseudonym Visconde de Montelo—in multiple books, pamphlets, and periodicals. But at this point in his career he affected a scrupulously skeptical attitude. He was among those present near the Cova for the September 13 event but saw nothing he cared to attribute to divine influence. "I did not approach the place of the apparitions," he remembered, "and I hardly spoke to anyone, but stayed on the road approximately thirty meters away and only noticed a dimming of the sunlight, which seemed insignificant to me and probably due to the high mountain altitude."

But now, at the end of September, he had come back to Fatima, charged by church officials in Lisbon to interview the three children who had created so much commotion by claiming to have seen the Lady. Even though he himself had witnessed nothing extraordinary on September 13, his own vocational beliefs, his experiences at Lourdes, and the reaction of the pilgrims he had seen that day had convinced him that "a buoyant hope of heavenly blessings" was more than a possibility. Nevertheless, he conducted a series of interrogations of the children that were, judging by the transcripts he later published, as rigorous as a trial lawyer's.

He met the children first in Aljustrel on September 27, when expectations were running feverishly high about the next and final promised apparition, on October 13, when the Lady had told Lucia she would perform a miracle. Formigão interviewed the younger children first—Francisco and then Jacinta. He did not think the two young Marto siblings looked particularly well nourished, though that may have had more to do with the cascading stress of the last few months than with their diet.

His questions for Francisco and Jacinta were pointed and specific. He wanted to know exactly how the Lady was dressed, how she held her hands, what color her hair was, whether she wore earrings, whether she held her rosary in her right or left hand, whether she ever cried or smiled.

A half hour after he questioned Francisco and Jacinta he met with Lucia, who sat herself down at a chair by his side. She displayed "an unselfconsciousness which contrasted in a marked manner with the shyness and timidity of Jacinta . . . She willingly consented to be questioned on the events of which she was the principal protagonist in spite of the fact that she was visibly fatigued and depressed by the incessant visits and the repeated and lengthy questioning to which she was subjected."

If we can judge by Formigão's reports and by Lucia's own accounts, she might have been close to a breaking point. Her claim to have seen the Virgin, her refusal to admit it was a series of fantasies, had destroyed the Cova, undermined her father's equilibrium, subjected her to threats and kidnapping, and made her a figure of resentment in her own family.

After his initial interview with the children, Formigão made inquiries around Fatima about the families in which the children had been raised. The parents of Francisco and Jacinta, he learned, "are very good people, profoundly religious and well thought of by everybody." The reactions were more guarded when it came to Lucia's father. Although Maria Rosa was regarded as pious and hardworking, the best that was said about Antonio was that he was "not at all a bad man." They pointed out his "fecklessness" and the fact that after the second apparition, in June, his friends had gotten him so stumblingly drunk that a bystander at the Cova had pushed him to the ground.

Lucia was aware not only of her father's growing drinking problem but of her mother's increasingly tenuous health. The back pain that had been tormenting her had worsened during the tumultuous months of the apparitions, and the treatment she needed was a long walk or horseback ride away, which only aggravated her condition, "with the result that she got worse until a day came when it seemed that her days on earth were numbered." In her memoirs, Lucia gives the impression that that day came sometime between September and October, though in reality it happened later, after the apparitions had concluded. But the assaults on the family's privacy and well-being were constant, and at some point Maria Rosa was given the last rites by the parish priest, the same Father Ferreira to whom she had brought Lucia for questioning back in June.

Lucia represents this scene as one of high drama: Maria Rosa on her deathbed clasping Lucia in her arms and calling out, "My poor little girl! What will become of you without your mother? I am dying with you stuck in my heart"; then Lucia's sister forcing the child out of the room and telling her, "Our mother is dying of sorrow because of you and all the trouble you have caused."

But Maria Rosa didn't die. Lucia went to the Cova, knelt in

front of the stripped-away oak where the Lady had been appearing, and begged her to spare her mother's life. When she got home, Maria Rosa was sitting up in bed feeling much better and eating chicken soup.

She had been well enough, when Formigão showed up again in Aljustrel sometime before the October apparition, to answer a few questions the priest had about her daughter, specifically about whether the book about the appearance of the Virgin at La Salette that Maria Rosa read to Lucia had "made a great impression on her mind."

Maria Rosa thought it had not, an impression that was confirmed by Lucia herself, when Formigão interrogated her again that same day. She told him that she had "never thought" about the story of La Salette or talked about it to anyone. Having gotten nowhere with the idea that Lucia might have been inspired by other shepherd children to whom a mysterious lady appeared to create her own version of the story, Formigão shifted the subject to October 13, the upcoming sixth apparition and day of reckoning.

"What did she say that she would do in order that people might believe?"

"She said that she would perform a miracle."

"Are you not afraid of what the people will do if nothing extraordinary happens on that day?"

"I am not at all afraid."

———

For two days before the promised apparition, the roads were filled with pilgrims from all over the Serra and beyond making their way to the Cova da Iria. The weather was foul—damp, drizzly, cold. Some of the people were on horseback or riding donkeys, others in carriages or on bicycles, the well-to-do in automobiles. Thousands were on foot. "The cotton skirts of the women," wrote one witness, "dripped and hung like lead around their ankles . . . Boots and bare feet splashed through the muddy puddles . . . and up on the mountain there was what appeared to be a large dark stain—thousands upon thousands of God's creatures waiting for a miracle . . ."

They slept out in the open, many of them, and were up before sunrise saying the Rosary.

Others, like Avelino de Almeida, a journalist covering the event for *O Século*, were there out of professional curiosity. He wrote about the traffic on the road—oxcarts, motorcars, victorias, braying donkeys—and about the men and women walking barefoot, carrying their shoes in bags to spare them from the mud, praying in unison as they advanced along the Leiria road toward the Cova. Almeida, wondering where all this would lead, provided his readers with a remarkably clear glimpse of the Fatima that was to come: "And there are even people who dream of a great and magnificent church, always full, of large hotels nearby with every modern comfort, of shops well stocked with a thousand and one different objects of piety and souvenirs of Our Lady of Fatima."

But the atmosphere that day was tense, at least in the memories of Lucia and other members of her family. There was the threat of violence. Perhaps it would come from antireligious republican agitators who were mixed in with the rural believers and were rumored to be planning to throw a bomb. The children might be trampled by the press of people desperate to see and touch them. Or they might be attacked by those same people when the promised miracle didn't take place.

"My parents . . . were very much afraid," Lucia wrote, "and for the first time they wished to accompany me, saying that if their daughter was going to die, they wanted to die by her side." That morning, Lucia and her parents went to the Marto house, where, Francisco and Jacinta's father said, "the people filled the house so that you couldn't move. Outside it was pouring with rain so that one could hardly see through it and the ground was thick with mud."

Manuel Marto remembered that Francisco and Jacinta were calm, and that a woman from a nearby village brought new dresses for the girls to wear to the expected apparition. "Lucia's was blue and Jacinta's white, and she put white wreaths on their heads so that they looked like the little angels in processions."

But it was no orderly procession. The children and their parents had to fight their way to the Cova in the driving rain and the mud through a tightly packed crowd. Jacinta cried when she saw people pushing her father. But after a while the people began to recognize the *pastorinhos* and back away to create a path for them to approach the destroyed tree and the crude ceremonial archway.

When Lucia, Francisco, and Jacinta reached the spot it was mid-morning. What happened soon after was the usual experience between the children and the being they said was visiting them, a private spiritual conversation that was unheard and unwitnessed by the people packed in the churned-up field of mud that had once been the bounteous orchard and grazing land of the Santos family. But there would also be a public dimension to this last visitation, something in the sky that thousands of people would witness or seem to witness at the same time and conclude was the promised miracle.

Lucia, "moved by an interior impulse," as she remembered the scene in her fourth memoir, called out for the onlookers to close their umbrellas and to begin praying the Rosary. A little later, she wrote, she and her cousins saw the flash of light that signaled the Lady was coming, and then there she was once again, in her usual position at the top of the tree. In Lucia's recounting, she asked the Lady what she wanted of her. She replied that she wanted "a chapel to be built here in my honor. I am the Lady of the Rosary. Continue always to pray the Rosary every day. The war is going to end, and the soldiers will soon return to their homes."

Lucia wrote that she once again asked the Lady about curing sick people and got the same answer, that she would cure some and not others; that she looked sad and cautioned the world not to offend God anymore, "because He is already so much offended."

The vision disappeared, and then Lucia cried out for everyone to look at the sun. It had stopped raining by then, and from the various eyewitness reports that were published later the sky seemed to have taken on an after-storm radiance and clarity. "The sky," wrote the reporter for the Lisbon newspaper *O Dia*, "pearly gray in colour, illuminated the vast arid landscape with a strange light." The sun, in the memory of another witness, looked like "a disc with a clean-cut rim, luminous and shining." Manuel Marto, standing near his daughter Jacinta, remembered that it was possible to stare directly at the sun without being blinded by its brilliance, an effect that may have had something to do with the peculiar flat light described by other witnesses. "It looked like a plaque of dull silver," Avelino de Almeida wrote in his account in *O Século*, "and it was possible to look at it without the least discomfort."

Then, to the (perhaps) sixty thousand or more people gathered in the Cova da Iria, the sun moved, or—in that peculiar afternoon sky—gave the appearance of moving. It "spun like a fire wheel," one woman wrote in a letter. It seemed to detach itself from its place in the sky, "nervously agitated as if driven by electricity," one witness wrote. The crowd saw the sun spin and then hurtle toward the earth like a fiery meteor. Some people dropped to their knees in prayer; others scattered in terror. The apparent fireball never reached the ground, but it created an eerie shifting of the color spectrum that one spectator thought at first was the result of a detached retina. Suddenly everything was purple, or orange, or blue, or—in the words of another witness—"the colour of old yellow damask. People looked as if they were suffering from jaundice."

Lucia maintained that the children saw none of this. She related that they were locked into a private vision of their own, in which they saw a series of confusing tableau-like visions: Jesus as an infant, with Saint Joseph and Mary beside him, and then the adult Jesus making the sign of the cross as if "to bless the world."

But the crowd that had gathered to see a miracle believed they had seen one—had seen the sun spinning wildly in the sky, casting a kaleidoscopic color spectrum upon the earth. They were awed, terrified, electrified, and after about ten minutes had passed and the heavenly pulsations had subsided, many of them rushed toward Lucia and her cousins, the young seers whose spiritual credibility they could no longer doubt. Before they could be overwhelmed by all the people wanting answers and blessings, the children were lifted into the arms of protective adults and taken home to Aljustrel. When they got there, Lucia discovered that her kerchief had been stolen and that the long braids that reached below her waist had been cut off by some frenzied bystander and stolen as souvenirs.

———

Formigão subjected the children to a debriefing that evening, and then came back to Aljustrel a week or so later to question them further. He arrived at the Marto house to find Francisco and Jacinta enduring yet another interrogation, by a priest who was the chaplain of the Portuguese Expeditionary Force. All three children, Formigão soon discovered, were traumatized and depleted by the commotion that had befallen them after the events of October 13. Lucia appeared numb and robotic, hollowed out by exhaustion. "If the children," Formigão wrote, "are not spared the fatigue of these frequent and long inquiries, there is a serious risk to their health."

Nevertheless, the priest-inquisitor drilled down, making them endure his most stringent examination yet. Much of it had to do with Lucia's proclamation that the Virgin had told her that World War I was coming to an end, a prophecy of obvious concern to a country that had sent almost a hundred thousand young men to fight in Africa or in the trenches of the Western Front.

"On the thirteenth of this month," Formigão asked Lucia, "Our Lady said that the war would finish on that same day? What were the words she used?"

"She said: 'The war will end today. You can expect the soldiers very shortly.'"

"But listen, Lucia, the war is still going on. The papers give news of battles after the thirteenth. How can you explain that if Our Lady said the war would end that day?"

Reading the transcript of Formigão's October 19 interviews with the children, you can easily sense how flustered and tired and scared they all were, cornered again and again by people demanding information, authority figures trying either to confirm they were telling the truth or to trick them into admitting they were lying. At one point in the transcript, Formigão, in his exasperation with Lucia's wandering answers, simply records, "No coherent reply."

———

Although Lucia and her cousins were too young to fully realize it, much was at stake. Their claims about the apparitions of the Vir-

gin Mary, the anticipation they had created of a miracle and the
seeming fulfillment of their prediction, were helping to bring the
cultural and religious tensions between Catholic and republican
Portugal once again into open conflict.

"Citizens!" warned a Masonic pamphlet. "As if the pernicious
propaganda of reactionaries were not enough, we now see a *miracle*
trotted out in order further to degrade the people into fanaticism
and superstition. There has been staged . . . an indecorous comedy
in Fatima at which thousands of people have assisted, a ridiculous
spectacle in which the simple people have ingeniously deceived by
means of collective suggestion into a belief in a supposed Apparition of the Mother of Jesus of Nazareth to three children jockeyed
into this shameful spectacle . . ."

The pamphlet regarded the children as "poor little dupes,"
unwitting players in a larger scheme to undermine the "realms of
Truth, Reason, and Science," and not incidentally to bilk the public for financial gain. It was, in the opinion of an editorial writer
in *O Século*, a transparent attempt to create a thriving tourist trap,
"whose revenue source is any mineral spring existing in the depths
of the mountains that has been discovered by someone who, in
the name of religion, wants to transform the Serra de Aire into a
miraculous resort like Lourdes."

The reaction from secular society wasn't just rhetorical. The
seven-year-old Portuguese Republic, already undermined by debt,
food shortages, labor unrest, and a ruinous war, was facing a resurgence of Catholic sentiment and a degree of monarchist nostalgia.
The religious commotion at Fatima was the last thing the republicans needed, and one night, ten days after the "Miracle of the Sun,"
a group of fed-up pragmatists from nearby towns got into a motor-
car and drove to the Cova, where they took away the arch with its
lanterns, several homemade crosses, and the table that served as
an altar. They also chopped down what they thought was the holm
oak upon which the Virgin had appeared, but it turned out—at least
according to Lucia and other believers—that it was the wrong tree.
If they missed the real one, it was probably because it was only a
stump now, whose limbs and branches had already been stripped
away by the faithful for holy relics. The republican marauders created a spectacle of the artifacts they had stolen, parading them

sarcastically through the streets of Santarém. The reaction of believers to this desecration was, of course, outrage—"the whole population," wrote a prominent Catholic doctor to the minister of the interior, ". . . was disgusted at this degrading action on the part of a few people who can only be called pustules of society."

But there was also a more widespread revulsion that crept into the pages of secular newspapers like *O Século*, which viewed the episode as a "disgrace" and pointed out that it was a bad look for the same authorities who had suppressed Catholic processions to allow one for the purpose of religious mockery. It was an attitude that was becoming more indicative of the country as a whole, and the pilgrim crowds that kept returning to Fatima after the events of October 13 were vivid evidence that the republic had gone too far and was vulnerable to a political recoil.

That happened less than two months after the final apparitions, when a right-wing populist named Sidónio Pais overthrew the government in a brief, bloody coup and proclaimed a "Crusade of Regeneration." Part of the regeneration involved reallowing open Catholic practice into Portuguese life and reabsorbing the idea that Portugal was "born under Our Lady's mantle." Pais himself, as a self-infatuated dictator, seems to have flirted pretty strongly with that idea. One of his guards reported that the new "president-king" believed himself to be protected by the Virgin. If that was true, the Virgin must have decided to stand down. Pais was assassinated just over a year after he stormed into office, and Portugal continued along the path of civil war and upheaval that led to the government changing hands forty-four times until 1926, when a military coup set the stage for the long-running dictatorship of António Salazar.

All this was part of a momentous cycle of changes that no doubt would have still happened if a ten-year-old girl had not believed she had seen the Virgin Mary, or if tens of thousands of people had not been reported to have seen the sun spinning in the sky. But it's safe to say that it would not have happened in the same way. And it was not the first time that the revelations of Fatima would deeply insinuate themselves into world events.

7

The Hypnotic Current

Father John de Marchi, in his influential account of the sun's aerial gyrations at the Cova da Iria on October 13, emphasized something else that happened just afterward. "The people, who had been soaked by the rain, found themselves suddenly and completely dry." This was evidence to de Marchi that the Blessed Virgin had not just made the sun dance but "had multiplied her miracles in order absolutely to confirm the veracity of the children."

"No one," he continued, "can escape from these hard facts inexplicable by the ordinary laws of nature."

Like many Catholic children of my time, I grew up not just believing in miracles, but expecting them. "Hard facts" were so richly interwoven with issues of faith that there was no compelling impulse to separate them. But when it comes to the Fatima story, the Miracle of the Sun is the event that forces you to take sides. Was there a miracle or not? Nobody but Lucia, Francisco, and Jacinta claimed to have seen or heard the Virgin Mary, but there were plenty of onlookers at the Cova that day who insisted they had beheld the spinning sun with their own eyes and experienced the way the ground and their clothes had unnaturally transitioned in an instant from sodden to dry.

But, as a number of skeptical writers have pointed out, there is no clear visual evidence of the sun's strange behavior. Newspaper photographers, like Judah Bento Ruah, were on the scene that day. Ruah, on assignment from *O Século*, had come from Lisbon with Avelino de Almeida. The thirteen powerful photographs he took that morning of October 13, particularly the images of pilgrims kneeling and staring up in wonder at the sky, make up the scant but iconic visual record of the Miracle of the Sun. No doubt there were other professional or amateur photographers there as well, but if any of them were able, with the cameras available in 1917, to record a sudden atmospheric occurrence, none of the results have survived. Other photos that are often offered as evidence of the miracle are either clearly fabrications or, in the case of the most widely circulated one, an image of a solar eclipse taken not at Fatima in 1917 but near the town of Torres Novas in 1921. And nothing beyond the words of the witnesses testifies to the sudden-evaporation phenomenon that was said to have happened in that rain-drenched landscape, though at least one Miracle of the Sun scholar points to the blurry shadows on the "nose, eye and naso-labial fold" of a girl in one of Ruah's photos as evidence (that I've tried fruitlessly to follow) that the drying could not have been the work of the sun or the wind.

Had the sun actually moved so erratically in the sky, or had there been an eclipse or some other hard astronomical fact, it would have been seen the world over, but no observatories made note of it. A prominent Portuguese poet, Afonso Lopes Vieira, was at his seaside veranda about twenty-five miles from Fatima and reported that he saw "a remarkable spectacle in the sky." At the village of Alburitel, almost ten miles away, a young boy—later to become a priest—testified that the "people were shouting and weeping and pointing to the sun." But there are few other indications that anyone other than the people gathered at the Cova da Iria witnessed anything unusual. The bishop of Leiria, in a pastoral letter, seized on the fact that the movement of the sun was a local-ized spectacle, not a world-ranging one, as proof that it could not have been a natural event, and therefore had to be a miracle. And he had it both ways by insisting that the reports of some people who saw the phenomenon from a distance constituted "a fact which destroys any theory of collective hallucination."

One of the most indefatigable Fatima chroniclers I've come across (and that's saying something) is Frère Michel de la Sainte Trinité, a member of the Little Brothers of the Sacred Heart—a congregation that was established in Algeria by a former cavalry officer who published the first Tuareg-French dictionary before being assassinated in 1916. Frère Michel has written three massive and exhaustive volumes about the apparitions, the children, the mysterious Third Part of the Secret, and of course the Miracle of the Sun. The "solar prodigy" of October 13, 1917, he insists, "is an unquestionable fact, a solidly established historical event. It is more solidly established than the mass of facts firmly maintained by history, that it would never occur to anybody to suspect."

True enough, sort of. There are more firsthand accounts from people who said that the sun spun wildly in the sky that day at Fatima than there are for, say, the assassination of Julius Caesar. Beginning with what Avelino de Almeida described for *O Século*—how the sun "whirled on itself like a giant Catherine wheel"—there are dozens of similar descriptions, either set down close to the time of the incident or recalled many years later in interviews. "Up to the present," wrote Father de Marchi in his book, whose first edition was published in 1950, "we have not met a single person among the many we have questioned who has not confirmed this phenomenon."

But the estimates of the number of people who were at the Cova that day range from thirty thousand to one hundred thousand, which leaves tens of thousands of people who presumably saw the sun dancing in the sky but didn't report it, didn't remember it, didn't say anything about it to their children, didn't think it was divinely orchestrated, or didn't notice it in the first place.

The same is true of occurrences, to pick one example, like the one that took place in Lubbock, Texas, in 1988, where a crowd of twelve thousand people flocked to the grounds of a charismatic Catholic church. They were there because one of the church's parishioners claimed she had been in contact with the Virgin Mary and had predicted that a miracle would take place on the Feast of the Assumption. It was an overcast day, but in the middle of an outdoor Mass the sun broke through the clouds and people began to point excitedly to the sky, weeping and praying and declaring to one another that they saw Mary there, or Jesus, or the gates of heaven opening. But there were almost two hundred thousand other people living in Lubbock at the time, under the same sky, and to them it was an ordinary summer day.

Similar "miracles of the sun," in which crowds of expectant people believed they saw some blessed message in the sky, have taken place all over the world and, probably, all throughout human existence. During the twentieth century, in addition to Fatima and Lubbock, there were religiously charged solar occurrences in France, Belgium, Italy, Germany, and Rwanda. Auguste Meessen, a Belgian physicist and professor at the Catholic University of Louvain, sorted through these incidents and made a list of familiar characteristics, which included, as at Fatima, the impression of a solar disc hovering in the sky, throwing off beautiful colors, then seeming to rotate and plummet toward earth. "Most observers," he wrote, "had noted slight local changes in the luminosity of the solar disc, as if there were some kind of images, but they were unable to recognize what they could represent."

Believers, or at least people on the edge of belief, were naturally more likely at Fatima to attribute an unusual meteorological occurrence to the fulfillment of Lucia's prophecy that a miracle would occur. Avelino de Almeida, the journalist whose eyewitness account in *O Século*—the paper with the widest circulation in the country—created a sensation and helped lay the descriptive groundwork for the future testimony of other witnesses, is often cited as a dispassionate secular observer who had something of a conversion experience at the Cova da Iria. But Almeida was a former seminarian who, though he wrote for what one Catholic writer described as a "radical and Jacobinist" daily, was not hostile to religion and might have been susceptible himself to an observation he made in that year of war and upheaval: "Times of great calamities have always revived and renewed religious ideas." If he did have an epiphany, it may have been short-lived. "I looked hard," a friend remembered Almeida saying in contradiction to his own article, "but I admit that I did not see anything special."

The correspondent for a local newspaper in Ourém, six or seven miles away from Fatima, was less impressed from the start. "Mass suggestion immediately caught these thousands of believers and the curious . . . And thousands of 'suggested' people, and who knows if they were confused by the very light of the sun which appeared for the first time that day, fell to the ground, crying and holding out their instinctively joined hands."

If you're inclined, as I am, to rule out an actual miracle, mass suggestion is probably the simplest answer to the behavior of the crowd that day as they stared up in wonder at the sky. Whatever it was that might have triggered that response in the first place has never been nailed down. Just like the conspiracy theories that flow from the Kennedy assassination, there is an ocean of speculative literature that you could spend a lifetime paddling through without ever reaching solid earth.

Was the strange disclike presence in the sky the result of the sun's refraction, or of ice crystals, or of volcanic or Saharan dust? Was it a sun dog, also known as a parhelion, or was this a case of pareidolia, the human tendency to impose a human image on random visual patterns, like the sightings of the Virgin Mary on screen doors, or tree stumps, or even tortillas, that have created pop-up shrines and attracted thousands of worshippers?

"A clear-cut, sharp-edged, brilliantly shining disk . . . It looked like a polished ring cut out from the pearly insides of a shell." That's the way another eyewitness, José Maria de Almeida Garrett, described the sun, or the sunlike object, that he saw that day at the Cova da Iria. Garrett was a lawyer, not particularly religious, who was there out of curiosity and testified that he observed the events "coolly and calmly, without any emotion or fear."

It's that sort of description that has, naturally enough, created undying speculation that the erratic thing in the sky was not a miraculous demonstration but an alien spaceship. Here's how the authors Joaquim Fernandes and Fina d'Armada account for the appearance of the Virgin Mary in volume 1 of their three-volume "meticulous synthesis of history, science and Ufology": "A 'special cloud' appeared in the sky, approaching from the direction of Spain to the East. From that 'cloud,' which surrounded a portal bearing craft, a silver globe emerged . . . From this globe, a beam of focused light was emitted that served as a kind of transport sending the Being to the small oak tree."

═══════

Something unusual, it seems to me, did happen in the sky over the Cova da Iria that day, some refraction or other distortion of the sun's light in the aftermath of a downpour that Lucia noticed in her ecstatic state just after the Virgin Mary withdrew from her sight and retreated back into heaven. That's when she called out "Look at the sun!" and everyone around her followed her gaze, saw the now-cloudless sky and some peculiar meteorological effect in it, and cried out "Miracle, miracle! Wonderful, wonderful!" in a chain reaction of worshipful credulity.

The fact that Lucia had predicted three months earlier, after the July apparition, that the Lady would perform a miracle on this very day is further proof to believers that the mysterious sky formation could not have been a coincidence. But it's easy enough to argue the opposite: that Lucia's prediction had created an irresistible expectation among a beleaguered rural Catholic population for whom supernatural intervention in earthly life was part of the fabric of belief. It had happened before, at Lourdes, at La Salette, and at other places in Europe where children had seen the unseen and proclaimed themselves to be the custodians of divine messages and prophecies, and now there was every indication that it was going to happen again in Fatima Parish.

═══════

In 1975, fifteen years after the pope was supposed to release the contents of the Fatima Letter, and twenty-five years before he finally did, I met a man named Ray Stanford, who was the leader of a nonprofit corporation called the Association for the Understanding of Man (AUM). Stanford had written a book called *Fatima Prophecy*. He considered himself a medium, in touch with some sort of ur-intelligence called the Source, and his book was largely a transcription of things the Source had revealed to him while he was in a trance. Among other things, he was informed that the Miracle of the Sun was the work of "beings and manifestations of *levels of intelligence* from high regions within the astral, the etheric, the causal, that have been active in every age of human experience."

But it was not Fatima that brought me into contact with Stanford. I was writing a magazine article about a subsidiary initiative of AUM's called Project Starlight International (PSI), whose purpose was to signal passing UFOs, send them messages via a laser, and perhaps receive messages in return. On a dark, clear November night I joined the PSI team as they deployed their VECTOR (Video Experiment Console for Transitional Overt Response) to monitor the skies for any extraterrestrial beings that might want to be in touch. The team members wore identical white jumpsuits with the PSI logo stitched above the left pocket, radiation goggles, and a name tag. "This isn't a game," Stanford explained to me. "It's a dangerous undertaking. That's one reason we wear name tags out there—should we be killed, people will at least be able to identify us."

I didn't think I was in any danger. I didn't believe in UFOs, though I was delighted to entertain the idea that they might exist and that perhaps that very night one might fly past and spot the signal emanating from a lonely patch of Texas ranchland. As I was writing this chapter about the Miracle of the Sun, my mind returned to that long-ago night, standing with the PSI team as ninety-one spotlights, arranged in a circle, took turns flashing in a complicated messaging sequence, and as a magnetometer—to detect the supposed magnetic propulsion of alien spacecraft—emitted a series of eerie beeps.

As the night wore on, my reporter's mind observed and took notes from a skeptical and—I must admit—somewhat superior distance. But I was aware that there was a part of me that wasn't logically resisting but was magically yearning. I wanted to see the answering signal of a UFO high up in the night sky, and it would not have taken all that much to convince me that I had.

Had I been at the Cova da Iria on October 13, 1917, packed in around many thousands of people, straining to catch a glimpse of three young children on their knees in front of the remnants of an oak tree, watching their lips move as they spoke to an invisible presence, I doubt that I would have been any more resistant to the possibility of a supernatural occurrence than I was on that lonely night in 1975—especially when the punishing rain suddenly stopped and the after-storm optics imparted a beguiling clarity and movement to the sun or its refracted image. The testimony of a civil registry officer named Luís António Vieira de Magalhães e Vasconcelos, later to become the fourth Baron of Alvaiázere, carries—for an ex-but-never-quite-ex-enough Catholic like me—a haunting note of surrender.

Vieira de Magalhães had come to Fatima as a curious observer, not a pilgrim. When he arrived at the Cova, a place he found "wild and uninteresting," where the rain was still falling and the wind was howling down from the Serra, he ran into some friends who wanted to know what he thought. He told them that he thought it was all "blague," claptrap. He was a Catholic, but he wouldn't believe in a miracle unless it was something clear and unmistakable.

"I was absolutely convinced I would see nothing," he wrote. "I remembered the principle of Gustave Le Bon [the French author of a widely read book on crowd psychology], about the way a group of people can be dominated by a hypnotic current. I had to be careful to not let myself be influenced."

But whatever precautions he took turned out not to be enough. As soon as the clouds parted and he saw the "dull silver disk" that seemed to encircle the sun, his suppressed longing to witness a miracle tore through his barricade of rational thought, and he cried out, "I believe! I believe! I believe!"

8

Bearer of God

Those who were convinced they had witnessed a miracle at Fatima had no doubts about who had made it happen. It was the work of Mary, a real person who had once existed on the earth and given birth to Jesus, but who as Our Lady had transcended time and death and history and now resided eternally everywhere. She was not just the Mother of God but, in so many yearning and suffering human hearts, was felt to be the mother of us all.

So as startling as the apparitions were to the *pastorinhos* of Aljustrel, as miraculous as the movement in the sky seemed to the pilgrims at the Cova, there was nothing unfamiliar about the shimmering female presence who had descended from heaven. They all knew her; they all knew what she was supposed to look like. She was the relatable, unpunishing, sorrowing and forgiving female presence that had been at the heart of Christian worship since at least the year 431, when the Council of Ephesus, meeting in what is now Turkey, officially decreed that Jesus Christ's mother should be honored with the Greek description *Theotokos*, "Bearer of God."

The stylized image of the Virgin Mary—her blue cloak, her arms spread in welcome or benediction, her sword-pierced Immaculate Heart, her feet crushing Satan in his Garden of

Eden snake disguise—had been a powerful visual touchstone in the childhoods of Lucia, Francisco, and Jacinta. It had been the same for me in my own childhood, a half century later. The Virgin Mary—represented in prayerbook illustrations, on holy cards, in church statues and plastic figurines—was in almost every room we entered.

The images varied to some degree, but they were mostly benevolent and static, depictions not so much of a human woman but of a goddess who, at moments of her choosing, would slip from behind heaven's curtain to mysteriously present herself to the faithful.

I had my first real encounter with something more interesting than the standard iconography when I was fifteen. I was a Boy Scout, on my way to the National Jamboree in Valley Forge, Pennsylvania, when our troop made a brief detour and visited the 1964 World's Fair in Flushing Meadows, New York. One of the must-see attractions was Michelangelo's *Pietà*. The church had allowed the sculpture to leave Saint Peter's Basilica, where it had resided since the late fifteenth century, to cross the ocean in a specially constructed watertight container with an emergency locator beacon—in case it ended up at the bottom of the ocean—and be placed on exhibit in the Vatican Pavilion at the fair.

Inside that pavilion, you didn't just see the *Pietà*. You glided past it on a moving sidewalk to the droning rhythms of sacred music. The white Carrara marble of the statue shone brilliantly against a serene blue backdrop created by Jo Mielziner, the same Broadway stage designer who had created the scenery for *South Pacific* and *A Streetcar Named Desire*. The statue itself, in that setting, was distant and unapproachable, the object of an exercise in enforced awe. Even so, even as I felt that I was on a surreal slow-motion ride at Disneyland, I was startled by something vivid and real I had never seen in any other depiction of Mary. I was hypnotized by her face and bearing as she cradled the body of her crucified son.

I understood that in some sense it was all wrong. Mary was grieving over the death of a thirty-three-year-old man, but she herself had the look of a teenager. Michelangelo had been young himself when he carved the *Pietà*—still in his early twenties—and he was drawn to the idea of a virginal figure whose youth could never be taken away. But I experienced the *Pietà* that day, as millions of others have throughout the centuries, not as a distortion of reality but as an expression of authenticity. There was something seamlessly true about it. It defied reality at the same time it defined a reality of its own. The eerie setting—the moving sidewalks, the lighting and heaven-blue backdrop—made it seem as if it existed outside of time. And the face of Mary, strangely expressionless but also touchingly specific, portrayed a particular woman's sadness, serenity, strength, and beauty.

If Jesus Christ was once an actual person, as most scholars believe he was—not just because he's the focus of the Gospels, but because of more neutral and fleeting references to him from ancient historians like Flavius Josephus and Tacitus—then he had to have had a mother. He was, as Saint Paul said in his Epistle to the Galatians, in the earliest reference to Mary, "born of a woman." But who was this woman, and how did she become the Christian world's undying mother figure?

We know almost nothing about her. In the four Gospels of the New Testament, she is at best a minor character, referenced occasionally but never given the spotlight, except for the moment in Luke's Gospel when the angel Gabriel appears to a bewildered girl in Nazareth to tell her she's about to be made miraculously pregnant with the Son of God. That moment is known as the Annunciation. "Hail, full of grace," the angel declares, "the Lord is with thee; blessed art thou among women." I'm quoting the Douay-Rheims translation of the Bible here, revised and brought up to date by Bishop Richard Challoner in the mid-eighteenth century. It's the version of the Gospels that is most familiar to Catholics of my vintage, and it's the basis of the Hail Mary prayer that is encoded in our beings.

Mary was espoused but not yet married to Joseph, a carpenter who was descended, through many generations, from the House of David, and before that—according to the Gospel of Matthew—all the way back to Abraham. Luke traces his lineage even farther back, to Adam in the Garden of Eden.

In Matthew's telling, when Joseph learned that Mary was pregnant, he "was minded to put her away privately." But then an angel visited him in his sleep and told him not to worry. Mary was still a virgin, because the father of the baby she carried wasn't a man at all but the Holy Ghost. The angel said they were to call the baby Jesus and that he was going to "save people from their sins." So the marriage went ahead, and Joseph "knew her not till she brought forth her firstborn son." Matthew does not answer the intriguing question if he ever "knew" her after that, or if "firstborn son" implied that a second son came later, a matter that would be of some importance to the developing church lore that Mary was "ever-virgin."

If Joseph was initially suspicious of Mary and wanted to hide her away and call off the marriage, she herself was just as understandably perplexed when Gabriel visited her with the news that she was going to have a baby. "How shall this be done," Mary asked him, "because I know not man?" The answer, that "the Holy Ghost shall come upon thee, and the power of the most High shall overshadow thee," was enough for her to accept that she was now "the handmaid of the Lord." But Gabriel also told Mary that her cousin Elizabeth, well past childbearing age, had also miraculously conceived a son, though apparently through conventional means and not by the Holy Ghost. When Mary visits her cousin, Elizabeth feels her baby (who will be John the Baptist) "leap" in her womb. She greets Mary with words that became part of the Hail Mary: "Blessed art thou among women, and blessed is the fruit of thy womb."

The Annunciation is the most detailed of the scant biographical references to Mary in the New Testament. She is present, of course, for the birth of Jesus in Bethlehem, and in Luke's narrative she takes the baby to Jerusalem to be presented at the temple, where she and Joseph meet an old man named Simeon whom God had promised to keep alive until he could lay his eyes upon "the consolation of Israel," meaning the long-promised savior. Simeon is filled with rapturous excitement when he sees Mary's baby, but then turns to her and tells her, in a reference to the pain she will experience at the future crucifixion of this same child, that "thy own soul a sword shall pierce."

Luke recounts how Jesus, at the age of twelve, was taken again at Passover to the temple in Jerusalem and ended up being separated from his parents for three days. When they finally found him, he was in the process of beguiling a group of learned men with his probing questions. When Mary, frantic with worry, chastises her son for running off, he tells her, "Did you not know that I must be about my father's business?" Mary is confused and doesn't quite grasp what he means, but she "kept all these words in her heart" as her son grows up and stars in a narrative of prophecy and sacrifice in which she is rarely mentioned. We do glimpse her in John's Gospel at a wedding feast in the town of Cana, and get a forceful impression of her when, after she realizes that the wedding guests have run out of wine, she instructs her son to work his first miracle. Despite his protest that "my hour has not yet come," he bends to her maternal will and transforms the contents of six water pots into wine.

The Gospel of John is the only reference in the New Testament to Mary being present at the crucifixion, but the image of a mother who has witnessed the torture and death of her son, has been pierced with the sword of grief, is central to the world's understanding of Mary. Her sacred suffering has inspired countless works of art as mournfully sublime as the *Pietà* or the thirteenth-century Stabat Mater hymn that we still sang in Catholic school in the 1950s and whose lyrics expressed a very Catholic longing to experience a consuming, cleansing pain. "Holy Mother!" it pleads, "pierce me through; / In my heart each wound renew / Of my Savior crucified . . ."

In John's telling, Mary is at the foot of the cross as her son is dying his terrible death. He looks down at her, and at John, "the disciple . . . whom he loved," and tells Mary, "Woman, behold thy son," and then tells John, "Behold thy mother."

"And from that hour, the disciple took her to his own."

That moment—of Jesus placing his mother in the care of his most beloved disciple—is the last we hear about Mary in any of the four Gospels. She is mentioned once more in another New Testament book, the Acts of the Apostles, where she is included in a group of people who gather in an upper room to pray after Jesus has risen from the dead, but we're not told if she was among the eleven remaining apostles to whom he appeared before ascending into heaven.

There are multiple inspirational or biographical texts produced by early Christians that were not included in the Bible along with the books of Matthew, Mark, Luke, and John. These apocryphal—i.e., secret or hidden—Gospels include narratives like the Protevangelium of James. "Protevangelium" translates to "first gospel," but not in the sense that it was written before the canonical texts; it was probably composed many years later, sometime in the mid-to-late second century. It was "first" only in a chronological story sense, since it attempted to flesh out the skimpy backstory of the Mother of Christ.

In James's Gospel, we meet Mary's parents, Joachim and Anna, who are having difficulty conceiving a child until they are visited by an angel who tells them their prayers have been answered and they are going to have a baby after all. It's not a virgin birth. In fact, James is pretty graphic about childbirth and gynecological matters in general. After Anna gives birth to Mary, the gospel tells us, she "cleaned herself up from her discharges."

We read about Mary's first birthday party, her presentation at the temple, and her betrothal to Joseph, who in this version of the story is an old man who already has sons of his own. "She's a young girl," he tells the priest who has selected him to be Mary's husband. "I'll be the laughing-stock of the sons of Israel!" He's even more put out when he discovers that his sixteen-year-old bride-to-be is pregnant. "Who has ensnared me?" he howls. "Who has done this wicked thing in my house? Who has enticed this virgin away from me and defiled her?"

His mind is set at ease by another visit from an angel, who assures him that the girl is still a virgin and has been made pregnant by the Holy Spirit; but there is more drama to come, including the moment soon after Jesus is born when the midwife who had been assisting Mary tells another woman, named Salome, that "a virgin has given birth." Salome won't believe her "unless I insert my finger and examine the hymen." She does just that, and in punishment for her unbelief her hand is burned off—temporarily, because it's restored when, now a believer, she picks up the holy infant.

James's account has a different and more direct tone than the canonical Gospels. It reads more like a folktale, or like a spin-off designed to account for the origin story of revered characters. It's a brief book of twenty-five very short chapters, and after the gynecological exam that Salome subjects her to, we learn nothing more about Mary—nothing about her experiences as the mother of Jesus, or her life after his crucifixion.

Scholars have inferred from John's reference in his own Gospel to himself obeying Jesus's command and taking Mary "to his own," that he brought her with him to Ephesus, where she lived out her life. Whatever her remaining life held for her is a historical unknown, though its conclusion has been provided by centuries of tradition and dogma.

John may have become Mary's surrogate son, but what about James, who according to Saint Paul in his Epistle to the early Christians in the Roman province of Galatia, was the "brother of the Lord," and is the purported author of the Protevangelium? Was he Mary's stepson, one of the children of Joseph's previous marriage? Or was he indeed Christ's brother, not born of the Holy Spirit like Jesus, but humanly conceived by a man and a woman?

It was an awkward question for the church, which from early on placed a massive emphasis on the idea of Mary being, in the words of a fifth-century priest named Proclus, "the untarnished vessel of virginity." Mark refers to James in his Gospel, along with three others he identifies as brothers of Jesus—Joseph, Jude, and Simon. There are also unnamed sisters scattered throughout the New Testament. None of that has ever made much of a dent in the core Catholic belief that Mary was not only conceived without original sin (the Immaculate Conception) but remained the embodiment of purity throughout her life.

The author Miri Rubin puts the need for some kind of work-around succinctly in her book *Mother of God: A History of the Virgin Mary*. "If Jesus was more than he ever claimed to be in his lifetime—if he were a god—then a number of powerful truths followed: every aspect of his life had to agree with the claim of divinity. Jesus' life had to be worthy of his death and his emergent divinity. None of these assertions about Jesus' nature could be made without reference to the body that had borne him, the person who had nurtured him, Mary."

In giving birth to a god, Mary's body had to be incorruptible, untainted, a "closed gate" in the words of one fourth-century bishop. Another theologian of that century concluded that she would have been exempt from "the primeval curse" of menstruation, and that it was unthinkable that she would have had to experience any painful contractions or messy discharges while delivering her son in the stable of Bethlehem.

It was so important to keep her clear from potentially repellent bodily issues that the church created the dogma of the Assumption, the belief that upon her death Mary did not leave behind a corpse like the rest of humanity but was "assumed" into heaven. "She," wrote Pope Pius XII in 1950 in an encyclical called *Munificentissimus Deus,* "by an entirely unique privilege, completely overcame sin by her Immaculate Conception, and as a result she was not subject to the law of remaining in the corruption of the grave, and she did not have to wait until the end of time for the redemption of her body."

―――――

The theological speculation, dogma, and tradition that attached itself to Mary over time led to the creation of an immaterial, imaginary being who might have been free of birth pangs but was so vulnerable to her own exquisite sorrow that she embodied all the pain in the world. As the thinking about her expanded and evolved, the Virgin Mary became a goddess who could fulfill a human longing for mercy and intervention in a range of cultures throughout the reach of history. One of the earliest apparition stories arose from Walsingham, England, where at a disputed date sometime in the eleventh or twelfth century a noblewoman named Richeldis de Faverches claimed to have seen the Virgin and traveled with her to the Holy Land to visit the house in Nazareth where the Annunciation had taken place. During the Middle Ages in Europe, there were folkloric accounts of Mary dropping in to rub ointment on the sore knee of a nun who had spent too much time kneeling, or visiting a young girl who was so in danger of being seduced by "foolishness and games" that the Virgin decided she was better off dying and going to heaven, where no such temptations existed. In addition to Lourdes and La Salette in France, the Virgin made another nineteenth-century appearance in the western Ireland village of Knock, where in 1879 a group of twenty-five or so people believed they saw her, in the company of Saint Joseph and Saint John the Evangelist and various angels, shimmering upon the wall of the parish church. Among the many apparition claims that have taken place since Fatima was a series that began occurring in 1961 in the Spanish village of San Sebastián de Garabandal, where four eleven- and twelve-year-old girls said an angel appeared to them with news that they were about to receive a visit from the Virgin Mary, who appeared the next day and routinely for four years. And then there is the major contemporary site of Medjugorje, in Bosnia-Herzegovina. Like Fatima and so many other places where such phenomena have taken place, it is a remote European village that was in the midst of a tense, destabilizing time. On June 24, 1981, a variation of the familiar narrative began to unfold, this time sparked by six teenagers— four girls and two boys—who said they saw a vision of Gospa (the Virgin Mary) at a place known today as Apparition Mountain. She appeared before them the next day and is still claimed to do so every day, though only three of the now-middle-aged visionaries say they continue to see her. "Our Lady usually appears for Her daily apparitions," the Medjugorje website confidently reports, "every evening in Medjugorje at 6:40 p.m. or at 5:40 p.m. Daylight Savings Time."

As at Fatima, the visionaries said that Our Lady entrusted secrets to them—ten in all, which "when it is time" will be announced to the world. Of these, the most crucial seems to be the third secret, a deliberate echo of Fatima, and one that seems to promise a miracle, a "lasting sign" that will appear on Apparition Mountain and will be visible to everyone who goes to Medjugorje to see it—"a beautiful, indestructible, permanent sign."

Over a million people travel to Medjugorje every year from all over the world, five million to Fatima, even more to Lourdes. But it was in the New World, not in Europe, where the Virgin Mary made her most resounding visitation. This happened, or was said to have happened, in December of 1531, only ten years after the Spanish conquest of the Aztec Empire. The accounts are variable and suspect, made up of threads of folklore and church tradition, but the clearest distillation of the story centers around a man who in preconquest times was named Cuauhtlatoatzin. He was now a widower in his fifties, which meant that he had been well into his adulthood in 1519, when Hernán Cortés and the Spanish adventurers he led first encountered the wondrous Aztec city of Tenochtitlan, which to European eyes was an undreamed-of metropolis built upon a series of lakes in the Valley of Mexico.

Cuauhtlatoatzin would have been part of a world that was transformed in a way no one could have imagined by the victory of the Spanish invaders. Suddenly the statues of Meso-American gods like Huitzilopochtli were torn from their altars and replaced by images of the Virgin Mary. Great cathedrals were built from the stones of torn-down pyramids. In order to survive the new regime, or perhaps from some genuine conversion experience, people from Tenochtitlan and outlying cities allowed themselves to be baptized and took on Christian names. That's how Cuauhtlatoatzin became Juan Diego.

According to an account written in Nahuatl almost a century later, the Virgin Mary appeared to Juan Diego at the top of a hill known as Tepeyac. She was, she told Diego, "the mother of the very true deity God, the giver of life, the creator of people, the ever present, the lord of heaven and earth."

She wanted a church built for the benefit of the people of Mexico City. "There," she said, "I will listen to their weeping and their sorrows . . ."

Juan Diego was instructed to go see Juan de Zumárraga, the bishop of Mexico, and tell him of the Virgin's request. He did so, was interrogated by the bishop and told to return with a sign demonstrating that he was telling the truth.

"Am I, your Mother, not here?" the woman said to Juan Diego when she appeared to him again on the hill. She told him to gather

some flowers—roses, as the tradition has it, blooming unseason-
ably in winter—that he found on the summit of Tepeyac. He took
off the cape—the tilma—that he wore around his shoulders and
carried them back to Zumárraga. When he opened his cape, the
out-of-season flowers tumbled onto the floor. What was even
more astonishing to the bishop was the discovery that the image
of the Virgin—her skin dark, her mantle greenish blue, her eyes
closed in prayer and her hands folded—had magically appeared on
the inside of Juan Diego's tilma.

Over the centuries, that image has become a universal and
cherished symbol of religious faith and political autonomy. The
Virgin of Guadalupe, with a complexion that reflected the skin
tones of an indigenous population whose world was disrupted and
turned upside down by Cortés, became both a cultural balm and a
continuing inspiration to a racial underclass ruled by an elite that
prized pure European blood. The army of Miguel Hidalgo, who
in 1810 incited the Mexican War of Independence against Spain,
carried a banner of the Virgin of Guadalupe into battle, as did the
peasant forces of Emiliano Zapata a century later.

I first saw the original tilma image—or what has long been
accepted by believers as the original—on a trip to Mexico City
in 1969. At that time, it was displayed in the old basilica that was
erected in the late seventeenth century at the base of Tepeyac.
There was a line of pilgrims at the entrance to the church, shuffling forward on their knees as they began the journey to the
altar where the image was displayed. It was a starkly uphill climb
because of the way the old church had sunk forward into the sub-
siding surface of the ancient lake where Tenochtitlan had once
stood.

The old basilica is still there, but a new one—much larger and
much more stable—was built in the 1970s, and that's where the
tilma is displayed today. When I went back to Mexico City recently,
I found myself on yet another Virgin Mary moving sidewalk, this
one passing behind the altar of the new basilica and beneath the
image of Our Lady of Guadalupe. The ancient cloth on which it
had been painted by a human hand or magically imprinted by the
Virgin herself was high above us, out of reach, encased in a complex frame of silver and gold. Most of the many people on the side-

walk with me were Mexicans who had no doubt grown up among uncountable reproductions of this image; now they were being mechanically ushered past the original as they stared up in awe or took photos with their cell phones.

The moving sidewalk, because it passed behind the altar, was invisible to the congregants in the vast basilica itself, but the hundreds of people in attendance there could still see Juan Diego's cloak behind the priest who was saying Mass. To the right of the altar hung several dozen flags representing the countries where the Virgin had also revealed herself to other confused or suffering mortals like the semimythical Juan Diego or the all-too-real Lucia Santos and Jacinta and Francisco Marto.

I walked through the great plaza in front of the open doors of the new basilica, past the ancient sinking church where I had first seen the tilma, and followed the flow of tourists to a modern polychrome sculpture on the flank of Tepeyac Hill that depicted Our Lady of Guadalupe, pointedly dark-skinned, manifesting herself before a line of bronze worshippers that included a muscular Aztec lord. In the thinking of a sixteenth-century friar who was concerned about lingering pagan beliefs, the people of the Valley of Mexico had recognized, long before the Spaniards came, a womanly entity known as Tonantzin, a Nahuatl word that translates as "our mother."

"This appears," wrote this priest, Bernardino de Sahagún, "to be an invention of the devil to cover over idolatry under the ambiguity of this name Tonantzin."

When I climbed the stairs to the top of Tepeyac, where another church had been built long ago to commemorate the place where Juan Diego had gathered his winter flowers and put them in his cloak, I looked down over the plaza in front of the basilica, where pilgrims and tourists were milling about, and where indigenous dancers in bright costumes were gearing up for some sort of prayerful ritual.

This timeless, sacred oasis in the heaving metropolis of Mexico City is the most popular pilgrimage destination for Catholics in the world, drawing yearly visitors that some estimates have placed as high as twenty million. It seemed to me that, Father de Sahagún's fears aside, idolatry and ambiguity were at the heart of its appeal. It transcended the imperial regimes of the Aztecs and the Spanish, just as it transcended logic. Whether her name was Mary or Tonantzin, there was in human nature an inborn longing for someone aware of our misery and our aspirations, someone who would say to us, as she said to Juan Diego, "Am I, your Mother, not here?"

9

I Am to Suffer Very Much

Lucia's flustered, uncertain prophecy that World War I would end on October 13, the day of the Virgin's final apparition, was off by more than a year. The armistice that effectively concluded the war was not signed until November 11, 1918. That was a month before the new president, Sidónio Pais, was shot in the Rossio railroad station in Lisbon by an aggrieved left-wing activist.

At around the same time of Pais's death, the influenza pandemic that likely had its origins at an army camp in Haskell County, Kansas, and then reached Europe with the American soldiers deploying to France in the last year of the Great War, was already adding to Portugal's destabilizing order. The disease had first appeared in the southern part of the country in May of 1918 and quickly spread to urban centers like Lisbon and Porto, and from there to remote villages like Fatima and Aljustrel.

Lucia's mother, Maria Rosa, almost died in the months between the October 1917 apparition and the onset of the pandemic. Lucia records that she had a "displaced kidney" and some sort of vertebral disorder when she had to make the grueling trip to the town of São Mamede to have her spine treated with hot needles.

Lucia believed that the Virgin Mary had heard her prayers and saved her mother from the ailments that had seemed to place her on her deathbed. But a far more indiscriminate storm of illness was spreading over Portugal. Maria Rosa, after she recovered, exposed herself and her husband to the flu pandemic with her usual tireless ministrations. "Look here," Maria Rosa lectured Antonio when he tried to keep her away from the houses of the sick, "how can we leave those people to die, without anyone there to give them a glass of water?"

"Those people" included, most grievously, the Marto family, who would ultimately lose four children to the disease. In 1918, a year or so after the October afternoon when the sun had seemed to dance in the sky, the entire family, except for the father, Manuel Marto, came down with the flu. It was an unusual virus that sought out the young and the healthy, tricking their robust immune systems into mounting a counterattack so furious that it often left a patient's lungs in ruins. It could kill swiftly, with blood erupting from feverish victims' mouths and nostrils, even their eyes, and their faces turning a deep cyanotic blue as they groaned with pain that arose from inflamed joints or perforated eardrums, or from ruptured lungs infiltrated with air pockets that gave off a crackling sound when the patient was moved.

In the case of Francisco and Jacinta, the suffering was more chronic, and at least to some degree episodic. During the six months or so that Francisco lived after contracting the disease, he had periods of improvement from which he would helplessly relapse. One thing that didn't abate was the relentless demands of the people who kept seeking out the children, swarming into their houses to lay eyes on the shepherds and demand blessings and holy favors from them.

They kept coming to the Cova, too. Even though there was no spring or any other source to provide the kind of healing water they had heard about at Lourdes and La Salette, the pilgrims looked to the soil for miracles, digging up the dirt around what remained of the holm oak trunk and rubbing it on influenza victims or others who were sick. Even though she was very ill herself, at one point in 1919 Jacinta managed to join in a procession to the Cova to ask the Virgin to end the pandemic. A simple chapel would soon be erected there, but as yet there was nothing but the dry, denuded ground that had taken over the pasturelands where Jacinta and her cousins had once grazed their sheep herd.

"He was so good," recalled Francisco's mother of her son's worsening illness, "that we thought he would get better but he always said that all the medicines were useless because Our Lady was coming to take him to Heaven."

"Are you suffering a lot, Francisco?" Lucia writes that she asked him on his sickbed.

"Quite a lot," she has him answer, "but never mind! I am suffering to console Our Lord, and afterwards, within a short time, I am going to Heaven!"

Such is the record that was left to us of Francisco's last days—an unvarying and hardly believable catalog of serenity, cheerfulness, and holiness. The agony and fear that this ten-year-old child must have experienced as he was dying do not figure into the accounts, except as opportunities to portray him in a selfless and devoted light. All that mattered to him, according to Lucia, was to go to confession—he had once stolen a coin to buy a music box—and then to receive his first communion, and then to die and go to heaven and wait for Jacinta and Lucia to join him.

He died in the Marto family's house in Aljustrel on April 4, 1919. It was a Friday morning. "A smile passed over his lips, as he drew his last breath," wrote John de Marchi in a typical passage of devotional literature. "Sweetly and calmly, without agony or suffering, his soul passed . . ."

Lucia walked behind the coffin the next day as it was taken from the Fatima church to the cemetery. She was weeping. "This grief," she wrote, in a rare statement unadorned with religious consolation, "was a thorn that pierced my heart for years to come."

Jacinta was too sick to attend her brother's funeral. For months, she had been barely able to get out of bed. In a welter of pain, delirium, and boredom, she believed that the Virgin Mary came to visit her and Francisco soon before he died.

"I am to suffer very much," she told Lucia. Our Lady had informed her that she was to go to two hospitals before she died. She imagined a hospital as a "big dark house" where she would be left all alone.

In July, her father took her to Saint Augustine's Hospital in Ourém. She was there for almost two months, losing weight, growing weaker, enduring various brutal treatments. By the time she came home to Aljustrel at the end of August, she was, Father Formigão wrote, "like a skeleton and her arms are shockingly thin." She now had a chronic, suppurating wound in her side, and her lungs were destroyed by pneumonia, pleurisy, and tuberculosis.

In her memoirs, Lucia wrote that the Virgin Mary visited Jacinta once again and told the girl that she would now be going to the second hospital, in Lisbon, where she would die alone. Jacinta of course was terrified. "I tried to comfort her," Lucia wrote, "saying: What does it matter if you die alone, as long as Our Lady is coming to fetch you?"

Indeed, she did go to Lisbon. In January of 1920, Father Formigão arrived at Jacinta's sickbed in Aljustrel in the company of a prominent doctor, who examined her and convinced her parents that desperate measures were called for. The doctor, along with others, including Luis António Vieira de Magalhães e Vasconcelos—the aristocratic civil registry officer who had been so moved by the sight of the dancing sun—would pay for the trip to Lisbon.

It was, Lucia recalled, "a heartrending farewell." As Jacinta threw her arms around her cousin's neck and sobbed, she told her to "never tell the Secret to anyone, even if they kill you."

She was taken by train to Lisbon, first to an orphanage, where she was looked after by a well-known pediatrician who diagnosed her with purulent pleurisy, among other conditions, and by a kindly mother superior who believed that "a little angel had come into my house."

But she would not stay there for long. Early in February, she was taken to Lisbon's Dona Estefânia Hospital. She lingered there in a children's ward for over a week, waiting for an operation that she begged the doctors not to perform, telling them it was useless because the Virgin Mary had already told Jacinta she would soon be taken up to heaven. Her mother stayed with her as long as she could but had to leave before the operation to go home to Aljustrel to take care of her other desperately ill children.

The procedure was gruesome. Because she was so weak, the

surgeon couldn't risk anything but a local anesthetic as he removed two of Jacinta's infected ribs, "leaving a wound in which a hand could be inserted."

She survived the operation to face an agonizing ten more days of life, screaming out Our Lady's name during the excruciatingly painful daily wound dressings. On the evening of February 20, 1920, she asked for a priest to hear her confession. She wanted to take communion as well, but the priest delayed, saying he would return in the morning. By then she had died. There are contradictory accounts of whether a nurse was present in her last moments, but Frere Michel de la Sainte Trinité, in his inexhaustible three-volume account of Fatima, insists that the nurse was out of the room.

"Everything was accomplished," he wrote. "The prophecy of Our Lady had been fulfilled: Jacinta died alone, without parents or friend, and without anyone to attend her in her last moments . . . What a sacrifice!"

Jacinta's ravaged body was dressed in a borrowed white first-communion dress, along with a blue sash the color of the Virgin Mary's mantle. Her open coffin was placed in the sacristy of a local church. Hundreds of believers flocked to see Jacinta's body, and a crowd made up a procession a few days later as the coffin was placed on a train and delivered to Ourém, where Luis António Vieira de Magalhães e Vasconcelos had arranged for it to be interred in his royal family's own burial plot.

The baron had notified Jacinta's father by letter that his daughter was dead. "When I arrived in the town," Manuel Marto remembered, "and saw that group of people round the coffin of my Jacinta . . . I broke down and cried like a child . . . I felt it had all been no good, all useless; she had been in the hospital two months and then gone to Lisbon and in the end she died all alone."

———

In July of 1919, a few months after Francisco's death and while Jacinta was growing sicker in the hospital in Ourém, Lucia wrote that God "came knocking on my door to ask yet another sacrifice." She was referring to her beloved but troubled father, Antonio Santos, the only member of her family who had innocently taken her at her word that she was the recipient of a visitation from the Virgin Mary. He was healthy as usual one day, dead the next. Lucia writes that he died of double pneumonia. She doesn't mention the pandemic, but a swift and lethal lung complication sounds like one of the hallmarks of the virus that had already taken the lives of many of the people whose homes Antonio and Maria Rosa had been visiting in their efforts to alleviate suffering.

Lucia was shattered by her father's death. "He was the only one," she wrote, "who never failed to show himself to be my friend, and the only one who defended me from the disputes aroused at home on account of me."

From time to time after the apparitions, various relatives and patrons had offered to take Lucia away from Fatima and the never-ending, suffocating curiosity that surrounded her and her doomed cousins. Maria Rosa had allowed her to go on three or four of these recuperative visits with trusted acquaintances or respected members of the clergy or the medical profession. After her father died, Lucia and her mother visited kindly benefactors who took them to the beach at Nazaré and to the cliffside chapel where legend said the Virgin had saved the life of Fuas Roupinho as his horse galloped heedlessly toward the abyss.

On another occasion, Father Formigão arranged for them to go to Lisbon to stay with a wealthy woman who had a chauffeur and a butler and five maidservants. She also had a private chapel, with a folded flag of the old monarchy concealed beneath the altar stone. Lucia's benefactor had a heart condition that kept her mostly confined to the house, where she attended Mass every morning and said the Rosary every evening.

One day, the woman took Lucia and her mother to the orphanage where Jacinta had first stayed when she arrived in Lisbon, and then to the Dona Estefânia Hospital, where she had had her desperate surgery. Lucia was shown the bed where, all alone except for the heavenly mother she believed was there with her, Jacinta had suffered and died.

The events of October 13—the promised last apparition of the Virgin Mary, at which the onlookers at the Cova da Iria believed they had seen a miracle in the sky—had been far from an ending. The pilgrims kept coming to the Cova, and their yearning and devotion only accelerated when they learned of the deaths of Francisco and Jacinta. A rumor that Jacinta's body was going to be returned to Fatima (something that wouldn't happen until 1935) helped to spark intense interest in a procession scheduled for May 13, 1920, the third anniversary of the initial appearance of the Virgin. By that time, a small chapel—the Chapel of the Apparitions—had been built near the remains of the holm oak, where a new statue, *The Virgin of Fatima,* was to be installed.

The growing Fatima cult and its vivid demonstration of the sway that Catholicism still had among a segment of the population was a threat to the shaky republican government. The local authorities—led in part by Artur de Oliveira Santos, the notorious abductor of the three shepherd children—launched an intense effort to make sure the procession didn't happen. "I must put a stop to this ridiculous fairy tale," Santos told his secretary.

The district officials cut off all vehicular transport to the Cova, roughed up some of the believers who made it there anyway, and managed to ensure that no coherent commemoration took place. Believers were intimidated enough to hide the new statue of the Virgin so it couldn't be confiscated and destroyed, and they kept away from the chapel because there were rumors that the republicans were planning to blow it up. (That didn't happen, but two years later it did, when Freemasons planted bombs in the chapel and blew off its roof.)

"The projected parade," Santos wrote afterward, "whereby the ignorance of illiterate people was to be exploited once again, was brought to nothing . . . However," he cautioned, "these authentic enemies of the Republic and promoters of Fatima are not yet entirely disarmed for they propose to transfer with all their pomps, the body of an unfortunate child and pretended intermediary of the Virgin, who died in Lisbon, to another tomb. They also still make use of a so-called seer, Lucia, an ailing child of thirteen years, in order further to exploit the ignorance of the people."

The new bishop of Leiria, José Alves Correia da Silva, was a theologian and devout follower of the Virgin Mary who had been exiled by the republican government and only recently allowed to return to Portugal. He had no doubts about the authenticity of the apparitions at the Cova and quickly bought land around the site to build a basilica and promote Fatima as a holy pilgrimage site.

But Lucia, the only one of the three *pastorinhos* who had survived the pandemic, presented a problem. Fatima was rapidly growing into a major symbol of Catholic resurgence against a godless government. The fact that it all hinged on a thirteen-year-old girl, who could be kidnapped again at any moment, or who could—with the onset of puberty or frustration at the never-ending demands of strangers—change her mind and decide that her visions had been a childish fantasy after all, made the bishop very nervous.

His solution was to send her off in secrecy to a religious school in Porto, over a hundred miles away. It was a cruel development for an exhausted, emotionally vulnerable girl who had just lost her father and her two best friends, and now was expected to leave her mother and surviving family and the only home she had ever known. "These thoughts and reflections made me so sad that going to Porto seemed to me like being buried alive."

"I know no one in Porto," she told the priest who had informed her what was expected of her.

"Rev. Fr Vicar replied . . . that it was precisely because I knew no-one in Porto and no-one in Porto knew me that it was appropriate for me to go there; [he added that] in order not to be recognized I would change my name, I would not say where I came from nor whose daughter I was, nor would I speak about any other member of my family."

Somehow Maria Rosa agreed to this fate for her daughter and bought her a suitcase, which Lucia clung to for the rest of her life as one of her few possessions from her childhood. The two of them woke up one June morning at two a.m. and "set off by the pale light of Our Lady's candle, the moon, passing Cova da Iria on the way, where we stopped to say the rosary." At the train station in Leiria, Maria Rosa said goodbye to her terrified daughter with a final warning: "Off you go, child, and if you really did see Our Lady, she will look after you. I entrust you to Her. But if you were telling lies, I don't know what will happen to you."

At her boarding school on the outskirts of Porto, Lucia was given a new name to disguise her identity—Maria das Dores, which translates as Mary of the Sorrows. She was a strange new presence to the other students, described in probably hyperbolic accounts as "a mountain maid" or even "a wild animal." They bombarded her with questions about where she was from and who her parents were, questions she was forbidden to answer. Eventually some of them figured it out, but she seems to have gone through her four years at the school without calling any more attention to herself than necessary. "I wanted seclusion," she wrote.

She didn't just want seclusion. After three years of being interminably interrogated, gawked at, beseeched, revered, and reviled, she craved it. When she graduated from her Catholic school, it was a natural development for someone with her blazing religious temperament and her need for concealment to enter religious life. She became a postulant and then a novice and then, in 1934—in a convent in the Spanish town of Tuy, just across the border from Portugal—she took her perpetual vows as a "bride of Christ" in the Sisters of Saint Dorothy.

Years before that day, when she was still a postulant in nearby Pontevedra, Lucia claimed to have had another vision. It happened on a December day in 1925 when "suddenly the room lit up and it was the light of my dear Mother in Heaven who came with the Child Jesus on a luminous cloud."

The Virgin had a grievance. She showed Lucia her Immaculate Heart "surrounded with thorns with which ungrateful men pierce me every moment by their blasphemies and ingratitude." In order to rectify this, she said, she needed people to confess, take communion, and say the Rosary and meditate on its Mysteries every first Saturday of the month for five consecutive months. The next year Lucia was taking out the garbage when she encountered a little boy who she realized was Jesus, and who complained that a lot of people were slacking off on their first-Saturday observances and were saying the Rosary "in a tepid and indifferent manner."

And then in 1929, she said, she was visited once again, this time when she was at the convent in Tuy. She was alone close to midnight in the chapel, praying on her knees, then lying on the floor, then upright with her arms outstretched. There was a blast of light, followed by the vision of a glowing cross with Jesus nailed to it, blood dripping from his wounds into a chalice. Hovering beneath his right arm was Our Lady of Fatima, holding her Immaculate Heart in her left hand, aflame and pierced by thorns.

When she spoke, she told Lucia that the pope and all the bishops of the world must "make the consecration of Russia to my Immaculate Heart." If they didn't do it, according to what Lucia claimed God himself confided to her later in an "intimate communication," "Russia will have already spread her error through the world."

This was a reprise of the demand the Virgin had made over a decade earlier, when she had appeared to the three shepherd children at the third apparition and told them the Secret, the second part of which included the same demand to consecrate Russia.

Consecration is a powerful but nebulous concept. It means solemn dedication, wholehearted spiritual surrender to some urgent purpose. Mary's Immaculate Heart was an actual thing to Lucia, who glimpsed it in moments of religious rapture; but to nonbelievers or non-ecstatics it is just one more puzzling symbol of suffering or supplication.

Also real to Lucia and the Christian world in general was the threat of Russia. Two months before the first apparition of the Virgin to Lucia and her cousins in May 1917, Czar Nicholas II had been forced to abdicate, ending the Romanov dynasty in Russia and giving way to a provisional government that was itself overthrown a few months later by Vladimir Lenin's Bolsheviks. By the time Lucia had her midnight vision in the chapel, Lenin was dead, and Joseph Stalin was the leader and ruthless embodiment of the Soviet Union.

How much of this history Lucia knew is uncertain. She was a child in 1917 when the Russian Revolution began, and a cloistered nun for much of the rest of her life. But she had grown to consciousness in a country that had itself experienced a revolution and overthrown its monarchy, and that had tried to expose the Catholic Church as a sinister and repressive force that built its power and wealth off the credulity of the populace.

Things had greatly changed in Portugal by 1929, but that only threw the threat of global communism into greater relief. The Portuguese revolution had collapsed into a series of coups and counter-coups, assassinations and military dictatorships, until it finally stabilized under an authoritarian, right-wing regime led by the devout and celibate António Oliveira Salazar, who had once studied for the priesthood and who maintained a private shrine to the Virgin Mary.

Lucia now lived and prayed far away from the magical hills and pastures of her childhood. But in her absence the pilgrimages to the Cova da Iria had only grown larger and the devotion to Our Lady of Fatima more intense. Fatima was becoming, in the words of the sociologist Jeffrey S. Bennett, "the spiritual capital of the nation—a mystical, holy place that was somehow both more and less 'real' than the rest of the country."

Lucia was thought to have written Pope Pius XI about her apparition of Jesus and the Virgin in the convent chapel, but he never replied. The pope, born Ambrogio Damiano Achille Ratti, had been as a young man a scholar of historic handwriting and a mountaineer who had once climbed the Matterhorn, but now he was in his seventies and liked to be left alone at lunchtime so he could listen to the radio. Although the pope had passed out Fatima holy cards to students at the Pontifical Portuguese College in Rome, one Vatican source claimed that he had no interest in Fatima or in mystical visions in general. "They say that I am [God's] Vicar on earth. If He had something that He wished me to know, He would tell it to me directly."

Nevertheless, on October 13, 1930, twenty-three years after the Miracle of the Sun, the church gave its official approval for the faithful to worship the Virgin of Fatima. That next year, the highest-ranking Portuguese church official, Cardinal Manuel Gonçalves Cerejeira, addressed three hundred thousand pilgrims at the Cova as he read a proclamation consecrating the nation to Mary's Immaculate Heart. "Take it from our fragile hands," he begged Our Lady, "into Your own; defend it and guard it as Your own property; make Jesus reign, conquer and rule in it."

His speech then grew foreboding. "Intercede for Portugal, O Our Lady, in this grave hour when from the East blow furious winds, bringing cries of death against Your Son and against the civilization founded on His teachings . . ."

Those were the sort of ominous words that still echoed to Catholic kids like me on the other side of the Atlantic three decades or more later, as we said our Hail Marys and studied our catechisms. Martyrdom, we were pretty sure, would be coming our way. Would we be strong enough to endure it, as we did our best to prevent communist Russia from inflicting any more distress on Mary's Immaculate Heart?

PART TWO

So That You May Crucify Yourself

10

Fatimized

Bishop Fulton J. Sheen looked like Dracula. He had a sharp, thin-lipped face, a piercing gaze, and over his bishop's garb—which included a floor-length, full-buttoned cassock, a foot-wide cincture band, and the shoulder-draping garment known as the pellegrina—he wore a spectacular cape, which he deployed with dramatic precision.

His cape, cincture, and skull cap were all bright scarlet, though on a black-and-white television screen of the 1950s they registered as soft gray. Still, you couldn't miss the theatricality of his outfit, or of his Bela Lugosi poses. His voice was oracular and almost sinister, though it was lightened somewhat by the trace of an Irish accent and, every so often, an abrupt, disarming smile.

He was an Emmy Award–winning television pioneer whose weekly show, *Life Is Worth Living*, aired in prime time. Even in a devout Catholic household like ours, he came across as maybe too Catholic, a near-caricature of piety and imperiousness.

But he was hypnotic, and in fuzzy old clips available to see on the internet he is hypnotic still. In an episode from 1954 he takes Fatima as the subject of his television sermon. October 13, 1917, the day of the final apparition in the Cova da Iria, he proclaims, "might almost be called the birthday of the modern world.

Because it was on that day that the forces of good and evil seemed to reach their peak."

Sheen tells us that three years before, on October 13, 1951, he had been among the million people who had come to Fatima to commemorate the Miracle of the Sun, and who waved their white handkerchiefs in the air as the little statue of Our Lady of Fatima was carried through the pavement expanse in front of the great basilica where the Cova once had been. He points out the contrast between "the white square of Fatima and the Red Square of Moscow" and says that "in my imagination I could see a great change coming over the hammer and the sickle. I could see that hammer that had beaten down so many homes and profaned so many sanctuaries. I could see it being held aloft by millions of men and looking now like a cross. And that sickle, which the communists use to cut human life like unripe wheat, I now saw as changing its figure and its symbolism and becoming, as the Book of the Apocalypse said, the moon under Our Lady's feet."

Russia must be converted! That was the existential theme of my Catholic childhood in the middle of the twentieth century. I was still a young child, but I knew from pronouncements like those of Bishop Sheen that I was living on history's knife edge. Enough unconfessed sins, enough unsaid Rosaries, and the balance of the world would tip from Catholicism to communism.

"World War Three *need not* happen!" Sheen warned in that same broadcast. "And it will not happen, if we as a nation return to God. If there is a Cold War here or anywhere else it is because our hearts and souls are not *on flame* with love of God!"

The contents of the Fatima Letter, which Lucia had written in 1944, were still a great secret. What would the letter reveal about the future of the world when the pope finally opened it in 1960? The suspense over what Lucia might have written was, for Catholic children praying under their desks during duck-and-cover drills, a chronic, nerve-shredding condition, an extra layer of dread in the ominous atmosphere of the Cold War.

Maybe it was already too late. Among the apocalyptic Catholic literature of that time was a book called *Fatima or World Suicide*, which argued that after Mary came down to earth to speak to the children at Fatima, a faithless world had all but ignored her demands to pray the Rosary and pay attention to her Immaculate Heart. "This was the Peace plan from Heaven that would have saved the world," the author, a monsignor named William C. McGrath, concluded. But "her efforts ended in failure," and because of that the Second World War had happened.

————

What could be done? Another clerical Catholic writer from that time, Lester M. Dooley, exhorted the faithful to "fatimize your homes, your lives, and in this way, the Iron Curtain will be spiritually atomized and in God's own time it will assume the beautiful blue of the mantle of Mary, the Mother of God."

Dooley believed that the solution to the gathering menace was the family Rosary, which was "in a spiritual sense, the food and air and water of a family. If any father and mother failed to put a supper on the table for several consecutive evenings, their family would know there was something wrong in that house."

I doubt that my mother would have been aware of these obscure Catholic authors and their books, which were distributed by even more obscure publishers like Ave Maria Press and the Scarboro Foreign Mission Society. But Bishop Sheen, who was on national television every week, was a fervent proponent of the Rosary, and so were the nuns and priests at Saint Patrick's Elementary School, which I began attending in the middle of fifth grade when we moved to Corpus Christi in the late 1950s.

So it was that our own home was fatimized, with my mother decreeing that we say the family Rosary every night. I'm not sure how long this enterprise lasted—maybe a year, maybe more. Every night my parents would lie in their king-size bed, as my two brothers and my sister and I knelt around the perimeter and my mother led us in the Rosary, through the endless Hail Marys, ticking off, depending on the day of the week, the Joyful or Sorrowful or Glorious Mysteries.

It seems so strange, thinking about it now, in a more secular age, as a much more secular being. I don't remember regarding it as an odd ritual at the time, though we may have been the only family that we knew who said the Rosary together every night, and said it in exactly this way, with the kids on their knees and the adults recumbent and already half-asleep. For me, it was an exercise in mind-wandering stupor that had zero to do with religious contemplation. I murmured along with the decades of the Rosary, my knees restless against the patterned carpet, my eyes scanning, night after night, the titles on display in the bookshelf that formed the headboard of my parents' bed. They were mostly Reader's Digest Condensed Books, omnibus volumes that arrived every season, each volume with five or six abridged editions of that year's best-selling books. I stared at them for so long, in such boredom, that the titles displayed on the spines are burned into my memory: *Mrs. 'Arris Goes to Paris*, *Too Late the Phalarope*, *The Last Angry Man*. There were unabridged books on the shelf, too, with inscrutable or provocative titles like *As a Man Thinketh* and *The Ugly American*. There was also a brief biography of the Curé d'Ars, a nineteenth-century French pastor who became a saint, and a novel that looked like a textbook, published by a vanity press and written by a man our parents had once met at a dinner party.

Despite the boredom, I knew the family Rosary was an urgent exercise, our humble contribution to converting Russia and bringing peace to an increasingly frightening world where people were building fallout shelters in their backyards and kids were freezing in terror whenever there was a test of an air-raid siren.

If the Soviet Union dropped a hydrogen bomb, it would mean not just death, but—if you happened to be in a state of mortal sin—eternal torment in hell. I was pretty sure I was in a state of mortal sin from the onset of puberty, if not before. My offense to God was the mind crime known as "impure thoughts." I was very good at self-policing, keeping myself away from what we were warned, without any specific reference, to be the "near occasion of sin." For me, this meant mostly resisting the temptation to page through *Mad* magazine, which one of our nuns had told us was sinful to read, for reasons I could never quite figure out.

But it was one thing to stay away from magazines; it was another to expunge the thoughts that came unbidden into your own imagination, and for which you were morally responsible. The solution was to go to confession and be absolved, but I was so ashamed of myself for having modestly racy fantasies about what it might be like to, say, kiss a girl, or even stand close to one, that I couldn't bring myself to tell the priest in the confession booth that I had committed the sin of impure thoughts. We were told that giving a false confession—withholding our sins from the priest—was in itself a mortal sin, so there was a double-jeopardy component to every confession I made, and an ever more fatalistic understanding that I was headed to eternal fire as soon as the bombs started dropping. I still remember leaving the confession booth after losing the nerve to confess my major sins of impure thoughts and instead substituting minor infractions like talking back to my parents or stealing a candy bar—something I never actually did. The priest—who mercifully could not see me because our faces were hidden from each other by a screen—would instruct me to say ten Hail Marys and go in peace, but I knew that ten Hail Marys was far too light a sentence for someone who had just lied about the state of his soul. I imagined what it would be like to walk out of confession after making an honest accounting and giving an honest penance, to feel cleansed and confident that if I were to die at that moment I would not be condemned to hell but welcomed by the Blessed Mother herself into heaven. But the reality was so grievously different. I was a preadolescent boy staggering under a mental load of guilt, self-loathing, and existential dread. My waking life was like a nightmare in which I harbored a secret that I had committed an unspeakable crime.

―――――

In the Lisbon orphanage where Jacinta was sent for a time before being transferred to the Dona Estefânia Hospital, there was a Franciscan nun named Mother Godinho who was kind to the dying girl and allowed her to sit at an open window where she could look down at a garden and breathe fresh air into her ravaged lungs.

Mother Godinho was also somewhat star-struck that one of the shepherds of Fatima was in her institution. She made extensive notes of the conversations she said she had with Jacinta, in which the girl shared her thoughts on sin, penance, charity, and the dangers of communism.

One of the things that Jacinta purportedly said to Mother

Godinho was that "the sins which cause most souls to go to hell are the sins of the flesh."

If she indeed said this, Jacinta was still only nine years old at the time. She would die a month before reaching her tenth birthday. Like so many of the pious observations that were attributed to the three children of Fatima, often committed to posterity by Lucia herself, this statement reads like the product of an older consciousness conditioned to be wary of, and perhaps revolted by, human sexuality. It's likely that Jacinta was confused about this sin to begin with, since her mother recalled her thinking "sins of the flesh" referred to the Catholic prohibition against eating meat on Fridays.

In any case, had Jacinta lived she probably wouldn't have been spared, as she grew into adolescence, the essential shame that Catholicism taught its children about the human body and its awkward relevance to reproduction. "Taught" is probably the wrong word, since in my experience we were told almost nothing out loud or in print, just provided with glancing warnings about impure thoughts and deeds. From an early age I was already crushed with embarrassment about feelings I was too young to feel, aware that lurking in my future was some unknown and ungodly urge that could contaminate my soul, horrify the Virgin Mary, and land me in hell.

In the seventh grade we were subjected to a skittish attempt at sex education by a deeply embarrassed priest. It was only for boys—the girls were sent to a different classroom for their own lecture. I don't remember much about this brief acknowledgment of sexual desire except for the fact that it was, more than anything else, a warning against the whole idea. We were advised to steer clear of our "private parts" and told, by our scarlet-faced, celibate expert in human carnality, "a naked woman is not beautiful."

How would I know? I had never seen a naked woman, and my rule-following about avoiding occasions of sin was so absolute that I had never even seen a photo of one. Once, glancing up at the magazine rack in the Co-op Fun Shop, a store that sold magic tricks and comic books, I had had a glimpse of the cover of an adult publication, on which there was a woman with a nearly open blouse. I returned my eyes to the floor and broke out into a sweat, astonished by what I had seen and frightened by the almost irresistible impulse to look up again. The chasm of her cleavage had given me a sensation like vertigo.

Movies—or at least the movies we were supposed to watch— never presented such dangers. This was during a time when the Legion of Decency posted a Catholic guide to motion pictures every week next to the holy water font in the back of our church. I was a passionate moviegoer from an early age and scrutinized the list far more religiously than I paid attention to Mass. There were three broad categories: A for unobjectionable, B for objectionable in part, C for condemned. But within the A group there were subcategories, from A-I to A-IV, that set the parameters for which movies people should be allowed to see at different stages of their lives.

Most of the films that were condemned, French New Wave titles by Godard or Truffaut, or Italian sex comedies, were never even on my radar, since they had no chance of being shown in the first place in a conventional movie theater in Corpus Christi, Texas. The movies I cared about—westerns and historical epics— were reliably rated A-I or A-II, and the "morally objectionable in part" B films were never much of a temptation until *Dr. No*, the first James Bond movie, came out in 1962. I suppose my parents would have let me see it if I had been bold enough to insist, but I was an unrebellious child who lived by the code of the Legion of Decency.

In 1965, when I was seventeen, I awakened to the realization that I might be old enough to view something that was rated A-III, "morally unobjectionable for adults," without jeopardizing my soul. The movie was *The War Lord*, an eleventh-century drama with Charlton Heston about a knight who falls in love with a young village woman betrothed to one of his subjects and exercises his droit du seigneur to sleep with her on her wedding night. The woman was played by Rosemary Forsyth. In her first scene the knight's rampaging underlings ripped off her sackcloth dress and threw her into a pond. There was not all that much to see. Her nude body was discreetly obscured by the murky water, and the film was discreetly cut not to reveal it when Heston arrived to save her and give her back her dress. But she didn't pull the dress on; she just held it in front of her. The fact that her bare flanks were visible was the most disturbing, wondrous, and paradigm-shattering moment I had ever experienced in a movie theater. There was no going back—from then on, I was living in an A-III world.

But such a mental leap, and such a provocative movie scene, were an undreamed-of phenomenon when I was still a boy saying the Rosary at the foot of my parents' bed, praying for the conversion of Russia, and wrestling with my anxiety about would happen in 1960 when the contents of the Fatima Letter were revealed.

Heaven's Secrets

Portugal's northern border with Spain is the Minho River, which rises in the Galician highlands and flows southwestward to the Atlantic, through Spanish and Portuguese wine country and past ancient cathedral towns and fortified villages dating back to Roman times and before.

During her decades as a Dorothean nun, Lucia—Sister Maria das Dores—was assigned back and forth between convents in Pontevedra, about thirty miles north into Spain, and Tuy, which sits on the river itself, opposite the Portuguese town of Valença. Lucia would later become a Carmelite sister and live in cloistered seclusion in Portugal, but during her time in Spain she was not confined to the convent and made frequent excursions outside. From Tuy she could see across the broad river to Portugal, the country that was said to be born under Our Lady's mantle and that Lucia had left in 1925 to begin her postulancy. She had been eighteen then. By 1943, she was in her mid-thirties, and still an exile. She had not been home to Fatima or Aljustrel since Bishop Silva had arranged for her to be sent away to school in Porto twenty-two years earlier.

She saw her mother for the last time in 1934. Maria Rosa had come to Tuy to watch Lucia take her perpetual vows. Afterward, Lucia had asked Maria Rosa if she now believed that she had been telling the truth when she claimed to have seen Our Lady at the Cova da Iria.

"Oh daughter," she replied, not willing to say the words Lucia longed to hear. "I do not know." Later, leaving to go back to Aljustrel, she said, "Goodbye, until we meet in Heaven."

When Maria Rosa was on her deathbed in 1942, she wrote to Lucia asking her to come visit her. Lucia desperately wanted to go, but her superiors told her that "such a thing was out of the question." She appealed to Bishop Silva, but he denied her request as well. And when her mother had Lucia's sister call the convent so that she could at least say goodbye to her daughter over the phone, "this too could not be allowed.

"My sister had no way of concealing this further refusal from my mother, because she was there beside her, waiting to stretch out her hand and take hold of the receiver in order to say her last farewell to me on this earth."

By the time of her mother's death, Lucia had experienced numerous other emotional milestones—from tragic to ecstatic—and had been caught up like the rest of the world in the relentless onrush of the twentieth century. From Spain, she had witnessed yet another monarchical collapse and the rise of a republican government, one that in turn was destroyed after the horrors of the Spanish Civil War.

And a new global war had followed. This was the conflict—World War II—that Lucia maintained Our Lady of Fatima had prophesied during the third apparition of July 1917, when she said a "worse" war would be coming if "world devotion" to her Immaculate Heart wasn't established. "When you see a night illumined by an unknown light," Lucia reported the Virgin telling the children, "know that this is the great sign given you by God that He is about to punish the world for its crimes, by means of war, famine, and persecutions of the Church and of the Holy Father."

This warning was a component of the three-part secret that Lucia said the children had received at the Cova. But by the time she wrote it down in 1941, in her third memoir, World War II was already decisively underway, so it was another "post eventum" prediction that could only be taken on faith. The same could be said of the "night illuminated by an unknown light" that Lucia said would be an omen of a coming global disaster. In January of 1938, there was a massive geomagnetic storm that caused an aurora borealis to be visible across much of the world, startling and scaring people who lived at latitudes where such a phenomenon is rarely, if ever, seen.

"God manifested that sign," Lucia wrote, "which astronomers chose to call an aurora borealis. I don't know for certain, but I think if they investigate the matter, they would discover that, in the form in which it appeared, it could not possibly have been an aurora borealis. Be that as it may, God made use of this to make me understand that His justice was about to strike the guilty nations."

This ominous atmospheric display has, over the years, come to be known as the Fatima Storm, an event seized upon by UFO researchers, doomsday prognosticators, theologians, and filmmakers to preach that something truly horrible had happened or was about to happen and that nobody would listen. "What I'm discovering now really scares the hell out of me," says Martin Sheen as a physicist in a faith-based 1985 movie called *A State of Emergency*, as he worries that an upcoming nuclear test will set off a chain reaction that will end the world. "If that was the great sign in the sky back in 1938, why should it look so much like an atomic blast a good seven years before one was set off?"

But Lucia had yet to reveal, or at least write down, her most famous oracular pronouncement, the Third Part of the three-part secret that she said had been given to her and her cousins by the Virgin Mary. She had already reluctantly revealed the first two parts—the vision of hell and the threat of communist Russia—at the request of Bishop Silva in the pages of her third memoir, written in 1941. But the Third Part of the Secret, which would later become known to terrified Catholic children like me as the Fatima Letter, was still unshared, as she had promised the Virgin it would be.

"Her glance is serene," a priest named José Galamba de Oliveira, who visited her frequently around this time, described the woman Lucia Santos had become. "There is nothing about her which could, even from afar, give us the idea of a neurotic, excitable person or a visionary.

"She expresses herself with a great facility and a natural elegance remarkable for a person deprived of all literary formation."

Galamba de Oliveira had a vested interest in preserving Lucia's credibility. He was a devout believer in Fatima and had written a biography of Jacinta, based on Lucia's memories of her cousin. But his admiring portrait doesn't seem off the mark.

Much had happened in Lucia's life that had tempered her personality but hadn't undermined her visionary convictions. ("I feel myself in a mystery of light," she wrote to Bishop Silva.) She had adjusted to a new existence in a new country and had survived the privations of the Spanish Civil War. She was chronically homesick but accepted her longing for the pastures and craggy hillsides of the Serra de Aire as just another test the Lord had sent her. "I am not surprised," she wrote, "that the pain is so costly." The fervor of the Fatima cult grew without her, and she was not present in 1942 for the twenty-fifth-anniversary celebration of the first apparition on May 13. She offered instead her "poor and humble prayers of consecration to many souls gathered there."

She was tough. One year when she and some of the other Dorothean nuns had been given a vacation at the beach, she saw two children swept out to sea in a tidal surge. She jumped into the water and pulled them both to shore. After the children had vomited up sea water and it was clear they would survive, their mother tried to thank her but was told by Lucia to thank Our Lady instead, since she was the one who had truly saved them.

She also had the emotional grit to view the photographs that were taken when Jacinta's body was exhumed in 1935 from the Baron of Alvaiázere's family cemetery in Ourém and reburied in the cemetery of the Fatima parish church, next to Francisco. Jacinta had been dead for almost twenty years, but the photographs show that her face, when the burial shroud was pulled back, was more or less intact. It was still a heartbreaking sight, the blank visage of a long-dead child, but the fact that it was still identifiable as Jacinta's face was believed—and is believed still—to be a sign of miraculous incorruptibility.

If Lucia found the photographs disturbing or even ghoulish, she was able to quickly move on to spiritual consolation. "I was so enraptured!" she wrote. "My joy at seeing the closest friend of my childhood again was so great. I cherish the hope that the Lord, for the glory of the most Blessed Virgin, may grant her the aureola of holiness. She was a child only in years."

In 1943, Lucia herself almost died. She came down with pneumonia, which developed into pleurisy. She rallied and relapsed several times, believing the end had come, and writing to Bishop Silva that she was happy that "my mission on earth is being completed."

Silva visited her while she was bedridden in Tuy. Like other clerics, in particular Father Galamba, he was worried that she would die and take the final part of the secret with her to her grave. Accounts differ about whether Silva ordered her to write it down, or merely strongly suggested it. In either case Lucia hesitated, both because she was still very ill and because she was confused about whose will to follow: the bishop's, who urged her to record the secret, or the Virgin Mary's, who had originally told her not to tell it to anyone.

At one point during her extended illness, she was well enough to walk across the international bridge to Valença for another meeting with the bishop and Galamba de Oliveira at a Franciscan women's college, where she was pressured again to write down the secret. She apparently agreed, though she agonized about it, not convinced yet that she had Our Lady's permission. She was soon sick again, this time with a dangerous leg infection that required an operation. In the operating room, she protested against receiving anesthesia, preferring to endure the pain rather than risk being unconscious and inadvertently blurting out the secret. But the doctors prevailed, and when she woke up after the surgery and was told she had said or revealed nothing, "I was at peace."

But not for long. She was still tormented by indecision, by her fear that writing down the secret, while it might be convenient to the church, would violate the vow she had made to Mary at the Cova that it never be revealed. She asked for an unambiguous command from Bishop Silva. He supplied it, but still, as she wrote, "this order made me shudder."

For several months she tried and failed to comply, to write down the final part of the secret. But her hand trembled when she took up her pen, and she began to imagine that the order from Silva that she had asked for might be the work of the devil.

Then, just after the turn of the year, on January 3, 1944, she went to the convent chapel. She said that the Mother of God appeared to her there while she was alone, touched her on the shoulder, and spoke the familiar words that Lucia had first heard over a quarter century earlier: "Do not be afraid."

"Be at peace," she remembered the Virgin telling her, "and write what they order you, but not what has been given you to understand its meaning. After writing it, place it in an envelope, close and seal it and write on the outside that this can be opened in 1960 by the Cardinal Patriarch of Lisbon or by the Bishop of Leiria."

Relieved, inspired, Lucia went to her room, and—on her knees, using her bed as a writing table—in one ecstatic rush committed the secret she had held inside since she was a little girl to paper. She put the paper in an envelope, sealed the envelope with wax, then set it within the pages of a loose-leaf notebook. She did not dare trust the post office to deliver it to Bishop Silva, so she had to wait several weeks until she had an opportunity to pass it on to a trusted messenger who could then personally hand it to the bishop at his country home.

Lucia had written on the outside of the envelope, as she believed she was instructed to by the Virgin, that the message could not be opened until 1960. Why 1960? "Because then it will seem clearer," Lucia reportedly told Cardinal Alfredo Ottaviani in 1955. She later wrote to the pope, in 1958, predicting that within the next two years "communism will reach its maximum height."

But it's also reasonable to assume that Lucia—after so much internal conflict over revealing the secret in the first place, and after being close to death the summer before, coughing up blood from her infected lungs and willing to undergo surgery without an anesthetic rather than risk blurting out a divine confidence— expected to die soon enough, and was eager to push the whole problem of what she thought the Virgin had told her at Fatima far into a future she didn't expect to see.

Bishop Silva took the sealed envelope that contained Lucia's Fatima Letter, placed it in a larger sealed envelope, and set it in his safe, where it remained until shortly before his death in 1957. Every once in a great while he would take the envelope out and show it to visitors. But he never opened it. His discretion tested the patience of Father Galamba de Oliveira, who believed that the bishop had every right to read what Lucia had written.

"I asked him many times why he would not open it," Galamba de Oliveira remembered. "He always answered, 'It's not my duty to interfere in the matter. Heaven's secrets are not for me, nor do I need to burden myself with this responsibility.'"

The bishop was old, almost blind, and near the end of his life. He might have been relieved when he received a message from the papal nuncio in Lisbon requesting that he send photocopies of all of Lucia's papers to the Vatican. "Especially the Secret!" the nuncio emphasized.

But the secret was in a double-sealed envelope and could not be copied without breaking the seal, so da Silva sent the original. Unlike the rest of Lucia's photocopied documents it was not placed in the Vatican archives, but stored in the personal living quarters of the eighty-one-year-old Pope Pius XII. Eugenio Pacelli had been elected to the papacy in 1939 after the death of his predecessor and namesake Pope Pius XI. He came from a family of Holy See insiders and had previously served as the nuncio to Germany and as the Vatican's secretary of state. He had strong emotional ties to the Virgin Mary and to Fatima as well, possibly because his consecration as an archbishop had taken place in the Sistine Chapel on the same day in 1917 as the first of the Fatima apparitions. He was the first pope to directly mention Fatima in a formal papal document, and in an apostolic letter in 1952 he made an early gesture of following through on what Lucia said was the Virgin's big ask: to consecrate Russia to her Immaculate Heart. In the letter he addressed the wayward people of the Soviet Union directly, asking the "most clement Mother" to help "you victoriously overcome all impiety and error."

Two years earlier, in 1950, as he was in the process of officially proclaiming the dogma of the Assumption, the belief that Mary had been "assumed" upon her death—floating up into Heaven instead of corroding in the ground—he was walking in the Vatican gardens and happened to look up at the sky. He reported that the sun "looked like a pale, opaque sphere, entirely surrounded by a luminous circle." It seemed to spin and to move erratically around in the sky as it had during the final apparition at Fatima. "I have seen the 'miracle of the sun,'" he wrote, "this is the pure truth."

But for all his Marian devotion and his fascination with Fatima, Pacelli appears never to have had the curiosity to read Lucia's Third Part of the Secret text. He kept it in a small wooden safe bearing the words "Secretum Sancti Officii" (Secret of the Holy Office).

When he died, a little over a year and a half after it was put into his keeping, the Fatima Letter was still sealed, still in the little safe, still unread. It was October of 1959, and 1960—the year that the Virgin Mary's final secret was to be revealed—was now only months away.

12

Dark, Black Depths

In 1954, a Trappist monk at the Tre Fontane Abbey in Rome slugged one of his superiors in the nose and was kicked out of the monastery. Afterward, that monk, Laurence Downey, made his way to Fatima, where he became a tour guide at the massive pilgrimage site that had replaced the pastures of the Cova da Iria. He apparently didn't last long there, either, returning to his native Australia, where he lived until he moved to Ireland in 1978, on the run from charges of assault and land fraud.

Three years later, in May of 1981, Downey boarded an Aer Lingus flight from Dublin to London. He was in his fifties, with thinning gray hair. He wore a lumberjack shirt and sipped cognac during the flight. A few minutes before the plane was scheduled to land in London, he ignored the Fasten Seat Belts sign, stood up, and locked himself in the bathroom, then emerged and walked up to the unsecured cockpit carrying two small plastic bottles and a lighter. Reports differ about whether he had doused himself with gasoline in the lavatory, or merely rinsed his hands with it, or was just lying when he told the pilots he was a human bomb. He said that the two bottles contained cyanide gas, though he later admitted that they had just been filled with water.

Downey ordered the pilots to fly to Tehran. He had just written a new constitution for Iran that he wanted to personally
deliver. He was told they didn't have enough fuel, so the plane
ended up being diverted to northern France, to the city of Le Tou-
quet. While they were on the ground waiting to refuel, just before
French authorities managed to board the plane and arrest him,
Downey ordered the pilot to open the cockpit window and throw
a nine-page document onto the tarmac.

The document was a manifesto, a demand that the Vatican release the letter that Lucia had written and that was still in
the pope's possession, still unopened. Even more than Downey
wanted to set the government of Iran straight, he wanted to learn
what the Third Part of the Secret of Fatima was.

This happened twenty-one years after 1960, the year when the
contents of Lucia's message were supposed to be revealed.
Downey's hijacking of Aer Lingus 164 was only the most extreme
example of obsessive curiosity about what it might say. Nineteen
sixty was supposed to have brought an end to, as Frère Michel de la
Sainte Trinité phrased it, the "anguished wait of the entire Catholic universe."

I was eleven years old when the world's meter rolled over
from 1959 to 1960. To a child of that age, or at least the child I
was, the beginning of a new decade was an awesome demarcation.
The decades of the twentieth century were not like the decades
of the rosary. They were linear, not circular, advancing toward the
unimaginably distant horizon of the next century. In my mental
diagram, the beginning of a decade was like the summit of a long
slope. When I looked back from that summit, I could see the
years that had already taken place receding down the slope, growing smaller and smaller, until the first year of the decade was barely
visible in the valley floor below.

The coming of 1960 would have been a momentous and mysterious landmark in any case, but the fact that it was the year that
the contents of the Fatima Letter were going to be revealed made

it even more consequential—in my imagining of the peaks and valleys of time—than the new millennium looming far away in the future mist.

What we were finally told by Sister Martha in sixth grade—that the contents of the Fatima Letter were so horrible that the pope declared nobody could ever know what it said—turned out not to be true, though I wouldn't know that for many years, until I started writing this book.

In 1958, seventy-six-year-old Cardinal Angelo Giuseppe Roncalli had become Pope John XXIII. He was a reform-minded pope with a lot on his mind—mostly a sudden inspiration that, as he described it, "sprang up . . . as a flower that blooms in an unexpected springtime." The idea become known as "aggiornamento," a thorough updating of the Catholic Church, its liturgy, and its place in the world as a way of recalibrating its relevance to the twentieth century.

In August of 1959, the new pope had the Fatima Letter brought to him at his summer residence in Castel Gandolfo. Nineteen sixty was still four and a half months away, but John XXIII apparently made the decision to get an early start on what Lucia's message might contain. He broke the seal on the bishop of Leiria's envelope, removed Lucia's envelope that was inside it, and opened that as well. The document was written in Lucia's hand, in Portuguese. It's unclear whether the Italian pope read it at that moment or waited several days until he could have a Portuguese translator on hand to interpret what he termed the document's "abstruse locutions." In either case, he seems to have been unimpressed. "This makes no reference to my time," he said.

According to Alfredo Ottaviani, the cardinal that John XXIII had appointed as secretary of the Holy Office, the pope placed the letter in yet another envelope, "sealed it, and sent it to be placed in one of those archives that are like a well where the paper sinks deeply into the dark, black depths, and where no one can distinguish anything at all."

It became gradually clear to a crestfallen world that 1960 would not, after all, bring the revelation we had been anxiously waiting for. "It is most probable," wrote the Portuguese news agency ANI, "that the Secret of Fatima will remain, forever, under absolute seal."

Why? No one ever said, exactly. But maybe Cardinal Joseph Ratzinger came the closest. Ratzinger (later Pope Benedict XVI) was a theology professor at the University of Bonn when the letter was opened. In 1985, when he was prefect of the Congregation for the Doctrine of the Faith, he told a journalist that he had read Lucia's letter and believed that "to publish the 'third Secret' would mean exposing the Church to the danger of sensationalism, exploitation of the content."

To help understand what Ratzinger was talking about, this is probably as appropriate a place as any in this book to reveal exactly what the Fatima Letter said. The contents would not ultimately be made public until 2000, forty years after the timetable Lucia set. But this is what Pope John XXIII read and decided to put away into the dark, black depths of the Vatican archives.

The "J. M. J." heading should be immediately familiar to Catholics of my age who went to parochial school. The letters stand for "Jesus, Mary, and Joseph," and like Lucia we were obliged to write them at the top of every page of homework or any other school assignment. From then on, though, the letter is anything but commonplace:

J.M.J.

The third part of the secret revealed at the Cova da Iria–Fatima, on 13 July 1917.

I write in obedience to you, my God, who command me to do so through his Excellency the Bishop of Leiria and through your Most Holy Mother and mine.

After the two parts which I have already explained, at the left of Our Lady and a little above, we saw an Angel with a flaming sword in his left hand; flashing, it gave out flames that looked as though they would set the world on fire; but they died out in contact with the splendour that Our Lady radiated towards him from her right hand: pointing to the earth with his right hand, the Angel cried out in a loud voice: "Penance, Penance, Penance!" And we saw in an immense light that is God: "something similar to how people appear in a mirror when they pass in front of it" a Bishop dressed in White "we had the impression that it was the Holy Father." Other Bishops, Priests, men and women Religious going up a steep mountain, at the top of which there was a big Cross of rough-hewn trunks as of a cork-tree with the bark; before reaching there the Holy Father passed through a big city half in ruins and half trembling with halting step, afflicted with pain and sorrow, he prayed for the souls of the corpses he met on his way; having reached the top of the mountain, on his knees at the foot of the big Cross he was killed by a group of soldiers who fired bullets and arrows at him, and in the same way there died one after another the other Bishops, Priests, men and women Religious, and various lay people of different ranks and positions. Beneath the two arms of the Cross there were two Angels each with a crystal aspersorium in his hand, in which they gathered up the blood of the Martyrs and with it sprinkled the souls that were making their way to God.

Tuy–3-1-1944

So that was the Fatima Letter: a mystical word stew written by a nun who had a long history of visionary episodes and who had just survived a dangerous illness. It was, to be generous, open to interpretation, but on its face it seemed to be some sort of cautionary spasm about the end of the world or the end of Catholicism, featuring exactly the sort of apocalyptic imagery that seemed to belong to a medieval church, and not the one that Pope John XXIII and his allies in the Vatican were urgently trying to bring up to code with the modern world.

Their thinking about what exactly to do with this letter that the world was waiting for might have been influenced by the scholarship of a Belgian Jesuit named Edouard Dhanis. In the view of the anti-Jesuit, antiprogressive Fatima author Frère Michel de la Sainte Trinité, Dhanis was "the most unyielding and terrible adversary of Fatima."

His treachery, according to the growing ranks of Fatima traditionalists, sprang from an article in Flemish that he wrote in

1944, more than a half-century before Lucia's letter was finally published. The article modestly suggested that Lucia's memoirs, written long after the events of 1917 they described and with the benefit of several decades of world-historical hindsight, perhaps should not be taken at face value. Dhanis, it should be emphasized, was a believer. He had no problem accepting that the Virgin Mary appeared to three children at the Cova da Iria, or that she had created a miracle in the sky at the final apparition. Father Formigão's on-the-spot interviews with the children, contemporary newspaper coverage, and witness testimony all convinced him that those events took place. But Dhanis believed the memoirs that Lucia began writing in 1935 had the effect of retrofitting—and corrupting—the story with contemporary concerns like the rise of Soviet Russia and the coming of World War II.

"Let us observe," he gingerly suggested, "that a person can be sincere and prove to have good judgement in everyday life, but have a propensity for unconscious fabrication in a certain area, or in any case, a tendency to relate old memories of twenty years ago with embellishments and considerable modifications."

Internal and often bitter skirmishes among theologians and members of the Vatican curia about how to deal with Lucia's revelations did nothing to diminish the uncontainable curiosity ordinary Catholics had about the approach of 1960 and the expected revelations of the Third Part of the Secret. The overall anxiety reached a new high after a Mexican priest, Father Agustín Fuentes Anguiano, managed to meet with Lucia in December of 1957. Lucia was by that time at the Carmelite convent in Coimbra, Portugal, finally on her way to becoming what she had long dreamed to be, silent and shut away from a clamorous world, her mind liberated in prayer. Fuentes, however, had managed to secure a rare meeting with her. As a postulator appointed by the church, he was investigating a cause that would have been dear to Lucia's heart: the potential sainthood of her cousins Francisco and Jacinta.

Fuentes later wrote that he was struck by Lucia's demeanor—she was "very concerned, pale, far from well."

What had her upset, it seems, was the fact that "the Blessed Virgin is very sad." Nobody was heeding her message; nobody was paying attention to what she had said at Fatima. "Believe me, Father," she warned, "God is going to punish the world, and very soon. The chastisement of heaven is imminent. In less than two years 1960 will be here, and what will happen then? If we do not pray and do peace, it will be very grievous and for all of us. Our Lady has said repeatedly, 'Many nations will disappear from the face of the earth, and Russia will be the instrument of heaven's chastisement for the entire world, unless we obtain the conversion of that poor nation.'"

It appeared that Lucia, in 1957, was giving the world a sneak preview of what the Fatima Letter might contain. After Fuentes's interview was published, the bishop's office in Coimbra grew alarmed at the prospect of runaway doomsaying and the "storm of ridicule" against the church that might result. It issued a forceful condemnation and even published a recantation from Lucia herself, who was quoted as saying, "I know nothing, and could therefore say nothing, about such punishments . . ."

But no disavowal could turn back the tide of fretful curiosity about the Third Part of the Secret, and the pope's decision not to publish it when 1960 came around greatly amplified the mystery and created an opportunity for various international fraudsters to fill the void with their own fake Fatima Letters. One version, published in the German weekly *Neues Europa* in 1963, claimed that the Virgin had predicted to Lucia that "the greatest World War will happen in the second half of the twentieth century. Then fire and smoke will fall from the sky, and the waters of the oceans will be turned to steam . . . Millions and millions of men will lose their lives from one hour to the next, and those who remain living will envy those who are dead."

John XXIII was dead by the time the *Neues Europa* article appeared, and Paul VI was now pontiff. According to the bogus German exclusive, the new pope had read the Fatima Letter and had been so alarmed at what it said that he had strong-armed President Kennedy, Soviet Premier Khrushchev, and British Prime Minster Macmillan into getting together and signing the nuclear test-ban treaty of 1963.

"Our Lady is not a sensationalist. She doesn't raise fears." So decreed Joseph Ratzinger, the cardinal who was the Vatican's official interpreter of the faith. But he said this many years later, in 1996, and in 1960, at twelve years old, I was sure that the fate of the world was on a hair trigger, and that the Virgin Mary had issued a warning of unthinkable catastrophe that we were not allowed to hear. At twelve, I was unaware of fake Fatima Letters or of the intensifying struggle within the Catholic Church between traditionalism and modernism. All I knew was that the pope had some very bad but very secret news.

With the new decade came the election of John Fitzgerald Kennedy, the youngest and most glamorous president in the nation's history and also the first Catholic. Ours wasn't a particularly political household, but the idea of a Catholic in the White House was galvanizing. Kennedy represented not just the sweeping aside of the stodgy Eisenhower years but a broader confirmation that our religion—which was functionally the same as it had been when Lucia and Francisco and Jacinta had their visions in 1917—was emerging from its ancient shadows to boldly place itself in the sunshine of the now.

Corpus Christi was a city of less than two hundred thousand, only a hundred and fifty miles from the border. Almost half the people who lived there were of Mexican descent and had been imprinted with Catholicism to one degree or another. When we lived in Abilene, I had been vaguely aware that I belonged to an outlier religion, less established and maybe a bit suspect to the Protestant congregations for whom this part of the state had long been a more natural home base. In South Texas it was different. The Mexican cultural vibe might have struck me as a bit exotic at first, but it was offset by the familiarity of Catholic rituals and symbols. I felt, for the first time, that I belonged to a mainstream religion, and Kennedy's candidacy for president made me feel that even more.

I had no understanding of Kennedy's political positions, and no real curiosity about them other than a hope that he could save us from nuclear annihilation. But the tribal gravitation toward a Catholic presidential candidate was too strong to resist. So, along with a few other seventh-grade friends from Saint Patrick's, I went campaigning. We stopped in at the Kennedy for President storefront in downtown Corpus to supply ourselves with pamphlets and buttons that we would pass out on the street and bumper stickers that we affixed to every parked car we saw, not caring if the unseen owner planned to vote for Kennedy or not. Most people politely took the unsolicited campaign material we pressed into their hands, but there was one elderly woman who stiffened with anger as I handed her a pamphlet. "You boys want me to vote for Kennedy?" she snorted. "You want me to help put the pope in the White House?"

The idea that Kennedy was a stalking horse for a pope who would stop at nothing to turn America into a Catholic theocracy was a conspiracy theory I had heard referred to on television, but this was the first time I had encountered it in the real world. In this woman's eyes I wasn't just some clueless kid larking about in an exciting political campaign but a brainwashed member of a dangerous cult.

She stormed away and I grinned back at a friend who had witnessed the encounter. But I didn't quite shrug it off. Catholicism was scary to me, sure, with God's unblinking scrutiny watching my every action and judging my every thought, but it was a baseline phenomenon like the sky and the ocean. But in this woman's mind the Catholic Church wasn't just something that existed, it was an institution that had a motive. I didn't have anywhere in my imagination to file that thought. I had watched Kennedy's famous televised speech to the Greater Houston Ministerial Association that asserted his belief in the separation of church and state ("Contrary to common newspaper usage, I am not the Catholic candidate for President. I am the Democratic Party's candidate for President who happens also to be a Catholic") and of course believed every word he said. The encounter with the woman in the street, though, gave me an important glimpse into why that speech was needed in the first place, and how to people who belonged to other religions or none at all—like, say, the Portuguese secularists who wanted to shut down Lucia's visions—Catholicism was not an enfolding everything, but a strange and sinister force.

In 1962, Pope John XXIII's Second Vatican Council would begin remaking the church, eventually turning the Mass itself into an almost unrecognizable experience for Catholics like me who had grown up with the mustiness and majesty of the old rite. All the Latin phrases that I had been trained to repeat with an uncomprehending fluency—"Introibo ad altare Dei, ad Deum qui laetificat juventutem meam," "Agnus Dei, qui tollis peccata mundi"—would become useless knowledge, since in its efforts to make the Mass more relevant, Vatican II decreed that it be conducted in the local vernacular—in our case, English. The holy encrustations of the centuries—crowds of statues, elaborate clerical vestments, towering pulpits, tapestries—were gradually tapered down or stripped away. Ghastly depictions of a crucified Christ bleeding from his wounds and writhing in agony were likely to give way to simple Danish-modern crosses or to less disturbing images of a kindly looking Jesus, his arms spread in blessing, not hanging from the cross but sort of levitating in front of it. Latin hymns like Tantum Ergo Sacramentum or Panis Angelicus no longer filled the emptiness of cathedrals, and mighty organ music was replaced by plinky guitar chords accompanying newly written sacred songs with insipid lyrics and undetectable melodies.

In time, it would be a much different church than the one I remembered from childhood. Nowadays a nostalgia for the old Latin Mass is linked to rigid right-wing political beliefs, but you don't have to be a grouchy throwback to think that the church, after Vatican II, surrendered one of its most potent weapons: the enthralling inscrutability of a service performed in a dead language amid clouds of incense. There was something unapproachable and mysterious about that old ritual that entranced believers across the centuries in more or less the same way, and that made the visions of Portuguese shepherd children oddly relatable to a city kid from Texas forty years later.

I don't think that after the age of ten or so, I was ever really a believer. I might have been awed by the Latin Mass, but not as much as I was bored and bewildered by it. There were times when I was stirred by some somber hymn or lulled into a deep irrelevant reverie while listening to a Gregorian chant, but I never felt Lucia's ecstatic oneness with God—even though I knew that I should. I never paid attention to the component parts of the Mass, except to learn that certain gestures or prayers meant that it was closer to being over. This was a great disadvantage the one time I auditioned as an altar boy. The priest who was serving Mass just assumed that I knew what I was doing, but as soon as I walked out onto the altar I was seized with panic, an actor in a play who didn't know his lines. Somehow, I muddled through it, having picked up enough of the ritual osmotically to know that I was supposed to ring a little bell when the priest—his back to the congregation in those pre–Vatican II days—raised the host during the part of the Mass known as the consecration. This was the moment when we were meant to believe that what had a moment before been merely a thin white wafer was now the actual body of Jesus Christ. No amount of imaginative calisthenics could bring me any closer to an understanding of how this could possibly be true, but I rang the bell and sort of hit my marks until, in a cold sweat, I was finally able to withdraw with the priest and the other altar boy to the sacristy. I must have done better than I thought, and my co-server even worse, because without a word the priest turned and slapped him across the face.

It wasn't a powerful blow, but it was hard enough to be audible. The priest said nothing, no word of rebuke or explanation. Neither I nor the boy who had been slapped said anything, either. The priest took off his vestments and we did the same. The kid was a stranger to me, and I don't remember speaking to him as we left the church, and it never occurred to me to mention the incident to anyone.

At the time, I regarded this slap as just an example of the capricious anger that certain priests sometimes displayed. It was no big deal, except for the fact that I've remembered it all these years, and that it now seems to me to have a been a symptom of privileged authority, unquestioned by anyone, unchecked by any comparable female influence. To a degree that's probably still true, but back in those days priests, in their black cassocks or black suits with clerical collars, struck me as having a peculiar sort of male power. The energy shifted when they entered a room. They seemed bigger, hairier, busier than ordinary men, generals in an active war against Satan. Their celibacy—real or presumed—only made them seem more virile, with no time for nonsense like sex or romantic entanglements. We called them "Father," and it wasn't an accidental designation: they were the patriarchs of a system that echoed the vision of a masculine, all-powerful God, a world in which even the Virgin Mary herself was officially a secondary player.

My half-hearted attempt at becoming an altar boy happened at around the time the pope had decided to withhold from us any knowledge of what Lucia had written in the Fatima Letter, when every development on the world stage seemed to confirm my fears that the Third Part of the Secret was in essence a doomsday proclamation. Then, in 1962, came the Cuban Missile Crisis. During the tensest days of that frightening October, when Soviet ships—suspected of carrying nuclear missiles to deploy on Cuban soil—approached the American ships Kennedy had ordered to blockade the island, I was numb with dread. I was old enough by then to understand that my fears were rational and that a nuclear confrontation was a likelier outcome than not.

I was in the eighth grade that year, in Saint Patrick's School in Corpus Christi, home of the Fighting Shamrocks. It was my last year of elementary school and I was facing a decision about my future.

"Do you feel like you're special? Do you feel like God has a plan for you?"

Those were the sort of questions we were asked by the unfamiliar priests who would drop by the school in the spring of 1962. They were recruiters, looking for candidates who might, at the age of fourteen or fifteen, be willing to ship themselves off to a minor seminary. The recruiters were young and charismatic. They would remind me of the character played by Tom Tryon in *The Cardinal*, a movie that came out the next year that tracked the career of an idealistic young priest from his ordination to his elevation to the Vatican hierarchy.

We raised our hands when these dynamic priests asked those empowering questions. Of course we felt we were special. Of course we felt like God had a plan for us. There was nothing wrong with being ordinary, the priests explained. There was nothing wrong with getting married and having children, but if we thought we might have a *vocation*—if we thought that God had singled us out for a life of heroic privation and deep spiritual significance— then maybe we should consider going to the seminary instead of a normal high school.

I had seven friends at Saint Patrick's. All of them but me went to the local minor seminary when they graduated from the eighth grade, and none of them lasted more than a year. I'm not sure how I was able to excuse myself from the grandiose path that those recruiters laid out for us. I was just as susceptible to the idea of being a chosen one as my friends were, and even though I was starting to cautiously question a religion in which questions were not encouraged, I was still oddly devout, a hostage to prayers and observances whose organic power over me transcended a faith I couldn't feel. Also, going to the seminary meant leaving home, taking up residence in a brand-new, unlovely building in the middle of a South Texas cotton field. I knew I would be deathly homesick, that I would want to come home, and I sensed that I didn't want to take the chance of having to measure myself against an exalted destiny and—unlike Lucia Santos—come up short.

13

Wild Horses of Modernism

Though I didn't go to the minor seminary as so many of my friends did, I didn't land squarely in the secular world, either. My high-school years were spent at a Catholic boys' school on a bleak industrial thoroughfare named Corn Products Road, amid the refineries, grain elevators, and warehouses of the Corpus Christi Ship Channel. I never saw it happen myself, but there were students who swore that birds regularly fell out of the sky and thudded onto the parched football field, overcome by the noxious air we were all breathing.

There were two hundred students at Corpus Christi Academy. We were taught by Benedictine priests and brothers, followers of the sixth-century monk Saint Benedict, whose extensive religious philosophy was distilled into our school motto, Ora et Labora—Pray and Work. Most of our teachers came from a monastery in the town of Subiaco, Arkansas, which was named for the original Subiaco Abbey in Italy that Saint Benedict had founded. They wore full-length black robes with a hood hanging down in back, and heavy black shoes. Some of them were old, but most were earnest and intense young men in whom the struggles of celibacy were apparent even to me, still a few years away from being introduced to sexuality courtesy of Rosemary Forsyth in *The War Lord*.

I hadn't forgotten the Fatima Letter, though I don't recall any of our teachers talking about it by the time I was in high school, and the fact that we were all still alive after the Cuban Missile Crisis helped to slacken my curiosity about Lucia's still-unrevealed document of doom. I was a sophomore when President Kennedy was assassinated. When I look back on that unfathomable day, the thing that comes to mind is an ancient wooden intercom speaker hanging on a blank blue wall. It was through that speaker that we heard the distant, staticky voice of our principal breaking into an English class in which our teacher was trying fruitlessly to explain the sprung rhythm utilized by the Jesuit poet Gerard Manley Hopkins. "President Kennedy has been shot in Dallas," the voice said. We were in an algebra class about an hour later, across the hall from the principal's office. No one was teaching, no one was talking, as we listened to the radio playing through the open door of the office. I heard the announcer say the word "dead" and immediately pushed it aside, knowing if I let it into my mind it would eventually have to be accepted as real.

Kennedy's murder was a shock to the whole world, but the fact that he was the only Catholic president the country had ever had and that he had been killed in our home state was a force multiplier for those of us sitting in that Catholic classroom, in a city in Texas named for the Body of Christ.

Was Kennedy's assassination, I remember wondering, something that might have been prophesied in Lucia's still-undisclosed letter? It seemed plausible enough that the murder of a Catholic president could be the opening act of the apocalypse I had been waiting for throughout much of my childhood.

The Cold War, the reforms of Vatican II, and the refusal of either Pope John XXIII or his successor, Pope Paul VI, to allow the world to know the Third Part of the Secret all helped to ignite a bitter dispute within the church about what Fatima was all about and, to a significant degree, what Catholicism was all about. During my high-school life, though, my once-raging curiosity about the Fatima Letter began to slowly erode. So did, without me really noticing it, my compliant religious credulity. I still went to Mass with my family every Sunday and still participated uncomplainingly in the family Rosary, although that ritual mercifully began to trail off on its own as my three siblings and I grew older and harder to corral.

There was a Catholic girls' high school in Corpus, Incarnate Word Academy, and there was some minimal and highly structured interaction between the two institutions, but I rarely saw girls during those four years, never spoke to one, and was too cowed and abashed by the church's unspoken abhorrence of intermingled human bodies to admit that I wanted to.

Every once in a while, we would be taken to the gym to hear a priest lecture us about the threat of communism—one said he had been captured by the Red Chinese and forced to live in a pit for two years   and by the even more insidious threat of sex. Once, in my junior year, we listened to a ferociously opinionated guest lecturer as he told us about a time he had been driving on a highway and was passed by a speeding convertible. There were four young people in the car, and the couple in the backseat were luridly making out. The passing car zoomed recklessly out of sight, and the priest heard a collision up ahead. When he caught up to the scene of the wreck, he saw that all four of the youths in the convertible were dead.

"None of us can know the spiritual destination of the boy and girl in the front seat," he said. "But I can tell you with absolute certainty, without any possible doubt, that the souls of those two in the back went straight to hell. Do you want to know how I know this?"

He basked for a moment in a suspenseful silence, and then gave his thunderous answer.

"Because the lower halves of their bodies were locked in intercourse!"

It was a horrifying image, though I'm not sure that "image" is the right word, because even as a high-school junior I didn't yet have a mental picture of what "locked in intercourse" might mean. But it certainly sounded very unsettling and provocative. The priest went on to explain that he was sure those kids were in hell because they died in the middle of an act that—unless they were married—was almost the definition of a mortal sin, and there wouldn't have been time, as they saw their violent end approaching, to unlock their lower halves and mutter an emergency Act of Contrition. This was the prayer that began "O my God, I am heartily sorry," but which generations of children have misheard as "O my God, I am partly sorry."

One spring afternoon in 1966, in my senior year at Corpus Christi Academy, I was stretched out on the couch, too muscle-weary from football practice to do anything more strenuous than lift that week's copy of *Time* magazine. That's when I encountered its now-famous all-type cover which, in huge red letters against a black background, asked the unthinkable question "Is God Dead?"

The article inside was about trending thought experiments among radical theologians that the traditional idea of God had outlasted its relevance in a rapidly changing world. I don't remember actually reading the article itself but can't forget lying on the couch in our living room staring at those three words on the cover, intoxicated by their literalness, by the absolute brazenness of such a question.

I was taking a religion class that semester, so I brought the issue of *Time* to school the next day and showed it to Father Augustine, our elderly teacher, whom we more or less fondly called Augie Doggie (the name of a then-prominent cartoon character) behind his back. I naively thought he would thank me for introducing such a provocative question into the class, material that he could use to lead a rousing and challenging theological discussion among his students.

Instead, he stared at the cover of the magazine in confusion and then quiet outrage.

"God," he finally said, with a flash of anger, "is *not* dead!" He handed the magazine back to me without even opening it and went on to conduct the class as if I had never brought the heresy of God's demise to his attention.

His reaction was in keeping with a Catholic precept that either I had directly been taught or had been impressed upon me since childhood: my mind was not my own. It was not free to explore or question beyond limits that were real but undefined. You had to believe in certain things—the divinity of Christ, the reality of heaven and hell, the mystery of the Holy Trinity—and even if you didn't believe them you had to believe them anyway. The faith that you didn't feel demanded it of you.

I mostly kept my mouth shut, said the prayers, walked around with a rosary in my pocket, tried not to pull at all the multiplying threads of doubt, but I knew already that my time being an active, outwardly fervent Catholic was entering some kind of end stage, and that I would soon be floating free in a frightening void where I would begin to think for myself.

To some degree, my family was unknowingly nudging me in this direction. My mother was still as devout as ever, making the sign of the cross every time she drove past a church, ensuring that we all prayed before every meal ("Bless us, O Lord, and these thy gifts which we are about to receive from thy bounty, through Christ Our Lord, Amen.") and hustling us out the door every Sunday morning for Mass. But sometimes I was aware of the concern in her face when she glanced in my direction, the look of a mother worried that her child had learned his lessons too well—had taken things too seriously, too literally. A teenager who was afraid to have fun. Once she sent me to the family doctor for what I thought was a checkup but turned out to be a chat. How was I feeling? Everything going okay? Any thoughts of suicide?

Suicide! The word shocked me. I had never had the remotest idea of killing myself, but the morose, inert signal I had been putting out must have alarmed my mother enough to think that I might be spiraling down to some really dark places. In fact, I was relatively steady, just emotionally paralyzed, held in place by a web of Catholic rules and strictures that if broken would disappoint God and dishonor me.

My mother had been pregnant with me when her husband, an Air Force pilot, was killed in a plane crash on a gloomy mountain gorge in the North Cascades. Theirs had been a storied wartime romance between an army nurse and a fighter pilot, and she must have been sufficiently swept up both by love and by the disruption and excitement of the times not to worry about stepping outside the lines a bit and marrying a non-Catholic. Since childhood I've mused about the infinite ways my life might have turned out differently if I'd known my father. One of these alternative scenarios has been about how, with his Protestant upbringing, he might have diluted the strict Catholicism that was at the same time my spiritual home base and intellectual prison.

When I was five, my mother married Tom Harrigan. He was older than she was by almost twenty years and had spent a good part of his young adulthood working in South America in the scrappy days of early-twentieth-century oil exploration. He was slim and handsome and spoke fluent Spanish. His hair was prematurely white and he had lost a finger in an accident he never gave us a coherent accounting of. It was a rare sentence of his that did not contain a curse word, though in the presence of his wife and children the words were never any stronger than "hell" or "damn" or "sonofabitch." Despite his worldly demeanor he was an observant Catholic who might leave his downtown office to slip into church for a weekday Mass and seemed to hold a special respect for people he knew were "daily communicants."

But otherwise, he wore his Catholicism lightly. He had seen enough of the world not to confuse his private religious faith with an unyielding doctrine that all humanity must accept or be damned. In fact, I don't think I ever heard him express an overtly religious thought, nothing about Jesus or the Virgin Mary or guardian angels or all the other unseen presences that guided our lives.

In those years, the Catholic Church had not yet decommissioned the *Index Librorum Prohibitorum,* a list of forbidden books that it had begun keeping in the Middle Ages and kept updating all the way up until 1966, the year I graduated from high school. On the *Index* were works by famous disrupters like Galileo, Balzac, Flaubert, and Sartre.

After Mass one Sunday morning, when our family had invited the parish priest over for breakfast, Tom happened to mention that he had just read *The Grapes of Wrath.*

The priest paused as he ate his scrambled eggs and looked up at our father. "You know, Tom," he said, "that book is on the *Index.*"

"I know, Father," he said. "But I read it anyway."

The priest was mistaken. As far as I can tell, Steinbeck's novel, though highly controversial when it was published in 1939, never made it onto the list of the church's forbidden books. But that didn't matter. What mattered was the sly smile on Tom's face when he informed the priest that he preferred to make up his own mind about what he saw fit to read. It was an undramatic comment, a casual micro-declaration. But, as I look back on it now, it was a milestone in my own journey toward independence of thought.

———————

Unknown to me, there was no shortage of heterodox thinking within the Catholic Church at the time, and Fatima was playing a significant role in it. The Second Vatican Council had unleashed what one critic called the "wild horses of modernism." The updating of the church that Vatican II had called for was, in the eyes of an outraged old guard, a repudiation of everything that they understood Catholicism to be, and a repudiation of what they understood as the message of Fatima. As Father Paul Kramer summed it up in the introduction to his book *The Devil's Final Battle*, there were villains in the church hierarchy who had committed a "great crime" by not revealing to the faithful the contents of the Third Part of the Secret, because they were worried that it would get in the way of fast-tracking Pope John XXIII's urgent reforms.

"The perpetrators," he wrote, "recognize that the contents of the Message of Fatima, as understood in the traditional Catholic sense, cannot coexist with decisions made since the Second Vatican Council . . . decisions which they unswervingly carry out, to change the entire orientation of the Catholic Church." They had taken the modernist bait and fallen for an anodyne notion of "a utopian world 'brotherhood' between men of all religions or no religion at all." The reformers were gullible wimps, playing into the hands of the Kremlin, naively pursuing "groundless hopes for peace and world reconciliation."

The Fatima hard-liners had not forgotten Russia, or the Virgin's demand—as Lucia recorded it—that the church consecrate the godless country to her Immaculate Heart so that it could be converted. On May 13, 1931, the fourteenth anniversary of the first apparition, the bishops of Portugal had followed through, to some degree. At a ceremony in Fatima, witnessed by three hundred thousand people, they had consecrated their own country to the Immaculate Heart. According to Lucia in a letter she wrote to Pope Pius XII in 1940, after the start of World War II, this ceremony would ensure "that a special protection would be granted to our country in this war and this protection will be the proof of graces that would be granted to other nations if they are consecrated to her."

The Fatimists believed that the Virgin Mary took a heavenly role in elevating the abstemious pro-Catholic dictator António Salazar to power in Portugal, the very year after the country consecrated itself to her. They believed that Salazar's support of Francisco Franco in the revolution that took place next door in Spain rescued Portugal from communism, and that the neutral stance he maintained during the Second World War saved it from a reprise of the national trauma that had taken place after Portugal joined the Allied cause in 1916.

But to Lucia, the Portuguese Immaculate Heart pledge was only a trial run. In the vision she claimed to have had in the convent in Tuy in 1929, the Blessed Mother had told her that the pope, along with all the Catholic bishops, would need to "make the consecration of Russia to my Immaculate Heart." Not just Portugal, but the whole world would have to get its consecration act together and stop Russia from infecting all humanity with communism, annihilating nations, throwing souls into hell, and bringing about the end of the world.

As I graduated from high school in the spring of 1966, I was entering a world that seemed to be holding fire, a world in which Lucia's apocalypse had mercifully not yet happened and the Third Part of the Secret had frustratingly not yet been disclosed. But I had been living at the threshold of the end-times for as long as I could remember, and I knew that if the Fatima Letter were ever released, it would only confirm the dread I had been taught to feel about the cataclysmic reckoning I had been told was coming.

14

The Path of the Bullet

From 1960 until 2000, the contents of Lucia's letter were unknown to all the world except for a very few high-ranking church officials. Paul VI, who succeeded to the papacy after John XXIII died of stomach cancer in 1963, appears to have read the document. Loris Capovilla, a cardinal who had been John XXIII's personal secretary, said the new pope decided to follow his predecessor's "reserve" about the letter, neither revealing it to the public nor deploying it, as *Neues Europa* had reported, to bring about the 1963 test ban treaty. Paul VI died in 1978. His successor, sixty-five-year-old Cardinal Albino Luciani, who became John Paul I, was pope for only thirty-three days. "Your Holiness, you shouldn't pull such jokes on me," said one of the nuns who found him lifeless in his bed, his glasses still on his face and the reading light still illuminated above his headboard. Capovilla didn't know if the pope had read the secret letter during his short reign, though he had met Lucia a little over a year before, when he was still a cardinal, and had found her "as radical as the saints." Cardinal Luciani was unsettled when Lucia predicted he would become pope. "Since that day," he wrote, "I have never forgotten Fatima."

Karol Wojtyla, the Polish cardinal who become Pope John Paul II, was the first non-Italian pontiff since the sixteenth century—a literary, athletic, multilingual survivor of the German occupation of Poland. As a young man he had written plays and acted with an underground arts group in Krakow called the Rhapsodic Theater. As a seminarian and a member of a resistance union, he had made a hairsbreadth escape from the Gestapo as they swept through Krakow looking for dissidents after the Warsaw Uprising.

According to John Paul II's spokesman Joaquín Navarro-Valls, the pope read Lucia's letter and learned the Third Part of the Secret of Fatima within days after his ascent to the papacy. Assuming Navarro-Valls is right—others claimed John Paul II didn't read it until years later—the letter's dream imagery seems to have left him underwhelmed.

"If there is a message," he told the German magazine *Stimme des Glaubens* in 1980, "in which it is said that the oceans will flood entire sections of the earth; that, from one moment to the other, millions of people will perish . . . there is no longer any point in really wanting to publish this secret message. Many want to know merely out of curiosity, or because of their taste for sensationalism."

But there was something more profound about the message, and far more personal, that Pope John Paul II was to discover the next year. It was May 13, 1981, the fifty-fourth anniversary of the first apparition of Mary to the *pastorinhos* of Fatima. The pope was riding in an open white jeep along the colonnaded borders of Saint Peter's Square in Vatican City, a weekly ritual that would have culminated in a general address to the ten thousand or so people who had crowded there to see him. He stood upright in the "pope mobile" as it passed the eighty-four-foot-high ancient Egyptian obelisk in the center of the square.

One of the photographs taken that day shows the pope, in his white cassock and white skullcap, reaching forward to shake someone's hand on the right side of the vehicle. There is a tightly packed group of worshippers there, almost all of them reaching out a hand to touch his. One of these people is too far back in the crowd for his face to be visible. But his hand is. It's not open like the others, but clutched around the handle of a Browning 9mm automatic pistol.

The person holding the gun was a twenty-three-year-old Turkish man named Mehmet Ali Agca. With his cropped hair and sharp cheekbones, he looked like an assassin in a spy movie, and an assassin is what he was in real life. Agca was a slippery, shadowy figure who was linked to both Palestinian training camps in the Mideast and to the right-wing Turkish paramilitary organization known as the Grey Wolves. In 1979, he was arrested for murdering Abdi Ipekci, the highly respected editor of the Istanbul newspaper *Milliyet*. "I did it," he declared after his capture. "I killed Ipekci." But after his conviction he teasingly reversed himself. "I did not kill Ipekci," he said, "but I know who did."

He never bothered to follow through on naming the supposed real culprit. A few months after his conviction, he waltzed out of a high-security Turkish military prison. Somebody had given him an army uniform to wear, and the guards at the eight secure doors he passed through on his way to freedom never interfered.

The next day, he sent a letter to the newspaper whose editor he may or may not have actually murdered, informing the world that if John Paul II—"the Commander of the Crusades"—went through with a planned visit to Turkey, "I will without doubt kill the Pope-Chief."

Nobody has ever nailed down exactly who helped break Agca out of prison, or who was bankrolling him afterward as he traveled through a dozen countries, often staying at luxury hotels despite an in-absentia death sentence from Turkey. But he was clearly working for somebody. "Others have a cause," noted a Turkish justice official, "but not Agca."

Who and what brought Agca to Saint Peter's Square on the anniversary of the first apparition to the children of Fatima is, in the opinion of former CIA director Robert Gates, "the last great secret of our time." The most persistent theory, and a reasonably credible one, is that he had been enlisted by the Darzhavna Sigurnost, the Bulgarian secret service, to execute a dark assignment from Moscow.

Pope John Paul II was, by this time, a thorn in the side of the Soviet Union. His first foreign visit as pope, in June of 1979, was to his native country of Poland. The Polish People's Republic was a restive member of the Warsaw Pact, economically shaky and still—despite its communist government—longingly Catholic. The election of Karol Wojtyla to the papacy the year before had galvanized the country, and now when he kissed the ground at Okecie Airport church bells erupted all across Poland. When he said Mass at Warsaw's Victory Square, the communist heart of Poland, half a million people were there. By the end of his nine-day trip, a third of the country had seen him.

One of the places the pope visited in Poland was Jasna Góra, a monastery founded in the fourteenth century that was to Poland what Fatima had become to Portugal—a major pilgrimage site for believers in the Virgin Mary. At Jasna Góra there was a shrine housing a supposedly miraculous image of Mary called the Black Madonna that had been venerated in Poland for over six hundred years. The young Wojtyla had made a secret visit here during the German occupation of World War II and now he was back, rattling the cage of communist Poland for all the world to see.

"Our Lady of the Bright Mountain," he proclaimed at the shrine, "Mother of the Church! . . . I consecrate to you all men and women, my brothers and sisters. All the Peoples and the Nations. I consecrate to you Europe and all the continents. I consecrate to you Rome and Poland, united through your servant, by a fresh bond of love."

It would have been irritating enough to the Polish Politburo for the pope to declare, right under their noses, that he was consecrating their atheist country to the Virgin Mary. But there were more than bad manners at work.

In August of the next year, 1980, workers at the Lenin Shipyard in Gdansk launched a strike that led to the creation of Solidarity, the labor union that morphed into a pro-democracy movement and eventually ended communist rule in Poland. When Lech Walesa, an unemployed electrician and the future president of the country, led the strike in the shipyard, he was wearing a lapel pin of the Black Madonna. Others put up big images of the Madonna and of the pope on the shipyard gates.

A "malicious, lowly, perfidious, and backward toady of the American militarists" was the way one Soviet publication

described Pope John Paul II, the Vatican chief of state whose elec-
trifying visit to Poland had helped inspire the Solidarity revolution
that now threatened to destabilize the USSR. Wojciech Jaruzelski,
the Polish communist leader, recalled the alarm of Soviet General
Secretary Leonid Brezhnev. The Catholic Church, Brezhnev told
Jaruzelski, "was our enemy . . . sooner or later it would gag in our
throats, it would suffocate us."

The stakes were high enough that by December of 1980 eighteen Soviet and Warsaw Pact divisions were preparing to invade
Poland, shut down Solidarity, and arrest and execute its leaders.
And then there was the pope. "Use all possibilities available to
the Soviet Union," the Secretariat of the Central Committee had
directed a few weeks after John Paul II's visit, "to prevent the new
course of policies initiated by the Polish pope; if necessary with
additional measures beyond disinformation and discreditation."

The Soviets weighed the risks of an invasion and decided
to back down, but it's still a vibrant historical question whether
"additional measures" included the outright assassination of the
pope. There's no doubt, though, that Mehmet Ali Agca—a mysterious international operative of some sort, and one who had a sister
named Fatima—was the person holding the Browning pistol that
day in Saint Peter's Square. And after his arrest he recounted in
detail—but later retracted—the story of how he had been recruited
into an earlier, aborted, Bulgarian plot to kill Lech Walesa.

———

Stanislaw Dziwisz, a priest who was the personal secretary to John
Paul II, was riding in the jeep with the pontiff when Agca attacked.
He remembered that the pope had just picked up a young toddler
who was clutching a balloon. He kissed the girl and handed her
back to her parents. The sound of the first shot sent hundreds of
startled pigeons into the air.

"The second shot immediately followed. It was still echoing
in my ears when the Holy Father went limp on one side and then
collapsed into my arms."

The first bullet hit the pope in the abdomen, the second in
his right arm. The driver of the jeep took off with the stricken

pontiff slumped in the back. They sped through the crowds and around the back of Saint Peter's Basilica and stopped at a Vatican emergency room. John Paul was taken out of the popemobile and stretched out on the floor of the lobby, where his personal physician realized he was bleeding to death and ordered him taken by ambulance to Gemelli Hospital in Rome.

"His eyes were closed," Dziwisz remembered of that ambulance sprint to Gemelli. "He was in great pain and he kept repeating short exclamatory prayers. If I remember correctly, it was mainly: 'Mary, my mother! Mary, my mother!'"

There was no mystery that, in agony from the 9mm bullet that had penetrated his abdomen, colon, and small intestine, the pope would address his fears to the shining, soothing mother figure Catholics had turned to for solace for centuries. It was almost instinctive for him, in his distress, to call out to Mary as if she were the mother he had lost to illness when he was eight years old.

Karol Wojtyla had pondered the idea of the Mother of God for most of his life. When he was a young man working at a sodium factory, he had come across a book published in 1700 by a French theologian that was titled *Traité de la vraie dévotion à la Sainte Vierge*—A Treatise on True Devotion to the Blessed Virgin.

"I soon saw," he remembered, "that in spite of the book's baroque style it dealt with something fundamental. As a result, my devotion to the Mother of Christ in my childhood and adolescence yielded to a new attitude springing from the depths of my faith . . .

"My devotion to Mary . . . has lasted since then. It is an integral part of my inner life . . . I should add that my extremely personal and inward spiritual relation to the Mother of Christ had merged since my youth with the great stream of Marian devotion which has a long history in Poland and also many tributaries."

One of those tributaries, he would soon see clearly enough, was Fatima.

Things looked grim for the pontiff when he arrived at Gemelli. Just before he was to be operated on, Dziwisz was told to give him the "final anointing." John Paul survived the operation, but suffered a lot of pain afterward and was rehospitalized when his fever spiked to 104 degrees because of an infection caused by a virus circulating in a blood transfusion he had been given. At some point during his long recovery he started thinking hard about Fatima. "Two thirteenths of May!" wrote Dziwisz. "One in 1917, when the Virgin of Fatima appeared for the first time, and one in 1981, when they tried to kill him."

John Paul then asked to have Lucia's letter brought to him at Gemelli. If, as Navarro-Valls maintained, he had read it after he first became pope, it had not left much of an impression. But things were different after May 13, 1981. He had been shot, had suffered great pain, had almost died, and now, in Dziwisz's words, "he recognized his own destiny."

In the Fatima Letter he read about Lucia's vision of the angel with the flaming sword, a pope—"a Bishop dressed in White"—walking "with pain and sorrow" through a ruined city, passing corpses as he climbs a steep mountain toward a summit crowned with a big, rough-hewn cross. Then—on his knees at the foot of the cross—he is killed by soldiers firing bullets and arrows.

That wasn't John Paul II's destiny, of course. He was shot and survived, and the apocalyptic landscape Lucia described bore no resemblance to the architectural splendor of Saint Peter's Square. But for the pope the misshapen pieces fit into a coherent picture of a narrowly averted prophecy. The bullet that Agca fired had missed his main abdominal artery by only a whisper—a few millimeters. It was the Virgin Mary, the Blessed Virgin, Our Lady, and specifically Our Lady of Fatima, who had saved his life.

"One hand shot," he said, "and another guided the bullet."

─────

Agca was tried and sentenced to life imprisonment in July of 1981. Two years later, in 1983, the pope entered the maximum-security wing of Rome's Rebibbia Prison. He was there to meet and forgive the man who shot him. Agca wore a blue sweater and sneakers without laces. The pope was in a white cassock identical to the one Ahmet had bloodied in Saint Peter's Square. They sat on molded plastic chairs and talked for about twenty minutes or so, John Paul now and then reaching for the bewildered assassin's hand or giving him a reassuring grip on his arm. "At times," reported Lance

Morrow in *Time* magazine, "it looked almost as if the Pope were hearing the confession of Agca, a Turkish Muslim." A Vatican photographer and film crew were there, along with security agents, but the two men spoke out of their hearing in a corner of the cell, next to a radiator. Before he left, John Paul presented Agca with a rosary in a white box.

"What we talked about will have to remain a secret between him and me," the pope said after the visit. "I spoke to him as a brother whom I have pardoned, and who has my complete trust."

But neither Agca nor the pope kept their conversation much of a secret. John Paul related that Agca was very eager to know why he wasn't dead. "In the course of our conversation it became clear that Ali Agca was still wondering how the attempted assassination could possibly have failed. He had planned it meticulously, attending to every tiny detail. And yet his intended victim had escaped death. How could this have happened?"

That was no longer a mystery to John Paul II. "Could I forget that the event in Saint Peter's Square took place on the day and at the hour when the first appearance of the Mother of Christ to the poor little peasants has been remembered for over sixty years at Fatima in Portugal? For, in something that happened to me on that very day, I felt that extraordinary motherly protection and care, which turned out to be stronger than the deadly bullet."

John Paul wrote that Agca's confusion about how he, a professional assassin, had failed to kill his victim drove him to question the pope about the secret of Fatima. "That was his principal concern; more than anything else, he wanted to know this."

Did the pope tell the man who shot him what was in the Fatima Letter more than a decade and a half before the Vatican revealed its contents to the rest of the world? Not likely, although the story of Fatima did seem to be something Agca could relate to. That may have had something to do with the fact that Fatima was also the name of his sister, but probably it was Agca's own grandiose temperament and messianic sense of himself—reinforced by the pope's appearance in his prison cell—that caused him to pay attention.

Agca did not end up serving out his life sentence. At the

request of Pope John Paul II, he was pardoned by an Italian court, then deported to Turkey, where he was reimprisoned for, among other crimes, the murder of Abdi Ipekci. When he was finally paroled in 2010, he announced his willingness, if someone would pay him five million dollars, to cowrite a Vatican thriller with Dan Brown, the author of *The Da Vinci Code*.

Later, in 2014, he let it be known that he wouldn't object if the current pontiff, Pope Francis, made him a priest. His Fatima curiosity was undimmed, and he suggested that he and Francis could go there for the one hundredth anniversary of the Virgin Mary's first appearance to Lucia, Jacinta, and Francisco. While there, he would pray "to the Madonna, my spiritual mother."

———

Almost from the beginning of the Fatima apparitions in 1917, pilgrims had been leaving unsolicited donations, most of which ended up falling into the hands of a devout local woman named Maria Carreira. She wanted nothing to do with the money, and thought the best use of it was to build a small chapel at the site of the *azinheira* where the Virgin had first appeared to the children. The Cova by then was almost unrecognizable as the idyllic spot it had been before. "The people spoiled everything," Carreira remembered, "so that nothing would grow there. They spoiled the trees cutting branches—big branches, not twigs—right and left until there was nothing left growing near the tree of the Apparitions."

But a little chapel—a *capelinha*—was built there over the course of a few months in 1919 to mark the place of the miraculous appearances. A young Portuguese sculptor, José Ferreira Thedim, was hired to create a statue of the Virgin for the chapel. It was about three and a half feet tall, carved from Brazilian cedar, painted in soft blue and white and flesh tones. It depicted a very young, sad-looking woman leaning just a bit to her left, her hands folded in prayer, her bare feet resting on a swirling cloud which itself rests on a suggestion of the tree crown on which the children said she appeared.

When the box containing the statue was opened at the

capelinha on May 13, 1920, three years after the first apparition, thirteen-year-old Lucia was there to witness it and, according to de Marchi, she "leaned over [the statue] with tears running down her cheeks."

One night in 1922, anticlerical activists planted bombs in the *capelinha* and effectively blew it up, but the statue survived, because Maria Carreira took it home every night for safekeeping. The chapel was quickly rebuilt, and the statue that continued to reside within it grew more and more venerated. In the 1940s, a group of Portuguese women sent out a call for donations of gold pieces and precious stones and commissioned the famous Lisbon jewelers Casa Leitão & Irmão to create an elaborate crown, made of eight converging arches, for the statue.

Pope John Paul II knelt before this statue, and its gilded crown, in the expanded and modernized *capelinha* when he came to Fatima on May 13, 1982, a year after being shot. He was there to help fulfill Lucia's wish of consecrating the whole world to the Immaculate Heart of Mary, but also to ponder what he considered the near-miracle of his own narrow escape. "And so I come here today," he said, "because on this very day last year, in Saint Peter's Square in Rome, the attempt on the Pope's life was made, in mysterious coincidence with the anniversary of the first apparition at Fatima, which occurred on 13 May 1917. I seemed to recognize in the coincidence of the dates a special call to come to this place."

It turned out not to be the only assassination attempt that coincided with the Fatima apparitions. As the pope was making his way toward the outdoor altar in front of the basilica that day, a young priest surged out of the crowd. His name was Juan María Fernández y Krohn. He had been ordained by the uncompromising right-wing French archbishop Marcel Lefebvre, who would end up being excommunicated six years later. But even Lefebvre had turned out to be too soft for Fernández y Krohn, who was now a member of the radical Sedevacantist group, which considered every pope since Pius XII to be illegitimate.

Fernández y Krohn lunged at the pope with a bayonet, and managed to graze him and draw blood before security forces restrained him.

"I accuse you of destroying the Church," the assassin yelled at the pope as he struggled to get free. "Death to the Second Vatican Council!"

The pope was shaken, but not too shaken to go on with the ceremony and give his second attempted assassin his blessing.

15

The Gnawing Beast

Lucia was seventy-four years old when the pope was shot. She was no longer known as Sister Maria das Dores, the name she was given when she joined the Sisters of Saint Dorothy and lived in convents in Portugal and Spain. Since 1948 she had been Sister Maria Lucia of Jesus and the Immaculate Heart, a member of the Discalced Carmelite nuns living in a strictly cloistered convent in Coimbra, Portugal. "Discalced," derived from Latin, means "without shoes," and refers to the fact that Carmelites, along with several other religious orders, protect their feet only with sandals, a custom originated by saints like Francis of Assisi and his follower Clare.

The first pope Lucia saw was Paul VI, when he visited Fatima in 1967, on the fiftieth anniversary of the May 13 apparition. She was given permission to leave her convent and travel to Fatima so she could meet him. She had never before been in the presence of a pope, and the anticipation of a private encounter seemed to shake her loose from the severe rectitude that she had strived for so much of her life to achieve. "Is it true?" she wrote of the impending face-to-face with the pontiff. "I do not know! But I know that God is good, very good!"

Riding to Fatima by automobile, passing lines of pilgrims who were trudging along the muddy roads in the rain toward the great Basilica of Our Lady of the Rosary that was now the centerpiece of the sprawling pilgrimage site, she felt a keen desire to get out of the car. "If it were possible," she remembered feeling, "I would hide as a stranger, unknown among them, joining my voice to theirs, spending the night outside in the cold . . ."

But it wasn't possible. She knew that the moment she showed her face in Fatima she would be in the middle of a throng of believers who would want to speak to her and touch her and ask her to intercede with the Virgin on their behalf. It would be a much-multiplied version of the demanding fame that had dogged her since she was a little girl, that frightened her and threatened her identity as a humble servant of God.

At the same time, she was as susceptible to hero worship as any other human, and when she finally saw the pope—"the Vicar of Christ on earth whom I revere, obey and cherish as the representative of the same God"—she was almost overcome. She kissed his feet and his ring, and expected that when she asked to speak with him in private he would of course want to meet with the surviving *pastorinha* of Fatima. But according to Lucia's own account, he simply said "No." (The pope, in the opinion of his close friend Jean Guitton, "had a sort of generic aversion for visionaries.") But he did at least give her a rosary, and her bitterness at being rebuffed must have been tempered when, after the Mass, Paul VI went out onto the gallery of the basilica and looked out at the many thousands of people who had filled the esplanade of the shrine and were waving white handkerchiefs. They were yelling, "Show us Lucia!"

Recognizing the moment for what it was, the pope took Lucia's hand and called out to the sea of pilgrims who were straining to get a look at her, "Here she is!"

The black-and-white video you can see online of that day shows just a glimpse of Lucia's face as she rises from her seat and stands next to the pope, looking out at the tightly packed crowd of people standing on the sea of pavement where her father's crops once grew and where she and Jacinta and Francisco once tended sheep and played childhood games. The sixty-year-old nun, in her severe black-and-white-and-brown Carmelite habit, is doing her best to remain expressionless and suppress any outward sign of happiness or satisfaction, but she can't quite succeed. ("In truth," she had once written to one of her confessors about her battles with her ego, "I do not know how to destroy this gnawing beast which gets into everything.") The unwelcome fame that had driven her into the cloister seems, in this moment, something she is almost willing to embrace.

———

When John Paul II made his own visit to Fatima in 1982, a year after Agca's attack, the papal outreach to Lucia was far more of a priority. Not only did the pope believe that Our Lady had decided to prevent the central vision of the Third Part of the Secret of Fatima—the death of the Bishop in White from gunfire—from becoming a reality. He had also studied all the documents relating to the Fatima apparitions and, as he told a bishop when he left the hospital, "I have come to understand that the only way to save the world from war, to save it from atheism, is the conversion of Russia according to the message of Fatima."

So there was a sense of urgency and fellow feeling when John Paul met Lucia for the first time in Fatima.

"We have to talk fast," he told her, "because the time is short."

At this point Lucia and the pope were only two of a handful of people who knew the contents of the letter in which she had revealed the Third Part of the Secret of Fatima, and she recalled that the two of them "agree that it was more prudent to keep it silent as before."

Lucia also wanted to speak to John Paul about the beatification of Jacinta and Francisco. Beatification is a step short of sainthood, an official recognition by the church that a dead person is reliably in heaven and therefore in a position to be prayed to and to intercede with God or other beings in the celestial hierarchy.

The pope told Lucia that he, too, wanted the two dead shepherd children to be beatified and that he would do his best to make it happen. While he was in Fatima, he made a point of praying before the tombs of Francisco and Jacinta. The bodies of both children had been reinterred by that time in the transepts of the basilica. He encountered Lucia there, also kneeling, praying for her young cousins.

"Happy are you, my daughter," he said, as he bent down to kiss Lucia's veil.

The pope told Lucia he would fulfill the request she said the Virgin Mary had made when, one late night in 1929, she had visited the young nun in her convent chapel: "The moment has come in which God asks the Holy Father, in union with all the Bishops of the world, to make the consecration of Russia to my Immaculate Heart, promising to save it by this means."

The pope did this, or at least thought he did, during that same 1982 visit to Fatima, when he proclaimed that "the power of this consecration lasts for all time and embraces all individuals, peoples and nations. It overcomes every evil that the spirit of darkness is able to awaken . . ."

There was a problem, though, because in Lucia's mind neither Pope Paul VI nor Pope Pius XII before him had met the strict requirement she had heard from Our Lady that the consecration take place "in union with all the Bishops of the world." As it turned out, all the bishops of the world had not been notified in 1982 in time to be aware that the consecration was going to happen, so they couldn't have been "in union" with it. Lucia complained with such conviction about this technical breach that two years later the pope decided to do it all over again.

This time the consecration took place in Rome, in Saint Peter's Square. And for the occasion the cherished statue of Our Lady of Fatima, with the golden, jewel-encrusted crown that had been the gift of the women of Portugal, was flown to the Vatican. The night before the ceremony, the pope asked for the chapel to be cleared, and he stayed there all alone, kneeling in front of the little statue, thanking the Virgin for saving his life.

The day after the consecration, at a private dinner with trusted church officials, the pope wanted to know if they thought the request of Our Lady to Lucia had finally been properly fulfilled. They agreed that it had. Afterward, in his private chapel, John Paul II turned to Alberto Cosme do Amaral, the bishop of Leiria, and said, "This is a gift for Our Lady."

In the pope's open hand was a bullet that had been fired from Mehmet Ali Agca's gun, and that Monsignor Dziwisz had retrieved from the floor of the jeep after it had passed through the pope's body without, somehow, causing his death.

"None of us were able to say a word," recalled one of the priests who were present in the chapel. "All of us had eyes filled with tears."

But what to do with such a precious object? After some thought and consultation, they decided there was only one place for it. So it was sent off to Portugal's most venerable jewelers, Casa Leitão & Irmão, to be welded into the golden crown of the statue of Our Lady of Fatima.

16

Nobody There

Lucia's encounters with Paul VI and John Paul II were not her only return visits to Fatima. She first went back in 1946, having been away from her home for a quarter of a century. She had been a fourteen-year-old girl when, under orders from the Bishop Silva, she had said a sorrowful goodbye to her mother and boarded the train to Porto. When she saw Fatima next, she was a thirty-nine-year-old woman, again under bishop's orders, instructed to lead a group of priests and convent mothers to the pastureland that had now become holy ground. She took them to the still-rocky places where she and her young cousins had believed they saw an angel, and to Valinhos, where the Virgin had appeared to them after they had been detained and imprisoned by the administrator at Ourém. They walked through an olive grove that had belonged to Lucia's parents, "and where each stone reminded me of my conversations with Jacinta and Francisco." She saw the graves of the two young shepherds, still buried then in the local cemetery along with her mother and father and the many victims of the worldwide pandemic.

And she went to the Cova da Iria, of course. The tree where the Virgin had appeared to her was long gone, but the little Chapel of the Apparitions stood now in its place, and the others left her alone as she knelt there and prayed. "While kneeling down there after so many years," she remembered, "I felt a strong impression, such as that of a shiver, but managed to control myself without the Mothers knowing. Then with an inner energy I was filled with the memory of events that took place, and then the Mother touched me on the shoulder to go home and I was completely serene."

But at that time in Lucia's life serenity was a moving target. She dearly wanted to go even deeper into a life of seclusion and prayer, to become a Carmelite nun. "It is not that I intend to find in Carmel a life of roses," she explained to a friend. "No. I think that if anything it will perhaps reap more painful thorns . . . but what I try to find in Carmel and what I do not have here, or cannot have, are the enclosed walls that protect me from the large stream of curious and indiscreet views."

She was almost forty years old but was still thought of by at least one of her superiors as "very simple . . . a child of the mountains."

She struck a visiting Dominican priest, Father Thomas McGlynn, as more interesting. "There seemed to be both passive and active qualities in her attitude. She humbly attended on the completion of any question yet keenly studied the person and words of the questioner. Agility and strength of mind were reflected in her mobile, expressive mouth and large chin."

McGlynn was intrigued by her alternating moods of humor and rectitude. He was not just a priest but a sculptor, who had come to consult with Lucia in 1947 about a new statue of Our Lady of Fatima. Unlike José Ferreira Thedim's much-adored wooden statue in the *capelinha*, this one would be a colossal thirteen-ton image, carved in marble, bound for a commanding niche at the front of the basilica. The statue was to be based on the memories of what Lucia said she had seen in 1917. Father McGlynn had brought a model for her inspection. "Wrinkles formed on her brow," the nervous artist recalled of her stark reaction to his preliminary rendering, "(and in my soul)."

No, Lucia told him, the Virgin's feet had not rested upon a cloud, as so many people said, but upon the leaves of the holm oak itself. The tree was young, and it had been no taller than she had been as a ten-year-old girl. She instructed McGlynn that the gar-

ments in his model were too smooth. She said he needed to capture the way the light around her moved in waves and undulated
her clothing. The sculptor was surprised when Lucia told him that
the Lady's Immaculate Heart should be depicted as almost pop-
ping outside of her body. She also said the Virgin's face was too
old, and then demonstrated with her own body the prayerful position of the apparition's left and right hands. The only praise she
saw fit to offer was that seen from the side, the statue was a little
better.

Gamely absorbing Lucia's criticism, McGlynn started over,
creating another model with the shepherdess of Fatima as his col-
laborator. They worked on it for almost a week, and when it was
finished the priest packed it up to take to Rome, where he hoped
to see Pope Pius XII and have the pontiff bless his work.

When she heard this, Lucia asked him to deliver a sealed letter
"without anyone else knowing."

Unlike the famous letter she had written three years earlier,
in which she had set down in writing the Third Part of the Secret
of Fatima, this was a personal plea to the pope. For years, she had
been trying to find a way to seal herself more tightly away from
the world. She had not always gotten along with her fellow sisters
or superiors. She was as headstrong as she was humble, and sometimes felt singled out or exploited.

"Often on Sunday afternoons," she once vented in a letter to
her confessor, "I had to leave the Chapel so that the people who
were spying on me from the gallery would stop whispering and dis-
respecting Our Lord . . . Many times, the Rev. Mothers went as far
as taking people to the door and windows of the Clothes Room
to get a peep at me . . . There was no end to the holy pictures that
had to be signed."

In 1941, she had volunteered to become a missionary in Africa,
declaring that "I would be happier to be buried in leprosy reap-
ing the groans of humanity in decay, offer them to God as reparation for the sins of the world." Nothing came of the offer, or of her
repeated requests to join the Carmelites. But the chance of Father
McGlynn delivering her plea directly to the pope was a sign she
couldn't ignore. "The door is open," she realized now, "should I
enter? If I attempt to arrange things through my Superiors, I will

never be able to! If the Holy Father tells me yes, then no one would dare say no."

Several months later, Bishop Silva told her that the pope had agreed to her request to become a Carmelite nun. But it would be over a year, a fairly miserable year, before she could present herself at the Carmelite Convent of Saint Teresa in Coimbra. In October of 1947 she got sick again, this time catching the flu and developing a serious fever after sleeping in a drafty room. A dentist who saw her soon afterward decided that she needed to have all her teeth pulled, so the next months were spent enduring extractions and adjusting to the fitting of false teeth.

Mouth-sore, humbled yet again by illness, she arrived at her new home that next March, asking to enter the convent early in the morning so that no one would see her, and no unwanted attention would come her way. On the thirteenth of May, 1948, the forty-first anniversary of the first apparition, in a closed ceremony, she was officially clothed in the Carmelite habit and then shown to the cell where she would live. When she entered, she saw the big bare cross that adorned each nun's room. "Our Reverend Mother Prioress asked me: 'Do you know why this cross has no statue [corpus]?' And without giving me time to answer she added: 'It is so that you may crucify yourself on it.'"

Lucia had no qualms, no doubts. "What a beautiful idea to be crucified with Christ!" she remembered thinking. "Here lies the secret of my happiness."

And so she settled even deeper into a life of prayer, reflection, and hard-won anonymity. She was forty-one years old. She would remain there, at the Carmelite convent in Coimbra, living in the same cell, praying to a statue of the Immaculate Heart in the convent garden, for the next fifty-seven years.

———

The "enclosed walls" that Lucia sought for so much of her life meant the opposite of what they would have meant to me and to other restive Catholics later in the twentieth century. For her, a retreat from the physical world was a pathway to liberation, to mental and spiritual expansiveness.

"The temptations of the devil," she conceded in a book she composed about the meanings of the apparitions, "penetrate even into the cloister." But it's hard to imagine her being much tempted by anything more than a normal human longing to be at peace. The peace she sought was the goal she ascribed to all "consecrated souls"—to experience God's presence and "plunge themselves into His immense Being."

God's immense being became for me, over time, a suffocating blanket. After four years of an all-boys Catholic high school, I wasn't quite ready to take my place in the secular world, so I went for my first year of college to St. Edward's University. It was a small school in what was at that time the South Austin hinterlands, four or five miles from the bustling, beckoning University of Texas in the heart of town. This was 1966, six years after the date the Fatima Letter was supposed to be, but was not, revealed. But the mysterious contents of the letter, the Third Part of the Secret of Fatima, no longer had much of a grip on my imagination. It had receded to about the same low-humming curiosity level with which I wondered if there were really UFOs in the sky or a monster swimming through Loch Ness. And there were more immediate worries: America's deepening involvement in the Vietnam War; its increasingly edgy confrontation with its racial realities; a bitter, unprecedented divide between the generations; and an incipient sense that the country could very well fall apart.

I went to St. Edward's the first year it was no longer an all-male school, though girls were technically part of a different college on the same campus grounds, called Maryhill, a reference to the Blessed Mother and perhaps a hopeful nod—as the sexual revolution was surging forward—to her ever-virgin state.

Some of the classes were taught by priests and brothers of the Congregation of Holy Cross, but our teachers were mostly lay professors, and how much or how little you wanted to tune in to the Catholic vibe was pretty much left up to you. There was a chapel on campus—Our Lady Queen of Peace—and I began my college days dutifully attending Mass there every Sunday.

On one Sunday morning, though, I overslept. I had grown up believing—or at least being told—that missing Mass on Sunday was a mortal sin. And of course a mortal sin was a ticket to hell. I no longer consciously thought there was any such thing as hell, or that a supposedly benevolent God could have created an unending prison of pain that was more cruel, more evil, than the human sins that so offended him. But going to Mass still registered somewhere in my mind as an obligation, so I hurriedly got dressed and made it to the chapel just as the offertory—the part of the Mass where the priest prepares the bread and wine for communion—was concluding.

I was there by myself, and feeling a little odd about the fact that I was the only freshman in my dorm who had felt the need to crawl out of bed, get dressed, and drag himself to church. After the Mass was over and I left, dodging the skateboarders on the empty street in front of the chapel, I was struck with an unwelcome memory. Somewhere along my journey as a Catholic kid, I had been told that if you arrived so late as to miss the offertory, it meant you had to go to Mass all over again.

I don't think this was ever an official church teaching, but that didn't mean that some nun or priest had not told me that it was, and that I had believed them. I was angry with myself for going to so much trouble to go to Mass and not getting credit for it. I had a choice to make. I could attend the next service or go on with my life knowing that I had not fulfilled my Sunday obligation and that, come midnight, I would be in a state of mortal sin and my eternal soul would be imperiled. Or I could just say to myself, as I had been secretly longing to do: forget it, I'm through.

The door to liberation had unexpectedly swung open. I knew I was not going back to Mass, and I knew it was laughable to think I would be going to hell because of it. Just like that, it was over. That fall morning in 1966 was my last day as a practicing Catholic. I never went to Mass on my own initiative again.

I don't remember being tortured about that decision, any wrestling with the question of whether or not God existed, or whether he was a caring god or merely a celestial clockmaker, or how the universe could possibly exist without some kind of designer. It was just . . . over.

Atheism? No, nothing so declarative or insistent. It was more like the pleasingly exhausted feeling of waking up from a nap. I had lived too long in a world where my thoughts and actions were squeezed down by rules like the one I had just violated: no missing the offertory, no eating meat on Friday, no elbows on the pews. And once the random scaffolding holding up the great mystery of the existence of God began to fall, the answer struck me as self-evident: nobody was there, nobody was ruling, nobody was observing. But it was a revelation that only cleared the way for an existence filled with greater and more interesting mysteries. I didn't feel conflicted, or afraid, or worried that without the super-structure of my religion I would slide into depravity or sin. I was *happy*.

It was only that simple for a little while. Disentangling myself from my religion, from the rituals and strictures that had formed my identity, has been—as this book bears witness—a lifelong proj-ect. I'm aware that Catholicism can be a more capacious, more intellectually nourishing expression of belief than the narrow version I experienced growing up, and I suppose I'm open to the charge of not giving it a chance and allowing some broader con-cept of God to expand along with my developing consciousness.

In my Catholic life, there had never been much of an intel-lectual component. The religion class where Father Augustine had declared that God was not dead no matter what *Time* maga-zine said was a clear enough demonstration that probing ques-tions were not welcome. Later I would have Catholic friends who had been educated by Jesuits and who were accustomed to robust academic bull sessions that welcomed doubt and hereti-cal thought. It was hard to pin these friends down on what they specifically believed or didn't believe. They had read Thomas Aquinas and Teilhard de Chardin and Thomas Merton and took a deep satisfaction in pondering how God manifested himself in the world while questioning whether such a thing as God really existed. They weren't unsettled by the disconnect between their traditional religious observances and their vaporous, metaphori-cal beliefs. But it all seemed like wasted mental gymnastics to me. Theology bored and confused me. If there was a God, why would he need so much explication? Wouldn't he have the power to make himself known and understood? If there wasn't a God—well, then there just wasn't, and what was the point of talking about it?

But I envied people who could wear their religion easily, who could balance it with what seemed to be an honest inquiry of thought. I see how life would have been easier on me and on my family if I had been able to do so, if I could have found a place for myself where familiar rituals—the Mass, the sign of the cross, the muttered prayers—were just that. Not a proclamation of faith, or a test of it, but a way to acknowledge that human nature is captive to the idea of something much larger than ourselves and that despite any real evidence we're determined to give it a name and a story.

But my Catholic childhood had shaped me into a rule follower, so just going through the motions like that would have felt like a transgression—a secular mortal sin.

None of that troubled me on that day in 1966 when I was eighteen years old and felt that sudden tailwind of freedom. My burden of worry about Fatima, and what it portended for the world, was now just a bad memory. Faith in God was a memory, too, though I would never quite lose a residual yearning for the cosmic motherly goodness exemplified by the Virgin Mary. I knew nothing about Lucia except for the fact that she had written a letter whose withheld contents had once scared the wits out of me but that now was just something I had cast off along with my other childhood nightmares. I didn't know that she was still alive, only a few months away from her meeting in Fatima with Pope Paul VI. I couldn't have understood that the exhilaration I felt that day as I slipped out of that chapel into the open world might not be all that different from the ecstasy that Sister Lucia sought in prayer, alone in her cell in Coimbra, as she waited for another visit from the Virgin Mary.

17

The Veil of the Future

The nine-year-old body of Jacinta Marto was exhumed twice. The first time was in 1935, when she was removed from the cemetery in Ourém and reburied in Fatima next to her brother, and fellow childhood visionary, Francisco. The fact that after fifteen years in a grave her face was still recognizable created a legend of saintly incorruptibility that is evident in artwork you can order today on the internet, purporting to be Jacinta's serene countenance in eternal repose.

Early in the 1950s, her coffin was disturbed once again, when both she and Francisco were exhumed and interred in the transept of the basilica that had been built only a hundred yards or so from the site of the apparitions. By that time Francisco's body had mostly crumbled to bones, and there's a heartbreaking photo of Jacinta in her coffin that demonstrates the limits of the cruel illusion that God had chosen to preserve her mortal remains. The little girl's face is corroded and mummified. But what's most haunting about the photograph is not Jacinta's corpse, it's the crowd of people looking down upon it, studying it with sorrowing expressions. They include a portly bishop, a young priest, and three doctors or forensic examiners in white lab coats. And with them are Jacinta's parents. Olimpia Marto has already reached her eighties;

her husband, Manuel, is four years younger. They have long out-
lived the four children they lost to the flu pandemic and are only a
few years from their own deaths. They are both staring hard, their
faces wrinkled, their mouths set tight in grief. You wonder, looking at this photo, how they could have allowed themselves to be
here, how they could have borne it.

They wouldn't have been able to deny the physical decay in
front of them, but they were not the sort of people who could
doubt that Jacinta's and Francisco's souls were untouched and forever in the heavenly custody of the Virgin Mary.

They would die long before that belief became a certified doc-
trinal fact, when Pope John Paul II returned to Fatima on May 13,
2000, to certify the beatification of Francisco and Jacinta Marto.
This first step on the way to their eventual canonization as saints
had been a process that took almost fifty years. It had required
decades of research by Vatican postulators and vice-postulators
and much theological debate by the Congregation for the Causes
of Saints about whether children of Francisco and Jacinta's age
had the maturity level to "heroically" exercise their faith. And the
children had to be credited with at least one miracle. This was
supplied by the case of a woman named Maria Emília Santos, who
had been bedridden for twenty-two years by what was described
as "a probable transverse myelitis." In 1989, after praying for the
intercession of Jacinta, she heard a buzzing noise in her head and a
voice telling her to sit up. She did, then progressed to a wheelchair,
and finally was able to walk again. The cure, according to the testimony of an ecclesiastical panel of doctors, was "rapid, complete,
lasting and scientifically inexplicable."

Six hundred thousand people came to Fatima to hear Pope
John Paul II declare Jacinta and Francisco blessed and to talk
about the "immense light which penetrated the inmost depths of
the three children." The pope by then was five days shy of eighty
years old. His health was grim. After almost being shot to death
nineteen years earlier, he had endured surgeries for a colon tumor,
a broken femur, and an inflamed appendix. Though it had not yet
been officially announced that he suffered from Parkinson's disease, his unsteadiness and rigid facial muscles made the condition
clear enough. The night before, in front of the many thousands of

people who had come to see him and were gathered at the Fatima Sanctuary, he had fallen to his knees alone in front of the statue in the *capelinha*. The devotion of the stricken pope to the Virgin Mary had moved the cheering, waving crowd into such sudden silence and stillness that the only sound that could be heard was the flapping and twittering of the sanctuary's resident birds.

———

Lucia was in Fatima as well that day, ninety-three years old. The elderly nun and the ailing pope met privately for a few minutes before joining nine cardinals, a thousand priests, and five hundred children at the altar outside the basilica where the rites were to take place. When the pope announced the beatification, bells rang throughout the great plaza and two gigantic black-and-white photographs—one of Francisco and one of Jacinta—were unveiled on either side of the basilica's two-hundred-foot-high bell tower. Lucia was among those staring at the photographs as a choir sang a newly composed hymn in honor of the two children. The colossal images were familiar to students of Fatima—nine-year-old Francisco in his voluminous stocking cap and rustic coat, Jacinta staring forward with a pout on her face, her left hand on her hip, her hair half covered by the headscarf known as a *lenço*. At the dawn of the twenty-first century, they were the embodiment of stopped time, whereas Lucia, still alive eighty-three years after she and her beatified cousins said they saw the Virgin Mary in the Cova da Iria, was living proof of its relentless momentum.

After the ceremony, Cardinal Angelo Sodano, the Vatican's secretary of state, stepped up to the microphone and made a startling announcement, one that the Catholic world had almost given up on hearing. Sodano told the multitudes gathered at the Fatima shrine that the pope had directed the Congregation for the Doctrine of the Faith, the division of the Roman curia that polices and promulgates Catholic beliefs, to finally reveal the contents of Lucia's letter, the Third Part of the Secret of Fatima.

The document, Sodano said, would be made public soon, after the church had had a chance to prepare an "appropriate commentary" to accompany it. But the cardinal himself gave a preview to the hundreds of thousands of people in front of him, pointing out that the mysterious message concerned a "Bishop clothed in White" murdered in front of a cross, and that it presaged the assassination attempt in 1981 on Pope John Paul II.

Lucia's text, Sodano said, "contains a prophetic vision similar to those found in Sacred Scripture, which do not describe with photographic clarity the details of future events, but rather synthesize and condense against a unified background events spread out over time in a succession and a duration which are not specified. As a result, the text must be interpreted in a symbolic key."

No "photographic clarity"? "Symbolic key"? The world had been waiting since 1917 for a direct pronouncement from Our Lady of Fatima, but what they got instead from Sodano's preemptive explanation of the Third Part of the Secret was a theological word thicket. And there was much more obfuscation and puzzlement to come.

The official unveiling of Lucia's letter came that next month, when the Vatican held a televised press conference at which it revealed the full text, along with commentary by Vatican notables like future secretary of state Archbishop Tarcisio Bertone and future pope Joseph Ratzinger, who was then the prefect of the Congregation for the Doctrine of the Faith.

Ratzinger wasted no time in squelching expectations about what many Catholics regarded as the greatest mystery of the twentieth century. The Third Part of the Secret, he wrote in his commentary, "will probably prove disappointing or surprising after all the speculation it has stirred. No great mystery is revealed; nor is the future unveiled . . . Those who expected exciting apocalyptic revelations about the end of the world or the future course of history are bound to be disappointed."

No kidding! Marco Tosatti, a veteran Vatican journalist and author, asked Ratzinger one of many obvious questions:

"Eminence, if you had to explain why the Church has not revealed this secret for fifty years, to a very simple person, what would you say?"

The profoundly unsatisfying answer: "It made no sense to offer to humanity an undecipherable image that would have created only speculations."

"The immediate reaction of millions of Catholics," wrote Father Paul Kramer in a book that came out two years later with the ominous title of *The Devil's Final Battle*, "could be summarized in two words: *That's it?*"

Kramer was one of the angry traditionalists who believed that Pope John XXIII's Vatican II reforms had betrayed the majesty and credibility of the Catholic Church and, in its dreams of "a utopian world 'brotherhood' between men of all religions or no religion at all" had appeased the same godless communism that Our Lady had warned against in her messages to the three shepherd children of Fatima. For years, such critics had warned, the church had been trying to sell the faithful a version of "Fatima lite . . . a Message of Fatima stripped of its divine warnings and reduced to generic pietism [as] the world moves ever closer to that great chastisement of which the Virgin has warned us again and again in this age of apostasy."

The most notorious of such voices was a Canadian priest named Nicholas Gruner, whose preaching and whose magazine, *The Fatima Crusader*, was convinced that with Vatican II the Church had sold itself out to the forces of atheism, that in reaching out to its religious cousins in the Orthodox Church it had unwittingly invited "KGB operatives in the garb of priests" into the heart of the Holy See. Not only had Pope John XXIII's reforms been predicated upon a "Vatican-Moscow" agreement, but "when it comes to Fatima," Gruner wrote in 1992, "we have been sold a bill of goods." He was determined to make the world understand that not even the pope's do-over consecration in 1984 had satisfied Our Lady's requirements, because he used weasel phrases like "all individuals and peoples" when the Virgin had pointedly told the shepherds that it was Russia that had to be consecrated and converted.

But it wasn't just the anti-Russian, anti-Vatican II, anti-world-brotherhood hardliners who thought there had to be more to the Third Part of the Secret than the confusing verbiage revealed at the press conference and the way that Ratzinger and the other ecclesiastical spin doctors tried to decode it.

In fact, there was widespread skepticism from the beginning that the church, for whatever reason, was withholding something.

Both Sodano and Ratzinger, not to mention Pope John Paul II himself, believed that Lucia's letter, with its vision of a pope being murdered, was a prophetic reference to the 1981 shooting of the pontiff in Saint Peter's Square.

But wait a minute: John Paul II, unlike the pope in Lucia's vision, wasn't brought down at the top of a mountain in an apocalyptic wasteland, kneeling at the foot of a big cross, "killed by a group of soldiers who fired bullets and arrows at him." He was shot in a moving vehicle in the middle of Saint Peter's Square, not by a group of soldiers but by a single would-be assassin, who fired only bullets, not arrows, and the pope didn't die but—as he testified himself—was saved by the Virgin Mary rerouting the deadly projectile.

The church blunted this objection, sort of, by declaring that the prophecy was symbolic, in line with the apocalyptic imagery in the Book of Revelation, the last book of the New Testament, with its nightmare depictions of things like seven-headed, seven-horned sea beasts and a great dragon that sweeps the stars out of the sky with its tail.

No, Ratzinger wrote, the Fatima Letter was not a prediction. "The image which the children saw is in no way a film preview of a future in which nothing can be changed. Indeed, the whole point of the vision is to bring freedom onto the scene and to steer freedom in a positive direction."

All this felt like a rhetorical smoke screen to people who had been expecting some sort of clear statement about the future of the world from the Blessed Mother herself. When he first tried to read the Fatima Letter in its original Portuguese, Pope John XXIII had complained of its "abstruse locutions." But now the abstruseness was reaching a new pitch of exquisite parsing and conspiracy theorizing.

For instance, "etc." This seemingly innocuous expression doesn't appear anywhere in the text of the Third Part of the Secret, but deep-dive Fatima scholars had had their eyes trained on it since 1941, when Lucia wrote her fourth memoir and recounted what she said the Virgin had confided to her and Francisco and Jacinta during the July 13 apparition in 1917. As we've seen, the shimmering figure on top of the holm oak tree had just shown the children a horrifying vision of hell—the "first secret," according to Lucia—and then conveyed to them the "second secret," which was a warning that if Russia was not consecrated to her Immaculate Heart the Red Menace would spread throughout the world, causing wars and persecutions and the annihilation of nations.

But Lucia reported that the Virgin predicted that "the Holy Father will consecrate Russia to me, and she will be converted, and a period of peace will be granted to the world. In Portugal, the dogma of the Faith will always be preserved; etc. . . ."

This "etc." was, in the words of the Italian journalist Antonio Socci, "a truly explosive little phrase."

Why? Well, it's hard to explain, mostly because at the level of subatomic scrutiny where such Fatima investigations take place, it's hard to understand. Here's how Father Kramer puts it, as succinctly though as confusingly as anybody: "The incomplete phrase, ending with 'etc.' . . . clearly introduces a heavenly prediction, containing further words of Our Lady not recorded."

So: the "etc." that appears in Lucia's account of the second secret is regarded as a hint that the Virgin Mary was about to say something else, something that should be expected to appear in the Third Part of the Secret. But since the document is written by Sister Lucia as a vision experienced by herself and not as a narration by the Virgin, there must be . . . a fourth secret?

Yes, the skeptics believe, somewhere in the dark, black depths of the secret Vatican archives there is another document, one that actually states what the "etc." implies, that is written in the words that the Virgin Mary herself spoke, and that is too compromising to the church hierarchy or too horrible to the world at large to be revealed.

A big part of the reason they believe this has to do with the number of pages, and the number of lines of Lucia's handwriting that make up the text of the Third Part of the Secret. The document had long been thought, based on the impression of a priest, Monsignor João Venancio, who in 1957 had supposedly held the double-sealed envelope that enclosed it up to the light, to have been a single sheet of paper with an estimated twenty to twenty-five handwritten lines. But the text unveiled by the Vatican at the press conference had sixty-two lines, and was written on four sheets of paper. So either the Venancio assessement, if it even occurred, was way off base, or the church, for reasons of its own, had withheld the real Fatima Letter and substituted one of its own.

"In traditionalist circles," Socci maintains in his book *The Fourth Secret*, "there is by now a widespread conviction that the Vatican is hiding from the world a tremendous and unspeakable secret."

But what secret, and why is the Vatican hiding it? If you read the work of the diehard Fatimists, you get the impression that Catholicism has been in the grip of the devil ever since the reforms of Vatican II. That in slackening its rituals, in abandoning the Latin Mass, in reaching out to the modern world, it sold its ancient soul and allowed godlessness to spread, horrors like 9/11 to occur, and scandals like pedophile priests to hollow out the moral authority of the church. They quote Cardinal Pacelli, who would become Pope Pius XII, stating in 1931 that the Blessed Virgin's message to Lucia and the children of Fatima was in effect a "divine warning against the suicide of altering the faith, in [the church's] liturgy, her theology and her soul." They quote Pope Paul VI worrying, ten years after Vatican II began, that "from somewhere or other the smoke of Satan has entered the temple of God. . . . It was believed that after the council a sunny day in the church's history would dawn, but instead there came a day of clouds, storms and darkness."

They don't buy Ratzinger's claim, in his theological interpretation of the Third Part of the Secret, that the events it describes "belong to the past" or especially Bertone's opinion that "the 'secret' of Fatima brings to an end a period of history marked by tragic human lust for power." They are convinced that the missing text—the fourth secret—is a suppressed transcript in which the Virgin Mary warned Lucia very directly about how the church was crumbling from within. "The Secret is wider," Socci concluded, "the prophecy still open and the martyrdom of a Pope and of the Church are still in our future."

Bertone, working under Ratzinger as the secretary of the Congregation for the Doctrine of the Faith, had visited Lucia at Coimbra a few days before the beatification ceremony for Francisco and Jacinta to let her know that the secret was about to be disclosed. He came back almost a year and a half later to do some damage control over the controversy that had erupted in the media after the press conference about the possibility of a hidden text, the "supposed *omissis*."

Bertone regarded Lucia as a "likeable old chatterbox," but reported that she had paused for dramatic effect when she told him that "everything has been published; there are no more secrets."

But the skeptics were far from being convinced, especially only a few months after 9/11 had presented the world with a new doom scenario that—who knows?—might have been predicted in the mysterious Fatima secret they claimed the Vatican was still keeping hidden. It didn't help that Bertone didn't record the two-hour meeting or produce a detailed record of what was said beyond Lucia's denial that there was more to reveal.

Lucia had tried for many years to enter the cloistered world of the Carmelites, and she had shown a pronounced distaste almost all her life for the badgering questions and demands of people who regarded her as a direct link to the Virgin Mary. But to those who questioned the Vatican's party line, she had not really sequestered herself of her own free will but had effectively been silenced by the Vatican since 1960 so that her visions wouldn't get in the way of the important business of church reform.

A more benign interpretation might be that every pope from John XXIII on had wanted to keep his distance from the Fatima Letter and the Third Part of the Secret because they knew it was a feverish, dreamlike vision that could be understood in whatever way anyone wanted to understand it. It was a "private revelation," as Ratzinger wrote in his commentary, something that was "not a question of normal exterior perception of the senses: the images and forms which are seen are not located spatially, as is the case for example with a tree or a house."

No tree, no house, but an inevitable fount of wild speculation and dark conspiracy. Even John Paul II, the pontiff who was most devoted to Our Lady of Fatima and believed that it was she who had guided the bullet away from a vital artery and saved his life, told Lucia in a private meeting in 1982 that he had not yet chosen

to share the secret with the world "because it could be badly interpreted."

I could fill up another chapter or two with more back-and-
forth about the number of lines in the text, the chain of custody of
the envelopes in which it was placed, or whether or not the consecration of Russia had actually taken place as Lucia had specified or
whether there had been a fake Lucia, a "ventriloquist's dummy of
the anti-Fatima forces," who merely said it had and was thus part
of the conspiracy to promote a "pro-Communist Vatican-Moscow
Ostpolitik."

There may indeed be a fourth secret, or at least some other
writing from Sister Lucia that the Vatican, for reasons that are
either practical or nefarious, has decided—just as they decided in
1960—not to let us see.

At this point I'm sort of curious, sort of not. I keep circling
back to the same question: How is it that rational people can be
comfortable with the idea that in 1917 the Mother of God had an
urgent message for the world, decided to deliver it to three children, allowed it to be undisclosed for eight decades while suspense over what it might say continued to build in the Catholic
world through the rest of the twentieth century—through a pandemic, the rise of communism, two world wars, a skyjacking, an
assassination attempt on the pope? And that when it was finally
released to the public, it was a document that said both nothing
and everything, that was so gnostic, recondite, and frustrating
that the people who took it upon themselves to explain what it
meant might as well have been a consortium of English professors
arguing over the meaning of *Finnegans Wake*?

But to all the believers arguing all sides of the question about
the authenticity of the Third Part of the Secret, such logic quib-
bles are irrelevant. The Virgin Mary told Lucia and her cousins
something in 1917, and Lucia wrote it down in 1944 in her Fatima
Letter. The fact that it could be "badly interpreted" has nothing
to do with God's questionable communication skills and everything to do with humankind's perverse inability to recognize its
own sinfulness and to see clearly the dark future that is so deeply
encoded in the mysterious document.

18

The Last Sheep of the Flock

"The idea I have of my soul," Lucia once wrote when she was still a young nun, tortured by her perceived failure to suppress her own human needs and wants, "is a small dead bird I found a while ago in the garden, covered in ants that had stripped it of flesh and feathers, and I immediately thought: That is the image of my soul covered in imperfections and stripped of virtues."

God, she wrote, demanded that she be led "to a total death to myself, to an absolute nonentity, and when will this be?

"It is such a terribly big ladder, and I am still *seated* on the first rung."

There was never a chance that Sister Lucia, the long-surviving seer of Fatima, could be a nonentity. In the Catholic universe, she was still the child who had spoken personally to the Virgin Mary and set the world on edge throughout much of the twentieth century with her close-held secret message.

All her life she had wrestled with fame and adulation. There were times she seemed to court it, or at least tolerate it, and there is no question she was gratified by the attention of church authorities, like John Paul II, who took her and her visions seriously. But she was also sincere about climbing the ladder of self-oblivion, trying to reach the top rung, where her healthy ego could finally be gloriously atomized.

Still, you can't help wondering what she thought when she had to miss viewing the high-profile, internationally televised Vatican news conference in June 2000 that revealed to the world at last the contents of the Third Part of the Secret.

"We watch TV," mysteriously explained Sister Maria do Carmo, the custodian of the Saint Teresa Convent in Coimbra, "but only on exceptional occasions. The press conference on the Secret of Fatima is not such an occasion."

This comes across as evidence to Fatima investigators who believe that Lucia had been placed in cold storage by a church fearing any further revelations from her that might contradict the official Vatican line that there was no more to the Third Part of the Secret, that it had been honestly revealed and authentically interpreted.

It does seem odd that the Carmelite sisters didn't gather to view the press conference, since it's hard to imagine a more "exceptional" occasion for them to watch TV. But maybe Lucia's superiors, or Lucia herself, decided that it all amounted to unnecessary clamor and confusion from the outside world at a time when she was failing in health.

The trip to Fatima for the beatification of Jacinta and Francisco had exhausted her. "After that," wrote one of her fellow Carmelites, Sister Maria Celina de Jesus Crucificado, in a biographical pamphlet, "she gradually became more frail, more dependent." Her legs were weak, she had severe pains in her foot, was almost deaf, and her hands were so crippled by arthritis that she had trouble holding the pliers to make the rosaries that had long been a kind of spiritual hobby for her, and which she had given away by the hundreds. She needed to use a wheelchair now to go to the convent garden to pray before a statue of Mary and her Immaculate Heart.

She referred to herself sometimes as "the last sheep of the flock," the only one of the three *pastorinhos* to live past childhood. And to the sisters who asked her about it, she was adamant that there was nothing left for her to disclose about what the Virgin had said in Fatima in 1917.

"If they know that there is another secret," she said of the chorus of doubters, "let them reveal it! I know of no other! Some people are never satisfied."

———

Lucia entered the Carmelite convent in Coimbra in 1948, the year I was born. Her life in that cell with its empty cross on which to crucify herself spanned the first fifty-seven years of my own life—from my birth and baptism, through my first confession and first communion, through countless family Rosaries at the feet of my parents' bed, through terror-filled nights worrying over the reality of hell and the impossibility of escaping it. Through moving to new cities and into new houses where my mother arranged for a priest to sprinkle holy water on the walls, blessing our new home and driving out any residual trace of Satan. Through unholy thoughts and impure thoughts, through thirteen years of Catholic education heavily grounded in indoctrination, through my epiphany of apostasy as a college freshman and the years beyond in which my mind was liberated but my spirit was still stunted, still reflexively wary about somehow offending a nonexistent God and besmirching an invisible something I still regarded as my soul.

I didn't leap into adulthood, as I saw my friends doing; I crept into it. I was habitually moralistic and ascetic, withdrawn and a bit judging. For a long time, it felt like the Virgin Mary was still watching my every move, registering disappointment and disapproval if I showed signs of behaving like a normal human being. There was still that residual, egotistical need that had been implanted in me by my Catholic education to be special, to be chosen, to hold myself apart. I confused caution with discipline, high-minded disapproval with rectitude. Without really noticing it happen, I developed a personality that was partially based on the things I didn't dare to do, notably drinking. This was easy. I couldn't stand the taste of alcohol, though I was well past the legal drinking age of twenty-one before I even ventured to take a ghastly first sip of beer. Growing up, I had a glimpse, through my extended family, of the heartbreaking effects of alcoholism, and had feared that a genetic marker for the disease might be lurking in me. In high school I was so wrapped up in wholesome activities like reading novels and going to Legion of Decency–approved movies and playing (badly) on the football team that I never went to a party, or ever even heard that a party was happening. So it was a shock, when I was a freshman in college, to witness a beer bash for the first time, to see my fellow classmates suddenly bellowing like beasts and heartily vomiting on the dorm floor. I had grown up in a house where my parents had never failed to observe a quiet cocktail hour for themselves, a ritual that was as boring to me as the family Rosary and did not prepare me for the horrifying abandon of underage binge drinking.

Part of my reaction was simple: I was a prude. Or maybe, to put a slightly more positive spin on it, I liked being in control and was caught off balance by the sight of people who were not. Also, I was in the process of breaking away from religion, and part of my rebellion was to rebel against anything else that might threaten to entrap me, that promised to create what I perceived as an ersatz ecstatic state.

———

Francisco and Jacinta died too young to face the dilemma that I did, and so many Catholics do, of how to explore the open terrain of adulthood. Lucia also never really had a chance to do so. Her visionary flights as a devout and deeply imaginative ten-year-old girl marked her as a seer and a conduit to the divine, and after that there was probably no escape from the fame, abuse, and unrelenting demands that ended up driving her out of her home and away from her family. She might very well have chosen to be a nun—a bride of Christ—in any case. But can a girl who is sent away at the age of fourteen by her bishop to a different city to live at a convent school under an assumed name really be said to have had a choice?

However it came about, she seemed content with the idea of a religious vocation, even though for much of her life she felt like an exile—"I long for my Homeland," she wrote in 1941, "like the thirsty deer longs for the running waters." Her insistent desire for self-mortification—wearing a hair shirt and a knotted rope around her waist, lying prostrate in the chapel from midnight to three a.m.—sometimes had the potential to concern her superiors, and there were instances of sharp-elbow encounters with patriarchal clergymen and even some of her fellow nuns.

"A short while ago," she confided in a 1942 letter, "a Sister, upset at being the last to be served by me, proclaimed, loud and clear, in the Refectory, that I was a spoiled brat, an imposter, filling the world with books full of lies. That she did not believe a word of it, etc. etc."

But it's hard to argue that Lucia's hermitic vocation and her lifelong devotion to the Blessed Mother—a being that to her was not a childhood figment but the entire key to the meaning of existence—didn't enlarge her life more than it constricted it.

That was the implicit promise made to me and my friends in the eighth grade when we were urged to join the minor seminary. I couldn't picture myself becoming a priest, but that didn't mean that I wasn't attracted to the idea of renouncing the world's static in order to monitor the frequency that could tune me in to a higher signal. At some level, I understood the cloistering instinct. And for a naturally shy and self-conscious kid, it was easy enough to confuse caution with a heroic spiritual quest.

All the same, it was liberating, almost intoxicating, to be a nonbeliever. The common phrase "lapsed Catholic" would have applied to me except that the word "lapsed" carried with it a connotation of failure. I didn't feel that I had failed. I had succeeded in finally breaking out of a maze of belief that had held my imagination hostage since birth.

Well, *somewhat* succeeded. The invisible strictures of Catholicism, if not its precepts, still ruled my reactions to the world around me during a period of sudden cultural upheaval. The late 1960s were an inopportune time to be well behaved, but I was who I was. The sexual revolution might as well have been taking place on another planet to someone who was still processing gruesome warnings by celibate priests about dead bodies locked in intercourse. I went to chaotic rock concerts and listened to records by Janis Joplin or Jefferson Airplane, but nothing ever completely clicked for me musically until the first time I heard Leonard Cohen singing songs like "Suzanne" and "Sisters of Mercy." It didn't register to me that Cohen was Jewish. His mournful, mystical lyrics and droning cadences convinced me that he had spent his childhood in the same pre–Vatican II somnolence that I had, mumbling along to O Salutaris Hostia.

I kept a wary distance from the drug culture, literally sitting outside the circle as friends and roommates, along with the questionable strangers someone was always inviting in off the street ("Hi, everybody, this is Red, and this is Crazy Robert"), passed around a joint and sat in stupefaction during long afternoons and deep into the night. After a while, I grew so tired of my righteous stance that I decided it was necessary to ingest some kind of drug just to intersect with the time in which I lived. So on four or five occasions, in a communionlike way with trusted companions, I joined in swallowing a pill that was said to be LSD or synthetic mescaline.

The first time, I sat in a ratty chair in an upstairs bedroom with three fellow voyagers, waiting so long for the effects to kick in that I had concluded I was impervious to them. "This isn't working," I remember saying out loud to the room. Richard and Mimi Fariña's album *Reflections in a Crystal Wind* was spinning on the cheap record player. We were all listening to "Bold Marauder," a harsh-sounding song with sinister lyrics ("And hi ho hey, I am the white destroyer") delivered to a feverish dobro accompaniment. I was staring at the album cover, which was propped up on the floor. It depicted Richard and Mimi Fariña in a conspiratorial embrace, staring at the viewer through a gilded antique window frame. A few short moments after I had made my comment that I wasn't experiencing anything, the eyes of the two singers started spinning, and then spiraled out at me like four red-tinged tornadoes. I jumped back, feeling for the moment the same terror I had felt as a nearsighted boy who had convinced himself that the murky tapestry at the side of the altar was the face of Satan.

But it didn't turn out to be a bad trip, just a jangly start. And when I embarked again, a few weeks later, we were at a rocky Texas lakeshore where the feathery mesquite leaves pulsed with a deep green, soul-calming energy. Close to twilight, I looked up at the sky to find that a random assortment of clouds had all taken on the same shape and purpose. Giant white gopherlike beings were now bounding across the heavens with a bewitching regularity, wave after wave of them in a great migration. I remember realizing at the time that they were just clouds, and that if I blinked my eyes or altered my perspective somehow, the hallucinogenic patterns would disappear and reality would settle in again. What's striking—thinking about it now—was how it was my own personal Miracle of the Sun, an optical effect caused by my wildly receptive perception of the way the failing light streamed across the sky.

Had I seen instead the dancing sun at the Cova da Iria, or the Blessed Mother herself alighting upon a tree, it might have felt like a variant of the same experience—the everyday world cracked open. There was nothing religious about my vision of a rodent-filled sky, and though I remember feeling that I was on the edge of understanding the mystery of time and the secrets of the universe, I'm not sure there was anything particularly spiritual about it, either. But the experience was thrilling and blindingly new, and looking back at that moment I can understand Lucia's lifelong yearning, through so many decades of rigorous prayer and isolation in the convent, to summon yet another apparition.

For me, though, a handful of acid trips was plenty. I had worked hard to purge myself of Catholic mysticism, and I was suspicious of miracle seeking. The psychotropic adventures I allowed myself to experience were, in their way, life altering—confirmation that the world I perceived was not the only world there was. But it was also increasingly obvious that the details of the world beyond would never be made satisfyingly plain. During the logy day-after of one of those psychedelic trips, when I was trying to process what I had seen and felt, I remembered what a nun had told us in elementary school. When we died, she said, and if our souls went to heaven, there would be an epic debriefing. Every question we had ever had about the universe, about infinity, about the history of earth and the planets of the distant galaxies would be answered all at once, and our souls (because we would only be souls then) would be filled with an oceanic, orgasmic knowledge.

On a coming-down morning I could still find myself fantasizing about such a breakthrough, but it was the newly emerged pragmatic and skeptical side of myself that was beginning to hold sway. I already knew enough hippie voyagers who had lost their bearings trying to find a destination in that limitless sea, and I didn't want to be one of them, any more than I had wanted to become a priest and embark on a quest for an unreachable something called God.

───────

There was precedent in our family for following the religious life. One of my great-uncles, after serving in the military in World War II, had entered the seminary in his forties and lived out his life as a Jesuit brother. My mother's first cousin, John J. Sullivan, was a charismatic priest who was appointed by Pope Paul VI as the bishop of Grand Island, Nebraska, and later of Kansas City. He was known in the family as Jack but also deferentially, even awesomely, as "the Bishop." He had officiated at my parents' wedding as a young priest, then at my sister's wedding and at the funerals of my grandparents. I flew to Kansas City to his own funeral after he died of Parkinson's disease in 2001 at the age of eighty. He asked to be buried in a plain pine box crafted by the monks of a local monastery. The monks had built the casket to the correct dimensions, but apparently nobody had told them he would be wearing his bishop's miter, so the rumor was that getting him into the coffin had required some scrunching. My mother laughed about this and thought that Jack, with his never-failing sense of humor, would have found it funny as well. But she had been close to her cousin, and his death had hit her hard.

Our family filled up several pews in Kansas City's gold-domed Cathedral of the Immaculate Conception as the funeral Mass took place. Despite the plain wooden casket, it was an occasion of jarring magnificence, with twenty fellow bishops in full vestments accompanying Jack's coffin up the aisle, followed by a platoon of sword-wielding, bicorn-hat-wearing members of the Knights of Columbus, who were in turn followed by the Knights of Malta, and then by the knights and dames of the Equestrian Order of the Holy Sepulchre of Jerusalem, the men in floppy medieval caps, the women in black witches' capes.

The over-the-top pageantry made me queasy and seemed out of character with the unpretentious, easygoing family hero I had known, who had always been much more at home mingling with his parishioners as a priest than ruling over a fiefdom as a bishop.

It also raised the stakes for what I knew would be coming next in the ceremony: communion.

In the Catholic church, communion is much more than a rite of fellowship; it's a spot check of faith and character. Catholics believe that the communion wafer isn't merely a symbolic reference to the body of Christ, it is the actual thing, his actual body, just as the wine sipped from the chalice is his actual blood. Transubstantiation—"a monstrous word for a monstrous idea," in the opinion of Martin Luther—was a concept that had been codified by the church in 1215 at the Fourth Lateran Council. It meant that what Jesus said to his apostles at the Last Supper when he shared bread and wine with them—"This is my body" and "This is my blood"—was literally true, and that at every Mass since then the substance of the communion host was invisibly transformed into Christ's body.

I remember being aware of this quasi-cannibalistic notion as early as my first communion, when we were warned to let the host slowly dissolve on our tongues, and never to let it touch our teeth, which would be the same as gnawing on Jesus himself.

Because it is leveraged with so much powerful juju, communion is off-limits to people of other religions, and also to Catholics who are not in good standing, either because their souls are burdened with unconfessed mortal sins or because they have fallen away from the faith. At that funeral Mass in Kansas City, I technically fell into both categories. I didn't feel like a sinner. I had no vices to speak of, and my main ethical transgressions were on the passive side—thoughtlessness, complacency, undeserved comfort. Of the Ten Commandments, I reckoned that I had really violated only one—"Remember to keep holy the Lord's Day." Keeping the day holy for a Catholic meant going to Mass every Sunday, and I had excused myself from that obligation long before, accumulating decade upon decade of compounding mortal sin.

The only times I had been to Mass during those years were at family gatherings of one sort or another. After Tom Harrigan died, in 1989, there were long years during which I regularly drove home from Austin to Corpus Christi to see my mother, or afterward to suburban Houston, where she moved to be closer to two of my siblings who lived there. These were weekends visits usually, spilling over into Sunday, when I had no excuse not to accompany her to church. Mass was an excruciating occasion, particularly at communion time, when I stayed in the pew and she went up to the altar alone. It would have broken her heart for me to just come right out and announce my apostasy, though of course a Catholic mother knows when her son strays off the grid. For decades she couldn't keep herself from probing, asking rhetorically if I was still going to Mass every Sunday, and I would shift uncomfortably in my chair or make some sort of mute nodlike gesture that she could, if she wanted to, interpret as a yes. And then there were years when it was too uncomfortable for both of us, and she no longer bothered to ask.

The pageantry of Jack's funeral called for a different response. With communion underway and people beginning to file toward the altar, I decided I didn't like the look of things: me remaining seated in the pew, a brooding outcast, while my mother and the rest of the family left me behind to honor our departed relation. So I made up my own rule on the spot: at funerals and weddings, in order to avoid calling attention to myself and my errant ways, I would just pretend to be a practicing Catholic and go to communion as if it was a natural act. It was another mortal sin, but so what? If there was no God, there was nobody to care. If there was one, offending a supreme being felt like a lesser offense than embarrassing my mother.

———

My wife, Sue Ellen, was at home with our three children. Had she been there with me at the funeral Mass, things would have been even more complicated, with more awkward choices to be made about whether to remain seated in the pew with her or sally forth to the altar along with everyone else. At the time, we had been in what used to be called—in a whispered voice—a "mixed marriage" for twenty-six years.

Sue Ellen was born in Snyder, Texas, on the eastern edge of the Permian Basin. It was a little West Texas town whose population fluctuated with the price of oil and the production activity of nearby fields. Her father owned a small oil-jobbing company, buying fuel from refineries and selling it on the local retail market to gas stations, local farmers, and other businesses. Growing up in a town like that, working summers in her father's office, she developed a pragmatic understanding not just of how oil got from one place to another but about the social lubrication that kept a community operating. There was no anonymity when it came to which of the two grocery stores you shopped at, which bank you kept your money in, and—most visibly—where you went to church.

Sue Ellen's family were Baptists for much of her childhood, until when she was eleven or twelve they took their trade to the local Episcopal church, where the sermons were better and there was a lot less damnation talk.

She was my first serious girlfriend. We met a few years after college, and there was much to bring us together. We were only a year apart in age, shared many of the same childhood reference points, from forgotten TV shows to memories of a culturally isolated Texas upbringing. We were both far stricter moviegoers than we had ever been churchgoers and were both English majors listlessly afloat in the 1970s subeconomy of Austin. She worked in a bookstore. I mowed yards but was beginning to make some progress as a writer. I had sold a few magazine articles and was filling up composition books late into the night with the handwritten first draft of a first novel. I lived in an old house with two roommates—one of whom would soon star as Leatherface in *The Texas Chain Saw Massacre*—a few blocks west of the UT campus. I was approaching my mid-twenties, worried that my life was not yet in gear and terrified that unless I soon gathered some forward momentum I would be dragged deep into the Austin slacker netherworld. But I was too committed to the dream of being a writer to try to search out a steady job that would provide security but deprive my imagination of the free-ranging creative thought I enjoyed as I heaved my mower through my daily round of ten or twelve lawns. My Catholic upbringing had primed me to think that every step I took in life should have not just practical but moral stakes. A job was a job, but to be a writer was to have a vocation.

So I was content with my lifestyle of priestly asceticism—just enough money earned to pay the rent, just enough energy left from a long day of physical labor to turn my attention to my true calling. I still yearned for epiphanies, for some out-of-nowhere blast of glorious prose, but I had read enough biographies of famous writers and lived through enough of the countercultural 1960s to understand that such moments, if they came by way of drugs or alcohol, would feel, at least to me, suspect and unearned. I had to get used to the idea that writing was not ecstatic; it was mostly grunt work in search of a payoff. In a way, it reminded me of saying the Rosary: each word was a bead, each "decade" of beads was a paragraph. Giving in to the temptation to settle for an okay-enough insight or turn of phrase would have been like Lucia and her cousins blitzing through the Rosary by just saying "Hail Mary" over and over. It had been a long time since my childhood belief in the Virgin Mary, but as I sat at my desk I still felt monitored by an unseen presence.

———

I don't recall ever discussing religion with Sue Ellen, except to compare notes on our backgrounds, until we decided to get married. I knew how much it would mean to my mother if we were married "in the church," by a priest in a traditionally Catholic setting. Keeping up the fiction that I was still a believer for such a crucial ceremony would require an upgrade in hypocrisy on my part, but I was willing.

Sue Ellen seemed willing as well. Because I was such a coward when it came to declaring or denying religious beliefs, and because I thought she would make a better impression on her own than with her cringingly equivocal fiancé, I didn't accompany her to a get-acquainted meeting with a priest about what hoops she, as a non-Catholic, needed to jump through to make our coming marriage sacramentally up to code.

She came home steaming. For one thing, the priest had told her that the fact she was divorced meant that she would have to somehow have her previous marriage annulled. It had been an unhappy union that she felt no need to look back on and examine. The idea that she would have to drag her ex-husband to a tribunal to prove that he had somehow not entered wedlock in good faith outraged her, as did the patriarchal, patronizing tone of the priest who explained the rules. She came away from the interview with the impression that the Catholic Church was a snooty institution that thought it was too good for her, and let me know that my passive attempt to fold her into the family religion merely for the sake of making my life easier was not going to fly.

So we got married not in a Catholic Church but in an old house that rented itself out as a wedding venue, and not by a priest but by an easygoing Presbyterian minister who seemed happy to officiate for anybody of whatever faith. My mother very much approved of Sue Ellen, and if she disapproved of a thrown-together wedding that was more about a pledge between two people than a solemn covenant with God, she never said anything.

I was able to leave the yardwork behind and scrabble out a living as a freelance writer, back in the days when magazines were able to pay a decent fee. For ten years or so I had a steady income as a staff writer for *Texas Monthly*, a time in which I was able to branch out and establish some credentials as a novelist and as a screenwriter for mostly made-for-TV movies before going freelance again.

We had three daughters. All were baptized, though not as Catholics. Sue Ellen decreed that we have them christened in the Episcopal Church, which was familiar ground to her from her childhood. I remember the anxiety waves involved in that decision and every other decision we made about whether they were going to experience a life based at least partly in religion. I wanted to spare them my own memories of a Catholic childhood—the all-consuming fear of hell, the creeping shame of inhabiting a human body. Sue Ellen saw things a little differently. Despite her own experience with that dismissive priest and the way she witnessed me still emotionally writhing in the snares of Catholicism, she seemed to think that the church had shaped me more than warped me, that it had implanted not only rules but values.

So she wanted, more than I did, for our children to have some kind of religious upbringing. She thought that without it they would be unmoored in our culture, without the grounding to understand everyday references to Jesus or the Bible. And her upbringing in a small town had given her a sense that people needed to belong to something, to be part of a vital community. How much religion itself factored into her calculations I've never been able to figure out. Whenever I would try to pin her down about what exactly she believed or didn't believe, she would sidle away from the subject without making any sort of declaration one way or another.

For about ten years we were members, more or less, of an Episcopal church. Communion wasn't a problem like it was at a Catholic Mass. Deciding to partake in the observance never presented itself as an ethical decision one way or another. But I squirmed in my pew nonetheless. There was the strangeness of being a congregant in a Protestant denomination. In the insular Catholic world in which I grew up, Protestantism was thought of as a suspect foreign power. But then there was the strangeness of it not being strange.

The Episcopal Eucharist service had the same structure, and the same apparent spiritual valence, as the Catholic Mass I had grown up with. Yes, there were things to get used to—married priests and female priests were still only thought experiments to Catholics. But all the parts—the reading from the Gospels or Epistles, the sermon, the offertory, the communion, the priestly dismissal—added up to what seemed like the same whole. Except it wasn't. There was something that seemed too reasonable to me about the Episcopal service. There was an element missing, an element I had once been so used to that I felt a dark nostalgia at its absence: the ballast of sin and guilt and eternal punishment, the familiar sense that the fate of your soul was constantly in play.

I had become a nominal, nervous, recalcitrant, nonbelieving Protestant. It was an identity that fit me even less, made me even more uncomfortable, than my impossible-to-escape Catholicism, and I suppose it was my attitude more than anything else that finally caused our family's nonrigorous churchgoing to fall under its own weight around the time our daughters were in high school.

But my mother's religious journey never veered from a course that was, in its way, as straight and unquestioning as Lucia's. In 1973, she used her nurse's training to begin teaching natural family planning for the Diocese of Corpus Christi. NFP was a form of church-sanctioned birth control that replaced the old hit-and-miss rhythm method. The new version wasn't perfect—it required close, daily monitoring of a woman's ovulation cycle—but if done right it could considerably lower the incidence of pregnancy without the side effects of the pill or other birth-control methods of the time. It was also useful to some couples who wanted children but who were having difficulty conceiving them.

The 1970s were the decade of *Roe v. Wade*, of *Ms.* magazine, of the National Organization for Women and the fight to ratify the Equal Rights Amendment. Maybe an updated rhythm method for birth control seemed to belong to another time, but it was feminism, as much as Catholicism, that powered my mother's new career. Deep in her late seventies, widowed by then for a second time, she would load up the trunk of her car with binders and pamphlets explaining the Billings Ovulation Method and drive alone all throughout South Texas, empowering women with knowledge about their bodies' reproductive cycle to help them make their own decisions about how or when to get pregnant.

She managed to get funding for the program not just from the church but from the federal government, and over the years she had several meetings with Mother Teresa and once flew to Rome with a group—which included our fifteen-year-old daughter, Marjorie (named for her)—for an audience with Pope John Paul II. That was in 1992, eleven years after he was shot by Agca, and in the photos of the two Marjories shaking his hand you can see clearly the physical toll of the attack and of his onrushing Parkinson's.

My mother's faith ebbed, as far as I knew, only twice. The first time was after my father was killed, a few months before my birth in 1948. She was well into her eighties when she finally told me that when flying home to Oklahoma from Seattle after her husband's death, shocked and grieving and feeling hopeless, with a one-year-old son and another baby on the way, she had come harrowingly close to what Catholics regard as the "unforgivable" sin of despair and had prayed to God that the plane would crash and end her suffering. The second time was when her only daughter, my sister, Julie, contracted a hopeless form of cancer and died in 2005, far too young, at forty-nine. My mother was eighty-five by then, stoic throughout that year-long ordeal, praying ferociously for the impossible. After the funeral, and for weeks afterward, she didn't try to disguise her anger at God. "Why would he do that to her?" she kept asking. I tried to answer, to reassure her, but what could I say? I couldn't express aloud my own faith that God did not exist and could not be blamed—that terrible things just happened on their own. From my own childhood kneeling at the foot of her bed as she led us in ritual prayer during the Cold War, from all I had learned about Fatima and the horrors of the twentieth century, including the cruel childhood deaths of Francisco and Jacinta, I was content to believe that tragedies like the one that had visited our own family were exactly what the words of the Rosary meant: Sorrowful Mysteries.

It was a dark time for her, but ultimately not a dark night of the soul. She recovered sooner than I would have thought, returning to her fast-held beliefs, going faithfully to church every Sunday until she was bedridden. When I visited, I would sleep on the couch in the living room of her one-bedroom condo. Through her open door, all through the night, I could hear the TV she never turned off and that she swore helped deliver her into at least a fitful sleep. Much of the night it was tuned to TCM, to the fast-talking patter of film noir or forties comedies. But every hour or two those voices would disappear as my mother clicked the remote to the Catholic channel, and she and I would both be lulled to sleep, in our separate rooms and in our separate realities, by the soothing Gregorian chants of a televised High Mass, or of a learned nun explaining the meaning of the Immaculate Heart of Mary.

———

Lucia's own passage through old age and the end of life had been cushioned, like my mother's, by the serenity that came with faith, by the comfort that came from familiar, lifelong observances. "At the end," remembered Sister Maria Celina, "she lived in total abandonment in the hands of God. She did not complain of being so restricted. She thought it was natural. She used to say, 'No one wants to die, but it is difficult to be old!'"

Pain in her legs, possibly caused by a deformity in her spine, kept her confined mostly to bed, though she could still visit the garden in a wheelchair, where there was a statue of the Virgin that featured on its base a colorful tile illustration of the three little shepherds that Lucia would stare at wistfully, thinking of how Francisco and Jacinta "went off to heaven" in 1919 and 1920, such an unfathomably long time ago in the previous century. "Our Lady said I was to remain here for a while," she told one of the sisters, "but it has become a great long while!"

She fainted during Mass in November of 2000, an incident that Sister Maria Celina marked as "the beginning of a new, painful and difficult phase—the journey to Calvary."

She was plagued by gall-bladder problems, hearing problems, arthritis, and lack of appetite, especially for the daily banana that a doctor had prescribed and that she found repulsive and almost impossible to choke down. The only food that remotely appealed to her was the lupine seeds that she remembered her father bringing home from the fields in his pockets when she was a little girl. After a while, though, her tongue was so dry and cracked she could not get her false teeth into her mouth so that she could chew them. Lupine seeds, with their childhood echoes of the Cova da Iria, were the last thing she ever ate—except for the communion host she somehow managed to swallow.

Throughout her last illness, she never let go of a rosary that Pope John Paul II had sent her the year before. The Pope himself was nearing the end. On February 13, 2005, the day of Lucia's death, he had been out of the hospital for only three days and would soon develop a urinary-tract infection that would lead to complications that would kill him on April 2. (Mehmet Ali Agca, released from prison by then, would put flowers on his tomb.) John Paul II managed to send Lucia a farewell fax—"I come to affirm our affectionate union with a special remembrance of your personal union with God." The fax was read to her by her bishop, but she asked for her glasses so that she could read it herself.

The day before, Sister Lucia—unable to speak, beset by agonizing coughing fits—had pressed the pope's rosary into the hands of her prioress, "as if to say: 'You take it and pray it now, I no longer can.'" At midnight, one of the sisters brought her a picture of Our Lady of Fatima and held it close so that Lucia could kiss it.

After that, even though she no longer had the rosary, they watched her throughout her last night as she moved her hands in an unconscious pantomime, counting off the Hail Marys as she had done almost every day of her nearly ninety-eight years.

PART THREE

Pilgrimage

19

The Sanctuary

From the Baixa, Lisbon's historic and touristy downtown, it was a long and steady uphill trek along the busy Rua da Palma to find the street I was looking for. Jet-lagged and sweaty in the middle of a May afternoon, I picked my way carefully along a sidewalk paved with slippery limestone cobblestones before losing my way in a twisty network of side streets. Signage was hit-or-miss, and some of the streets changed names every block or two anyway, so I gave up consulting the map on my phone and just trusted dead reckoning.

After an hour of walking, I stopped at a minor intersection and looked up, hoping to find a street sign above one of the storefronts. And there it was: a stone tablet that read "Rua Jacinta Marto." The street sign also indicated that Jacinta Marto had been a *vidente* (witness) of Fatima and had lived from 1910 to 1920.

I followed the curving street that led uphill to the west until, after another block, I stood at the entrance to a pleasant-looking building of three stories, whose stucco facade was crowned with a scrollwork crest left over from the days of the Portuguese monarchy. The hospital was named for Portugal's German-born Queen Estefânia (Stephanie), who had married King Pedro V in 1858, and who had died of diphtheria at twenty-two a year later. A hospital for children had been a cherished project of the young queen during her brief reign, and the building that was opened in 1877, almost twenty years after her death, was named for her.

It was a children's hospital still, and it was where Jacinta had been brought for her hopeless last months in February 1920, where the surgeons had gone ahead despite her protests with an agonizing operation to remove two of her infected ribs.

From the outside, the hospital looked like a sanitarium from a nineteenth-century novel. It was situated in a parklike expanse, set back from iron gates at the end of a broad cobblestone driveway. Inside, it felt peaceful and unhurried, partly from the abundant sunlight flowing in through windows that looked out on a central courtyard.

It was on the second floor that I found the memorial to Jacinta that I had been looking for. It was discreet—just a dozen or so photographs and newspaper clippings mounted under plexiglass on the wall that medical personnel and patients hurried back and forth in front of without seeming to notice.

I knew that Jacinta had died in bed 60, but there was no indication from the memorial which room or ward bed 60 had been in, and the nurses I tried to ask in my phrase-book Portuguese just shook their heads in incomprehension. But it didn't matter, really. I was close enough. I took a seat on a couch in this second-floor corridor and thought of Jacinta Marto. She was Saint Jacinta Marto now, just as her brother was Saint Francisco Marto. Almost two decades after their beatification, they had been canonized by Pope Francis in Fatima on May 13, 2017, on the hundredth anniversary of the first apparition.

"It was night in the dingy hospital," William Thomas Walsh writes floridly in his Fatima history of the child who had died such an agonizing death here, "but it was forever dawn in the soul of Jacinta as the Mother of God bent over Bed 60 and gathered her into the arms that had enfolded the Christ in infancy and in death."

Walsh wrote that in death Jacinta had "a rosy flush on her cheeks, a half smile on her lips." That strikes me as just another example of the author's devotional hyperbole, along the same lines as an unsourced reference I found to tears of blood appearing on Jacinta's face after she died.

As I sat on that couch in Dona Estefânia Hospital, watching sick children being rolled down the hallways on gurneys with their anxious parents following, all I could think about was that poor child's lonely death over a hundred years ago. I wondered what, in this place, might possibly have given her comfort. If the hospital had been "dingy," as Walsh claimed, it wasn't anymore. It looked its age, but it was filled with natural light from all the windows facing the courtyard. And the walls of the corridors were painted a soothing light blue. Had they been that color—the color of May, the color of Our Lady—when Jacinta lay here dying? If so, her belief that what the Blessed Mother had told the children that day at the Cova da Iria—"I will never forsake you"—might still have seemed like a living promise.

———

The next day I boarded a bus at Lisbon's Sete Rios Station for the hour-and-a-half trip to Fatima. The A1 highway led north along the west bank of the broadening Tagus River, past the graceful winding arc of the Vasco da Gama Bridge, through undulating hills whose summits and valleys were crowded with residential and commercial developments and industrial outskirts. After a half hour or so the city had thinned out and the land was flatter, settling into an undramatic rural openness marked by low-lying trees and shrubs. Every few miles or so we passed another compact, ageless village of white walls and red-tiled roofs. Finally, up ahead just beyond the little town of Videla, reared an abrupt six-hundred-foot-high limestone massif that unmistakably announced the beginning of the Serra de Aire. Portuguese buses have excellent suspension, and as we climbed into the hill country there was a feeling of gliding upward, past more pocket villages nestled into the folds of the increasingly dense and contoured landscape. As we left the Portuguese plains behind and cruised deeper into the Serra de Aire, it was easy to imagine what an isolated and closed-off world this had been when Lucia was young, and why her fellow students in Porto had thought of her as a half-wild "mountain girl."

It was only about ten or twelve miles after the hills began that the bus took the Fatima exit off the A1. We looped around a traffic circle, past a McDonald's and a Burger King, and then turned into the bus station.

Fatima looked at first like a normal town, filled with apartment blocks and shops and hotels with red-tiled roofs, a shady boulevard flanked by an inviting pedestrian promenade. But as I gathered my luggage and walked toward the civic center along Avenida D. José Alves Correia da Silva—named for the bishop who had sent Lucia off as a girl to Porto and later ordered her to write down the Third Part of the Secret—I began to notice that the hotels had names like Aleluia, Cristo Rei, and Virgem Maria, and that there were more and more shops whose display windows were crowded with figurines of the Virgin Mary, the saints, the popes, and the three shepherd children. In terms of population, Fatima is a small town, with fewer than fifteen thousand permanent residents, but there are that many more guest beds available in hotels, residences, and church houses—enough to accommodate the 650,000 out of five million annual visitors who wish to spend the night.

That shrine—the pilgrimage site known as the Sanctuary of Our Lady of Fatima—was only a few hundred yards from the bus station, and I was a little surprised to come upon it suddenly. What I encountered first was the backside of what looked like a sports stadium. This was the new Basilica of the Most Holy Trinity, completed in 2007, that anchors one end of the sanctuary complex. It was only after I walked around this massive modern church obscuring my view that I finally stood there, at last, at the Cova da Iria.

Or at what it had become. I was now facing the esplanade—known as the *recinto*—that stretched from the new basilica behind me to the older and more ornate one at the other end, the Basilica of Our Lady of the Rosary, whose first stone had been laid on May 13, 1928, eleven years after the first apparition, and which had been completed and consecrated in 1953. Between the two basilicas was a sea of pavement—roughly eighteen hundred feet long and five hundred feet wide—sloping slightly downward at my end, rising slightly in the distance like a vast, lazy skateboard ramp. The original basilica was the opposite in architecture of the modernist one behind me and seemed like a relic from a different time and different faith. Its bell tower rose two hundred feet into the sky and was topped by a big cross mounted atop a golden crown. Father Thomas McGlynn's massive marble statue of the Immaculate Heart, the one that he had created under Lucia's persnickety supervision, rested in its niche above the entrance, and sweeping out from the church on either side was an expansive colonnade whose rooftop was guarded by evenly spaced statues of the saints.

It was hard, standing there and looking out over the esplanade, to process the reality that this was the place, the broad swath of hollow ground in the fields owned by Antonio Santos, where Lucia and Francisco and Jacinta had said the Blessed Mother had come down from heaven to appear before them above a small holm oak tree.

The tree was long gone—reduced to nothing by relic-hungry pilgrims a hundred years before. But where it had been, where a homemade arch had once stood, and where a little chapel had been built and then blown up by republican saboteurs, there was now an open-air church. From where I stood, this structure—known as the *capelinha,* or the Chapel of the Apparitions—was visible at the western edge of the esplanade.

I had come to Fatima in late May, deliberately timing my visit to avoid the hundreds of thousands of pilgrims who arrive here on the thirteenth of every month from May to October to worship on the days of the six apparitions. There were plenty of people here anyway, clustered around the *capelinha,* streaming in and out of both basilicas, buying candles—some as long as five feet—and then setting them in a big barbecue pit to watch them burn, carrying prayers and pleas upward with their waxy smoke. On a smooth marble strip in the pavement called the Penitent Way that ran the length of the *recinto,* a half-dozen elderly pilgrims, wearing fanny packs and knee pads, inched along on their knees, working their rosary beads in their hands as they slowly made their way to the *capelinha.*

I checked in at the Hotel Estrela on the eastern edge of the sanctuary. I arrived as a tour group from Korea was just leaving, loading their big roll-on suitcases into a bus parked out in front. From my room on the fourth floor I had a panoramic view of the whole sanctuary and the bustling religious commercial district of hotels, restaurants, gift shops, and retreat centers that spread into the hills beyond it. When Lucia and her cousins had grazed their sheep at the Cova there had been nothing in sight but pastures and rocky hills. Fatima had been a small parish church a mile or two off to the east, with a cluster of nearby houses that barely qualified as a village. Now it was one of the great destinations of the world for pilgrims, for spiritual-minded tourists, and for people like me who weren't a hundred percent sure what they were doing here.

I knew, though, that my first stop had to be the *capelinha*, which had been erected on the place where it had all begun. I walked across the *recinto* to find fifty or sixty people there of all ages, sitting on wooden benches on three sides of the open-air structure, all of them in absolute silence, most of them visibly praying. The place was shady and soothing, open to the elements and a faint breeze. There was a skylight in the pine ceiling just above the altar. And just behind the altar was the original chapel that had been much reconstructed since it was dynamited in 1922. The chapel, with its plain stucco front and tiled roof, had once been perceived as a threat to the integrity of the Portuguese Republic, but it looked not much bigger than a dollhouse.

In front of it, in the spot where the little holm oak had once been, there was a column with a glass case on top that contained José Ferreira Thedim's three-and-a-half-foot-high statue of Our Lady of Fatima, the same statue that Pope John Paul II had knelt before in silent prayer.

Catholics have long been accused of idolatry, of worshipping images of God and the saints rather than the invisible beings they are supposed to represent. This, of course, is forbidden by the Ten Commandments, where God warns against creating "graven images." The Catholic Church itself, at the Council of Trent in 1566, decreed that while it was okay to honor statues and paintings of "Christ, of the Virgin Mother of God, and of the other saints," it was a sin to confuse them with the real thing, "or that anything is to be asked of them."

I'm sure the worshippers in the *capelinha* that day knew that Thedim's statue wasn't the Virgin Mary herself, but you wouldn't have guessed that from the way everybody's eyes were focused longingly upon it. It did seem that here in this place, in front of this undersized but beloved image, you could get a little confused.

Growing up Catholic, I had been exposed to so many depictions of the Mother of God—in statues, in paintings, on miraculous medals and holy cards—that it had never occurred to me to think of them as individual works of art or to assess their relative merits. They were all the same—a celestial lady dressed in flowing robes, her hands folded in prayer, a sorrowful look on her face.

Was there something different about this one? I couldn't tell. But because I was here, in Fatima, within a few feet of the exact spot where Lucia said she and her fellow seers had beheld the Virgin Mary, I found it impossible even for me—a nonbeliever—not to respond to this image with my own kind of idolatry. For one thing, I was bewitched by the history that had flowed forth from this place, and Thedim's little statue was part of that history. For another, it was maybe the first time I had ever looked closely enough at a religious sculptor's work to understand that it took skill and feeling to carve such a gracefully mournful face.

The statue is so precious it is taken out of its glass case only on special occasions, most notably on the thirteenth day of each month from May to October, when it is placed on a flower-draped litter for a procession around the *recinto* in front of hundreds of thousands of praying and weeping people holding up lighted candles. Although the statue always wears a gilded crown, the original crown—the one with Mehmet Ali Agca's bullet inside—is used only on these occasions. The rest of the time it is housed for security in the Fatima Museum.

Even though the sculpture rarely leaves its position where the Blessed Mother supposedly descended from heaven, in the 1940s Thedim made another statue of Our Lady of Fatima that has been traveling around the world ever since, to over a hundred countries, where it is received with the same awestruck reverence as the original. And over the years it has been joined by twelve more.

"It seemed as if it were just the two of us," recalled a man who had seen this image, the International Pilgrim Virgin Statue, when it first came to the United States, in the Buffalo, New York, cathedral, where he went to pray for his gravely ill wife. "I looked at her and she looked at me . . . and smiled. I had a feeling at that moment, a feeling of certainty that my dying wife had been healed."

You don't have to believe in miraculous cures to understand that man's belief that a silent, personal communication had taken place between him and a wooden statue of the Virgin Mary that was not even the original one. The people who had gathered in the Cova da Iria in October of 1917 to witness the Miracle of the Sun had been in a similar state of hushed expectancy.

It was hard to resist it myself, especially when—after leaving the *capelinha,* and then pondering a thriving, towering holm oak a few yards away that had already been a mature tree when the *pastorinhos* had their vision in 1917—I walked along the western colonnade and entered the Basilica of Our Lady of the Rosary. As a church that had been consecrated in my lifetime, it didn't have the air of ancient mystery of so many other European cathedrals, but it still carried a charge. It was solemn and silent, rather spare in its immediate impact: a great nave of white marble, with golden pillars behind the altar that drew the eye upward to a relief sculpture of the coronation of Mary in heaven. A painting between the pillars, depicting the Virgin and the three young shepherds flanked by angels and bishops, struck me as busy, murky, and a little scary. But off to the side was Thedim's traveling statue, usually now in residence here in the basilica, and its calm presence offset some of the medieval menace of the painting.

The three *pastorinhos* were all buried upon their deaths in other cemeteries, but their bodies were eventually moved and all reinterred here in the basilica. Lucia and Jacinta's tombs are in the left transept, Francisco's on the right. I would have liked to have spent a few moments standing there, staring at their final resting places, but just then it was impractical. The church was quietly bustling, and most of the visitors were jammed in at the railings in front of the transepts, obstructing my sight of the tombs as they crowded in with their cell-phone cameras.

I decided to leave and come back later when I might have a better chance at a clear view and an unhurried moment. There was much else to see in Fatima in the meantime, at least for a deep-dive secular pilgrim like me. I visited a small museum on Rua de São Pedro, a few blocks west of the sanctuary, that focused on the short lives of Jacinta and Francisco. I was the only visitor there, and had all the time and room I needed to study the sad, resonant artifacts on display: the kerchief that Jacinta had worn over her head for Sunday Mass; a *carapuço*—the ubiquitous Portuguese stocking cap—that had been worn by Francisco; a fragment of a ligature that was used to treat Jacinta as she was dying; the baptismal gown that was worn not just by Jacinta and Francisco but by all the Marto children, and whose back was tattered because so many people, after the two seers died, had asked for strips of what they regarded as a sacred cloth. There was also a glass case containing a single bead from the rosary that had been put into the dead Francisco's hands, and that had been exhumed with him when his bones were moved from the parish graveyard of Fatima to the great basilica.

I stopped in at the Domus Pacis Hotel to meet Nuno Prazeres, the executive director of the International Secretariat of the World Apostolate of Fatima, whose mission is to spread and interpret the message of Fatima to the world. The World Apostolate was the idea of a New Jersey priest named Harold Colgan, who believed that the Virgin Mary had cured him of a near-fatal heart episode he had suffered in 1946. The next year he created a spiritual antidote to the unconverted Soviet Union—"We will be the Blue Army of Mary and Christ, against the red army of the world and of Satan." Colgan found a partner for his Blue Army in a dynamic lay person, a religious author and lecturer named John Haffert, and soon they had five million members in a hundred countries, with an airplane to ferry pilgrims to and from their world headquarters at this hotel in Fatima and Thedim's pilgrim statue of Our Lady traveling the globe.

The Blue Army changed its name to the World Apostolate in the 1980s, Nuno said, because the name had come to sound "too militant." We were talking in the lobby of the Domus Pacis, a sprawling hotel with a sky-blue onion dome poking above its red-tiled roof, a welcoming grace note to the pilgrims from Eastern Europe who could attend Mass in a Byzantine chapel, complete with a replica of the Icon of Kazan, on the second floor.

In the lobby, prominently displayed on one wall, was an unpleasant painting whose colorful sinuosity and somewhat nauseating surrealism struck me as oddly familiar.

"That's by Salvador Dalí," Nuno said. "It's Lucia's vision of hell."

What? Salvador Dalí? Lucia?

Yes, Fatima ensnared them both. They even met once, after John Haffert decided that Dalí was the perfect artist to render the image that the Virgin Mary had put into the shepherds' minds when she showed them the first of the three secrets—a vision of hell—during the July apparition in 1917. The commission came about in the early 1960s, after John XXIII had refused to allow the world to read Lucia's Fatima Letter, when the Cold War was at its zenith, and when Dalí was in an acute phase of middle-aged death-hauntedness and artistic flirtation with the Catholic imagery of his youth.

"It's up to you to present this Vision truthfully and vividly," Haffert told Dalí when he hired him. "You are being chosen to be Our Lady's artist."

Lucia was in the convent at Coimbra when Dalí met her and talked to her through the grillwork barricade in the parlor. There is no record of the conversation, but afterward Dalí went to confession—"the most moving, sincere and profound confession," according to the priest who heard it—and then went on to finish the painting, which depicts a parched, cracked landscape above which something that looks like a wrinkled white pillowcase is being stabbed by a phalanx of—escargot forks.

The painting in the Domus Pacis was not the original, which was bought by a Connecticut art collector after supposedly languishing under a nun's bed in a convent somewhere for thirty years. But the framed reproduction in the lobby was large enough and clear enough to see what a queasy, hypnagogic eruption it was. "I will paint what I see," Dalí had told Haffert, and one of the things he had seen were the little forks with which he ate his snails while the two men were having dinner. "The soul of a sinner is like a snail," he declared. "It curls and cowls up in the shell and the only way to retrieve it is by using an escargot fork!"

Nuno Prazeres seemed to regard the painting with good-humored perplexity. He was in his forties, energetic and engaging. He had studied philosophy and theology in London and Italy and had been a lay missionary in Mozambique for two years before going to work for the World Apostolate.

His vocation as an apostle was, in its way, a natural development. Not only was he born in Fatima, but his grandfather—Manuel Francisco—had been at the Cova da Iria on October 13, 1917, to witness the Miracle of the Sun.

Manuel was a boy at the time and was good friends with Francisco. "My grandfather told me Francisco was a normal boy. But after that first apparition he became much more prayerful. He would witness him praying for two or three hours on the floor of the parish church, prostrated."

He and other friends and family members had gone to the Cova that day not just out of faith or curiosity but to protect the three *pastorinhos*. Tensions were running high after Lucia had predicted that Our Lady would perform a miracle. They were afraid that if she didn't, the children would be killed.

The crowd was dense and the closest Nuno's grandfather could get to the children was a big tree—the luxuriant, spreading holm oak that still stands near the *capelinha*.

"He could see the children but couldn't hear what Lucia was saying," Nuno told me. "When the sun started dancing, he said, some people got scared. They thought it might be the end of the world. But what I retain from my grandfather telling me this is that he was not scared. He felt that it was from God. People were praying, confessing their sins. What he told me about what had impressed him the most was the fact that after that rainstorm, his clothes were so suddenly dry.

"After that day, on the thirteenth of each month he would not work but go to Mass instead and pray the Rosary. This man, who knew the little shepherds, never saw Our Lady, but it was almost as if he did."

―――――

"Almost." The word hovered in my imagination during the days and nights I spent at Fatima. The possibility of the impossible, the manifestation of the invisible. I had felt it keenly as a child, fearing the appearance of the devil, longing for his opposite—a Lady dressed in soft blue materializing out of the air to tell me not to be afraid. I saw the same expectation now in the adult pilgrims shuffling forward on their knees to the *capelinha*, in the flushed faces of the exhausted adventurers wearing backpacks and gripping hiking poles who had trekked here all the way along a pilgrim road, the Caminho de Fatima, from Lisbon.

I also saw it in the fellow members of my English-language guided tour of the Fatima Museum on the eastern side of the sanctuary. There were several dozen people on the tour, but most of them were from the Indian state of Goa, where Catholicism took root after the Portuguese general Afonso de Albuquerque conquered it in 1510.

The museum was primarily a series of rooms devoted to objects that have been given to the sanctuary in thanks or in hopes for the intercession of the Blessed Mother. Most of these things— giant monstrances, chalices, gilded rings, bejeweled vestments— had the effect of emphasizing the church's unseemly historical fondness for ornamental excess. But there were humbler things as well. They included a monogrammed handkerchief that Pope John Paul II had clutched on his deathbed and a bicycle that an eighty-two-year-old pilgrim had ridden all the way to Fatima from Germany.

But it was the homeliest and deadliest thing in the museum collection that we had all come to see: the 9mm bullet that had been removed from John Paul's body and set into the base of the Virgin's crown. The crown was small, sized to fit Thedim's miniature depiction of the Blessed Mother. I'd never paid much attention to jewelry, but I knew a knockout when I saw one. The little crown was a dazzling work of art, its eight golden arches bowing outward and converging perfectly at a center point, below a round dome of turquoise, all of it covered with the amethysts, sapphires, rubies, emeralds, and pearls that the women of Portugal had gathered from their own homes and sent to Fatima in thanksgiving for their country remaining neutral during World War II.

And there, visible just below the convergence point of the arches, was the teardrop-shaped gray slug that had almost killed the pope, whose fatal path he believed the Virgin Mary had diverted. You had to be looking for it to really notice it—but of course all of us were. It looked like it belonged there, had been part of the original 1940s design, along with the almost three thousand other precious stones that Casa Leitão & Irmão had used to create the crown.

"It had the exactly correct dimensions to receive the bullet," Jorge Leitão, the owner of his family's two-hundred-year-old jewelry company, had told me with a trace of wonder in his voice when I met him in Lisbon a few days before.

Leitão was an elegant, thoughtful man, dressed in a blue blazer and light-blue pants. We had met in the Leitão & Irmão store in the posh Chiado district, its display cases gleaming with large and small pieces made out of silver or vivid 18-karat gold. He led me down the side streets of Baixa until, after five minutes or so, we came to a forbidding-looking steel door set into a stone wall. Jorge punched a code into a keypad and led the way into the company's utilitarian workshop, a building dating back to the mid-1800s.

It was a busy little factory, staffed by artisans in blue coats who were busy in one way or another with the modeling, casting, or stamping process for all forms of gold and silver jewelry, from earrings to a new figure of Our Lady of Fatima for the hundredth anniversary of the apparitions that Jorge had commissioned from the nephew—also a sculptor—of José Ferreira Thedim.

Jorge's father and his uncle had supervised the creation of the Fatima crown. Twelve of the firm's master jewelers and goldsmiths, working together in 1946, had taken three months to complete it. Since all the jewels had been donated, the company got into the spirit and made the crown for free.

"I was born with the idea of the crown," Jorge told me. Though he didn't seem to have a doctrinaire sense of conventional Catholic belief—"Our capacity to think is too small to be able to understand what is God"—he had grown up under the spell of Fatima, in the shadow of its history, and had feelings about what the Virgin Mary meant to his country. She had, after all, been the Queen of Portugal—decreed so by King João IV in 1646. The Portuguese monarchy had effectively ended with the assassination of King Carlos I in 1908. "But they never shot Our Lady," Jorge told me as we toured the workshop, "and they never told Our Lady she was no longer the Queen."

When I was walking back to my hotel from the museum, I passed another testament to Fatima and its rich intersections with the twentieth century. Unlike the bullet in Our Lady's crown, this was no mini-monument. It was an eleven-foot-high, three-ton fragment of the Berlin Wall. It was an ugly concrete block but displayed like a holy relic in a circular glass enclosure. A sign in Portuguese next to it gave the dates of the erection and destruction of the wall, along with a prayer from John Paul II—"Thank you, Heavenly Shepherdess, for guiding with motherly affection your people to freedom."

The fall of the Berlin Wall in 1989, followed by the collapse of the Soviet Union in 1991, was proof to those who believed what Lucia said the Virgin had told her and her cousins as part of the second secret she had revealed during the third apparition: that if Russia was consecrated to her Immaculate Heart, it would be converted and peace would come to the world. Lucia had held that John Paul II's initial consecrations in 1981 and 1983 had been well-intentioned misfires because they weren't done in the presence of the whole church leadership. But the next year, she maintained, he had finally gotten it right and carried out the consecration in accordance with the Virgin Mary's request. Lucia confirmed this in 1989 and reiterated it much later, when she was ninety-five. "It was done!" she told a visitor, in what reads like an exasperated tone. "You can tell your friends."

But there are still those, like the late Father Gruner and his biographer, Christopher A. Ferrara, who are outraged at the idea—the fiction!—that the consecration was done and the Fatima prophecy was completed. This was, they argued, because the pope never uttered the word "Russia" during the ceremony. Also, it was not a public act, visible to the entire Catholic world, but a secret ceremony designed to put the whole Russia thing to rest and continue with the church's communist-appeasement policy that began with Vatican II.

"The whole world knows that it was not done in '84," Ferrara writes. "The most devout, attentive, loyal supporters of the Pope had not heard a thing about it . . . It was as if the FBI issued a news release in 1989 saying, 'Oh, by the way, Walt Disney killed Kennedy. We proved it back in '84.'"

Such strong opinions, about such very strange things. I wondered what ten-year-old Lucia knew about Russia in 1917, then in the throes of revolution, within the throes of World War I. She couldn't have known much more than what she might have heard from the conversations among the adults in her devout family or from the pulpit of her parish church: that we must be aware of a menacing godless state arising in the East.

Russia was no longer a communist country. There was no longer a Soviet Union. But on this day in May 2023, with the invasion of Ukraine in its fifteenth month, it would have been hard to convince anybody that Russia had been "converted."

In any case, I didn't have the impression that that was what people who came to Fatima were praying for. The busloads of pilgrims from all over the world—from Portugal itself, from Spain, from Italy, from the United States, from Poland and India and Brazil—did not seem to be embroiled in a rat's nest of conspiracy and apocalyptic thinking as they prayed at the *capelinha* or wandered through the hundreds of shops selling *artigos religiosos* where they bought rosaries or statues of Our Lady or—like me—souvenir figurines of Lucia, Francisco, and Jacinta.

"Nobody in Fatima is thinking about the Third Secret," Alexandre Marto Pereira, the owner of the Estrela, the hotel I was staying in, told me one night over dinner. "They just feel good here. They like to pray. They're searching not only for peace in the world. They're searching for internal peace."

———

Had Lucia been at peace? On another bus ride, from Fatima to Coimbra, the city where she had spent so much of her long life at the Carmelite Convent of Santa Teresa, I thought about the serenity of her early childhood: tending sheep in the Cova da Iria with her cousins, hearing her father's stories about Our Lady's lamp as she sat with him on the threshing floor. And then how different her life became soon after, when her childhood visions, or daydreams, or hallucinations, helped introduce a "poisonous caterpillar" into her life. She was at home with a disapproving mother, a father with a growing drinking problem. Her mother was doubting and contemptuous, the house almost empty after her sisters moved away, her father uncharacteristically distant. And then the real tempest of personal, familial, and political demands that came with the growing awareness of the apparitions—the abductions and recriminations, the exile to Porto, where for her own safety and the convenience of the church she had to change her name and pretend to be another girl.

If she was ever happy again, I thought, as I walked upward from the Coimbra bus station to the convent at the summit of one of the town's highest hills—upslope from the old Roman forum and the famous thirteenth-century university—it must have been here. There was a bronze statue of Lucia, complete with her Coke-bottle glasses, at the entrance to the convent near its forbidding-looking closed doors. But around the corner, across from a hillside park, there was a little museum in her memory that was open to the public. I paid the scant admission fee to a young man who looked like a student, and who asked me not to take any photos.

Once again, I was the only visitor. I wandered through the two floors of the museum, looking at the items in the glass cases. There was a photo of Lucia at age thirteen I had never seen, a solemn, dark-eyed girl, wearing a *lenço* over her head. Another photo showed her at age ninety-seven in her coffin, her face stern in death, a crucifix in her hands. There were family albums on display, and the pliers and loops of wire that were the tools she used to make the rosaries she sent as gifts all over the world. There was even a full-sized replica of her convent cell, furnished with a small wooden desk on which sat a portable typewriter, and a single bed with a plain brown bedspread. On the wall opposite the bed, visible to her as she would have fallen asleep night after night for almost six decades, was the big cross that she was told, when she joined the Carmelites, that she must crucify herself upon.

The object I stared at the longest, and thought the most about, was Lucia's suitcase, the one that had been given to her by her mother when she boarded the train to be secreted away at a girls' school in Porto and away from the life she was no longer able, or allowed, to live at home. She devoted a paragraph to this suitcase in her memoirs.

"[It] has accompanied me through my life," she wrote. "It is in that case that I keep a few personal possessions that I treasure. I made a gray cotton cover for it so that it would not get spoilt, and it is the case that I took to Fatima with me on the occasions when I went there."

The suitcase in the display cabinet was covered in the gray cotton that Lucia had mentioned. It had a wooden handle and was in surprisingly good shape for something that had been in use for more than eighty years. After all I had read about the exasperation and suspicion that Maria Rosa had shown toward her daughter over the apparitions, and her worry about the family's finances after their livelihood in the Cova da Iria had disappeared, I had assumed that the suitcase had been a cheap one, bought in a hurry on the way to get her troublemaking daughter out of town on the bishop's orders. But it wasn't cheap at all. It was substantial and sturdy, and lovingly maintained. "It reminds me," Lucia wrote about the suitcase, "of my beloved Mother."

"I entrust you to Her," her earthly mother had said to Lucia on the day she bought that suitcase and said goodbye to her on the train, passing the custody of her daughter into the hands of a heavenly vision she herself could never see.

20

The Month of Our Mother

At the far edge of Fatima there's a traffic roundabout whose grassy center is dominated by a quietly powerful statue of Lucia, Francisco, and Jacinta walking upward along an incline, with their sheep following. Just beyond it, the city seems to drop away. The hotels, souvenir shops, restaurants, drugstores, and nail salons that make up modern-day Fatima are left behind, and when you cross the traffic circle to the southeast, all that is in front of you is the immemorial landscape of the Serra de Aire.

A cobblestone path—the Caminho dos Pastorinhos—winds for about a mile and a half to Aljustrel, the little village where the three shepherd children were born and grew up, and where one of them—Francisco—died. Almost as soon as I set foot on the path, it felt like all the traffic behind me was shushed, replaced by birdsong. The grass that carpeted the rocky ground was high and green, and there were olive trees neatly ranked all along the path, and growing randomly beyond it into fields demarcated by ancient fences of stacked stone.

I was following, more or less, the route used by Lucia and her cousins when they came home every day after grazing the family's flocks in the Cova—the same meandering mountain paths they might have continued to take into their adult lives if their childish imaginations had not been inflamed that day by their belief that the Virgin Mary had visited them.

It was eight o'clock in the morning, and there were no other people in sight. I had the Caminho dos Pastorinhos—the Way of the Little Shepherds—all to myself except for what I took to be a large, black, misshapen dog lumbering along about fifty yards ahead of me, placing one paw painfully in front of the next. It was moving so slowly that it took only a few seconds for me to close the gap between us, to get a better view and to adjust my reality perception.

It wasn't a dog. It was a woman, with black hair, wearing a black T-shirt and black pants, on her hands and knees, crawling to Aljustrel. I passed her without looking down at her, my eyes ahead. It would have been rude to gawk, and it didn't seem right to interrupt her heroic devotion even to say good morning. I just kept walking, past the next station of the cross marker, past the little glen known as Valinhos where the Virgin had appeared to the children after they had missed their rendezvous at the Cova when Artur Santos arrested them. There was another statue of Mary there, residing in a chapel-like enclosure topped with stone doves.

Just ahead, the pathway joined a little street that led over a rise and into Aljustrel. It was a hamlet of a few dozen stone houses with a central road that its inhabitants shared with several purposeful-looking dogs. Of course, tourism hadn't escaped it. There was a gelato place, a snack bar, and the usual shops selling religious souvenirs taking up space in the ancestral buildings.

There was no need to check a map or to ask anyone where to find Lucia's house. There it was, just ahead of me: a solid stone structure with a flat whitewashed facade and a rippling tile roof. A sign on the door said, "Lucia de Jesus's House: Temporarily Closed for Restoration Works."

Well, okay. I wouldn't be seeing the rooms where Lucia and her family had lived, where she had argued with her mother about her fantasies of being visited by Our Lady. But here was her house all the same, and around the corner, beneath a capacious fig tree, were the stone pens where the family had kept its sheep, and a hundred yards away, down a slope leading to a well, was one of the places where an angel had supposedly appeared to the children a year or so before, Lucia said, they saw Our Lady. The spot was marked by some rather stiff statues of the children, on their knees before a towering figure that represented the angel, so swaddled in celestial garments he looked like he was being suffocated.

At a little information booth behind Lucia's house, I asked the young woman who sat at the desk if she knew where the threshing floor had been, where Lucia and her siblings had sat on stone seats listening to their father talk about the lamps lit in the heavens by Mary and the angels as he pointed up at the stars and moon in the open sky. From her description in her memoirs, I had the impression that the threshing floor was where she had been most content as a young girl before the chaos following the apparitions had torn the family apart.

The attendant said she was sorry, but she didn't know the place I meant. But not far from the information booth and the back of the house there was a sort of patio, an open square whose stone floor was bordered by a continuous low stone bench. It seemed as good a place to thresh wheat as anything else around, so I decided—with no other evidence—that this must have been it. I took a seat on the bench and looked up at the sky and at a nearby ridge crowned with wind turbines. It was morning, not night—no celestial bodies in sight or celestial beings at work—but the "quiet peace and joy" she had remembered from her childhood felt poignantly real.

From Lucia's house it was only a few minutes' walk up the main road of Aljustrel to the house where the Marto family had lived, and where Francisco and Jacinta had grown up. It was a small, low-ceilinged house, with a kitchen at its back and two bedrooms to the left. A sign in one of the bedrooms identified it as the room where Francisco, Jacinta, and their brothers and sisters had been born, and where Jacinta had lain ill until she was sent to Lisbon, where she died.

The other room looked much the same: a floor of pale planks, stuccoed walls, a wooden chest and chair and bed. It was roped off from the parlor, with a little sign in front that I didn't think to read until I had swept my eyes over the little room and was about to leave.

Neste quarto faleceu Francisco em 1918.

In this room Francisco died in 1918.

It wasn't the first time I had felt a disorienting, unseemly closeness to the children of Fatima. I had visited Dona Estefânia Hospital not as a pilgrim but as a reporter, a historian, a voyeur of a little girl's death at the dawn of the twentieth century, the horrible century that the Virgin Mary had foretold in her visitations to the little shepherds and pleaded with them to forestall. I had intruded upon the memory of Lucia's happiness as I sat there in the threshing floor. And now I was too close again, an uninvited unbeliever.

———

By the time I walked back along the Caminho dos Pastorinhos to the roundabout, and then past the souvenir shops along Rua Francisco Marto to the display of the Berlin Wall and the open space of the Sanctuary of Fatima it was mid-morning. I climbed the steps to the Basilica of Our Lady of the Rosary and was pleased to find that at this hour there wasn't a crowd in front of the *pastorinhos*' burying places. In the left transept, Lucia and Jacinta's smooth marble tombs were side by side. Francisco was all alone on the other side of the church, sad but somehow appropriate, since he was the only one of the three who never heard Our Lady's voice, who had been left outside the closed circle of female solidarity created by Lucia, Jacinta, and the Blessed Mother.

There was a kneeling rail in front of the tombs but I remained standing. Out of—what? Defiance? Pride in my hard-won secular freedom? Fear that if I bent my knees at this place—simply out of courtesy to the memory of these poor children—I would be sucked back into a vortex of superstition that was so familiar, so enclosing, I would not be able to escape it twice?

I left the basilica and walked outside where in 2000, at the beatification ceremony of Francisco and Jacinta, the world had learned that the Third Part of the Secret of Fatima would finally be revealed. I walked past the *capelinha* and the Virgin statue that stood where the holm oak had been, and then toward the modern basilica at the southern end of the sanctuary.

I could feel a light wind at my back, blowing up the paved-over but still apparent natural slope of the Cova da Iria. The breeze carried with it the smell of burning wax from the offering pyre near the *capelinha*. A few people were making a snail's progress on their knees along the Penitent Way, but nobody was literally crawling like that woman I had seen along the Caminho dos Pastorinhos to Aljustrel.

When I turned and looked back, I saw that the sky on this morning in May, the month of Our Mother, was a flawless pale blue, with a perfect swoosh of cirrus cloud behind the bell tower of the old basilica. Whenever, as a boy or as a man, people asked me what my favorite color was, I have always answered that it was blue. It always has been, and I had never given any thought to why. But maybe it had something to do with the light-blue mantle that the Virgin Mary had worn in all those hundreds of statues and images I had been bombarded with in Catholic school.

From the carillon in the tower, the six-thousand-pound main bell began to ring out with a melody that was so unnervingly familiar I almost lost my footing. It was one of the hymns we sang way back in the 1950s, a time that seemed every bit as distant now as the strange events of Fatima in 1917 seemed to me then. I would have been somewhere between the age of Lucia and her cousins, following a statue of Mary during our annual school procession in May, the sky just as blue in the Texas heat, singing:

> *Immaculate Mary,*
> *Our hearts are on fire*
> *That title so wondrous*
> *Fills all our desire . . .*

It was a hymn I had left behind me, along with my Catholic lore and faith. I hadn't heard it in many years, but I had the strangest possessive sensation: it was mine, it belonged to me. Just as all those cast-off beliefs—those holy relics of who I had once been— were mine as well and were part of the amalgam of who I was now and what my values were. I had liberated myself from religious doctrine, and was forever glad of it, but that liberation had come at a price: the tension that I suspect every outlaw of faith must feel, the sense that home is waiting for you but you can never go back to it.

What a foreign place this would seem to my friends back home, I thought—foreign even to my wife and children. Could they ever imagine how deeply I understood the yearning of those children so long ago in this sheep pasture for a vision of Our Blessed Mother? For the purposes of my sanity and self-respect I had long ago had to reject the literal story that Lucia had devoted her life to preserving—the apparitions of Mary, the Miracle of the Sun, the power of prayer.

But on this May morning, when my own path in life could not have been more distant and divergent from those of the three shepherds of Fatima, I chose not to reject the feeling that came over me when the bell tolled that sonorous, bone-deep hymn; and when I recalled its words about an unreachable mythical someone who, even while warning us of the terrors that lay ahead, wanted above all to set our hearts on fire and sweep away our fears.

Acknowledgments

I'm a bit wistful about writing these acknowledgments, since they must begin with a professional (though not personal) farewell to Ann Close, the great Knopf editor who retired in 2023 and with whom I worked on six books, including this one. Thank you, Ann, for sustaining my career. And thank you for passing me into the custody of another legendary editor, Peter Gethers, who gracefully and expertly ushered *Sorrowful Mysteries* into publication.

Speaking of legends, I have the honor to once again drop the name of Esther Newberg, my agent, advocate, and friend of—could it be forty-five years? I'm very lucky to have stumbled into such a rewarding partnership with such a remarkable figure in the history of publishing. Thanks also to Esther's colleagues Estie Berkowitz and Julianna Yablans.

When I told my friend Lawrence Wright that I was thinking about writing a magazine piece about the apparitions at Fatima and my queasy relationship with Catholicism, he immediately realized—having known me for so long—that there was too much material to be crammed into an article. He was right, as I almost instantly discovered. This book is the result of his insight and his friendship.

Larry's wasn't the only guiding hand while I was working on *Sorrowful Mysteries*. As always, there was Elizabeth Crook to provide her instinctive editorial understanding and, even more crucial, reassurance that I had embarked on a book that might have an appeal beyond my own memory chamber. Another great friend, Bill Broyles, read the manuscript and helped me think of my Catholic boyhood experiences in a much broader context.

I had already decided to write this book when I happened to have a conversation with my cousin Bob Berney, the CEO of Picturehouse and the distributor of such films as *Memento, Y tu mamá también, My Big Fat Greek Wedding,* and *Pan's Labyrinth.* When we asked each other what we were working on, I discovered that I wasn't the only member of the very Catholic Berney family who had turned his sights on Lucia Santos and her cousins. Bob and his wife Jeanne, the chief operating officer of Picturehouse, were in the process of distributing a movie—*Fatima*—about that very subject. Our projects were very different, but through Bob and Jeanne I met Natasha Howes, a producer on the film, who was extremely generous in sharing her hard-won contacts at the Sanctuary of Fatima and vouching for the good intentions of a nonbeliever like me who was interested in telling the Fatima story in good faith if not with actual faith.

I'm extremely grateful to Doctor Marco Daniel Duarte, the director of the Museum and Studies Department at the Sanctuary of Fatima, and to his colleague Sónia Vazão, for meeting with me while I was in Fatima and then afterward reading the manuscript, correcting errors throughout, but generously never contradicting my own experience or my interpretations of what may or may not have happened at the Cova da Iria in 1917.

I'm grateful as well to others in Portugal who offered me hospitality and shared their understanding of the profound events I was writing about: Nuno Parezes, the director of the International Secretariat of the World Apostolate of Fatima; Jorge Leitão, owner of the storied Portuguese jewelry firm Leitão & Irmão; and Alexandre Marto Pereira, CEO of the United Hotels of Portugal.

The publishing team at Knopf, which feels more like a family to me, is headed by Jordan Pavlin and includes such indispensable collaborators as Morgan Hamilton, who kept the sometimes bewildering process of creating a physical book moving flawlessly along; Patrick Dillon, whose copyediting skills came with a bonus, since as a graduate of Our Lady Queen of Martyrs Grade School Class of 1964 he knew the somewhat exotic territory of midcentury Catholicism and could fact-check my memory; Kevin Bourke, who was at the helm throughout as production editor; Janet Hansen, who designed the jacket; and to the publicity and marketing gurus Kathy Zuckerman, Angela Rose West, and Sara Eagle. Much gratitude as well to Reagan Arthur for her belief in *Sorrowful Mysteries* as a book for Knopf.

This book is dedicated to my wife, Sue Ellen, and in some ways was written for her, since she has struggled throughout our married life to make sense of the deep, confounding imprint my Catholic upbringing had on me. That upbringing no doubt has had ricochet effects on our three daughters, Marjorie, Dorothy, and Charlotte. And I hope my experience has helped them as they have guided their own children, in their own ways, toward some sort of spiritual understanding that doesn't require either miracles or visions of hell.

Notes

2 CONSOLE YOUR GOD

14 "Their parents": Barthas and Fonseca, p. 88.

14 "not a pretty child": de Marchi, p. 31.

14 "in spite of the repugnance I feel": Santos, *Fatima*, vol. 1, p. 34.

14 "My father was of a kind nature": Santos, *Fatima*, vol. 2, p. 15.

15 "That is how the days, months and years were spent": Ibid., p. 106.

15 "under the Mohammedan yoke": Barthas and Fonseca, p. 3.

16 "Maria Rosa Ferreira": Silva, p. 21.

16 "She was always very serious": Santos, *Fatima,* vol. 1, p. 68.

16 "I felt an unalterable serenity and peace": Ibid., p. 72.

16 "lost the taste and attraction for the things of the world": Ibid., p. 73.

17 "keep my heart always pure": Ibid.

17 "I don't know whether the facts I have related": Ibid., p. 74.

17 "A Mysterious Presage": Ibid., p. 75.

17 "like a statue made of snow": Ibid., p. 76.

17 "recalling that for some time after my First Communion": Ibid., p. 77.

17 "whiter than snow, transparent as crystal": Ibid., p. 78.

18 "My own opinion": Ibid., p. 139.

18 "light in colour": de Marchi, p. 39.

18 "She was naturally good": Ibid., p. 40.

18 "quite disagreeable": Santos, *Fatima,* vol. 1, p. 37.

18 "hold the little white lambs": Ibid., p. 44.

18 "Pray thus": Ibid., p. 78.

18   "Take and drink the Body and Blood of Jesus Christ": Ibid., p. 79.

19   "catechist": Ibid., p. 42.

19   "Only later did I come to understand": Santos, *Fatima*, vol. 2, p. 58.

19   "My God, where has all the joy of our home gone": Santos, *Fatima*, vol. 1, p. 81.

19   "Our house was like a desert": Santos, *Fatima*, vol. 2, p. 28.

19   "had fallen into bad company": Santos, *Fatima*, vol. 1, p. 80.

20   "When Mass finishes": Fox, p. 115.

20   "pagan custom": Santos, *Fatima*, vol. 1, p. 80.

20   "my voice was choked with sobs": Ibid., p. 81.

20   "was born under Our Lady's mantle": Silva, p. 71.

3 THE COVE OF PEACE

22   "The first thing I learned": Santos, *Fatima*, vol. 1, p. 67.

23   "knowledge of man": Luke 1:26–38 (New Jerusalem Bible).

24   "We worked out a fine way": Santos, *Fatima*, vol. 1, p. 43.

25   "flash of lightning": Ibid., p. 174.

25   "we beheld a lady": Ibid.

25   "I have come to ask you to come here": Ibid., p. 175.

25   "Throw a stone at it!": Martindale, p. 32.

25   "more beautiful than anyone I have ever seen": Ibid., p. 64.

26   "She will be in purgatory until the end of the world": Santos, *Fatima*, vol. 1, p. 175.

26   "undergo purification": Catechism of the Catholic Church, p. 268.

26   "we must believe . . . there is a purifying fire": Ibid., p. 269.

26   "Are you willing to offer yourselves to God": Santos, *Fatima*, vol. 1, p. 175.

27   "As she pronounced these last words": Ibid.

27   "poor and miserable instrument": Ibid., p. 137.

27   "lit by a single skylight": Ibid., p. 136.

27   "From the beginning of the world": de Marchi, p. 56.

27   "to consider": Santos, *Fatima*, vol. 1, p. 49.

28   "heroic march to the sewer": Bennett, p. 45.

29   "was far from defending the children": de Marchi, p. 61.

29   "an attitude of faith and trust": Santos, *Fatima*, vol. 2, p. 28.

29   "As usual": de Marchi, p. 65.

29   "about a metre high": Ibid., p. 66.

30   "something like a tiny little voice": Ibid.

30   "I will take Jacinta and Francisco soon": Santos, *Fatima*, vol. 1, p. 177.

30 "a heart encircled by thorns": Ibid.
31 "It sounded": de Marchi, p. 68.

4 THE THREE-PART SECRET

32 "Our Lady is coming!": de Marchi, p. 76.
32 "deathlike pallor": Walsh, p. 79.
32 "like a horse-fly": Ibid., p. 80.
32 "All this was for me": de Marchi, p. 76.
32 "contemptuous attitude": Santos, *Fatima*, vol. 1, p. 83.
33 "let him do whatever he likes with you": Ibid., p. 85.
33 "It doesn't seem to me like a revelation from heaven": Ibid.
33 "If the Lady asks for me": Ibid., p. 87.
33 "impelled by a strange force": Ibid.
33 "Continue to come here every month": Ibid., p. 178.
34 "This was the day": Ibid., p. 87.
34 "a secret made up of three distinct parts": Ibid., p. 123.
34 "the crowd seemed to sense": Walsh, p. 82.
35 "It's a secret": Ibid., p. 83.
35 "final secret . . . until the Queen of Heaven": Ibid., p. 82.
35 "This request": Santos, *Fatima*, vol. 1, p. 121.
35 "vision of hell": Ibid., p. 123.
35 "shrieks and groans of pain and despair": Ibid.
35 "devotion to my Immaculate Heart": Ibid.
35 "consecration of Russia": Ibid., p. 124.
36 "post eventum": Ibid., p. 131fn.
36 "If they asked us why it was a secret": Ibid., p. 146.
36 "Some people": Ibid., p. 125.
38 "Oh Hell! Hell!": Ibid.

5 OFFER IT UP

39 "Everything had been destroyed": Santos, *Fatima*, vol. 1, p. 130.
40 "false friends": Santos, *Fatima*, vol. 2, p. 135.
40 "He has made life black for me": Ibid.
40 "What hurt me most": Santos, *Fatima*, vol. 1, p. 90.
40 "What they wanted": de Marchi, p. 85.
41 "Let her answer for herself": Santos, *Fatima*, vol. 1, p. 89.
41 "was determined to force me": Ibid., p. 90.
41 "we think it's all women's stories": de Marchi, p. 90.

42 "If people who lie go to hell": Ibid., p. 92.

42 "This isn't the way to the Cova": Ibid.

42 "If there were a lot of people in July": Ibid., p. 93.

42 "rough poles of pale wood": (*toscos postes de madeira clara*) Santuário de Fátima, p. 157.

42 "we began to see a little cloud": de Marchi, pp. 93–94.

43 "I deny this infamous and insidious calumny": Ibid., p. 94.

43 "It was the secret which Arthur Santos wanted": Ibid., p. 98.

43 "they told us they were coming soon": Santos, *Fatima*, vol. 1, p. 52.

43 "In the presence of the children": de Marchi, p. 98.

43 "She's well fried": Ibid.

44 "recommended her soul": Ibid., p. 99.

44 "What is false": Silva, p. 122.

44 "By the man's face": Pelletier, p. 226.

44 "he died a lonely and embittered man": Ibid., p. 227.

44 "stop the speculation": Ibid., p. 122.

45 "O my Jesus!": Santos, *Fatima*, vol. 1, p. 52.

45 "Fanaticism in Action": Bennett, p. 105.

45 "surround and asphyxiate": Ibid.

45 "we felt something supernatural": Santos, *Fatima*, vol. 1, p. 180.

46 "I will cure some of them": Ibid.

46 "this instrument of penance": Ibid., p. 93.

46 "Look! Look!": Ibid.

47 "A scapular isn't a penance": "Your New Favorite Scapular," scapulars.com.

47 "They all wanted to see and question us": Santos, *Fatima*, vol. 1, p. 92.

48 "Come near, my children": Zimdars-Swartz, p. 29.

48 "A great famine will come": Ibid., p. 30.

48 "not unlike an ogival window": Zola, p. 90.

48 "the Mother of Angels": Zimdars-Swartz, p. 49.

49 "The priests have flocked to the place": (*Os padres teem afluido ao local*) Teixeira Fernandes, p. 46.

49 "For the love of God": Santos, *Fatima*, vol. 1, p. 181.

49 "no human respect whatsoever": Ibid., p. 180.

50 "the means of transport": de Marchi, p. 112.

50 "obtain the end of the war": Santos, *Fatima*, vol. 1, p. 181.

50 "Yes, I will cure some": Ibid., p. 182.

50 "I will perform a miracle": Ibid.

6 THE SPINNING SUN

51 "It was three o'clock in the afternoon . . .": (*Eram três horas da tard . . .*) Santuário de Fátima, p. 51.

51 "astonishing cures": Torgal, pp. 287–295.

51 "narrator, defender and bard": Ibid., p. 288.

52 "I did not approach the place of the apparitions": Ibid., p. 290.

52 "an unselfconsciousness": de Marchi, p. 118. (For the Portuguese original see Santuário de Fátima, pp. 55ff.)

53 "are very good people": Ibid., p. 121.

53 "not at all a bad man": Ibid.

53 "fecklessness": Ibid., p. 122.

53 "with the result that she got worse": Santos, *Fatima,* vol. 2, p. 151.

53 "My poor little girl!": Ibid., p. 152.

54 "made a great impression": de Marchi, p. 123.

54 "never thought": Ibid., p. 125.

54 "What did she say": Ibid., p. 124.

54 "The cotton skirts of the women": Ibid., p. 130.

55 "And there are even people who dream": Walsh, p. 141.

55 "My parents": Santos, *Fatima,* vol. 1, p. 98.

55 "the people filled the house": de Marchi, p. 133.

55 "Lucia's was blue": Ibid., p. 134.

56 "moved by an interior impulse": Santos, *Fatima,* vol. 1, p. 182.

56 "a chapel to be built": Ibid.

56 "because He is already so much offended": Ibid.

56 "The sky, pearly gray in colour": de Marchi, p. 136.

56 "a disc with a clean-cut rim": Ibid., p. 137.

57 "It looked like a plaque of dull silver": Ibid.

57 "spun like a fire wheel": Ibid., p. 139.

57 "nervously agitated as if driven by electricity": Jaki, p. 107.

57 "the colour of old yellow damask": Ibid., p. 138.

57 "to bless the world": Santos, *Fatima,* vol. 1, p. 183.

58 "If the children": de Marchi, p. 149.

58 "On the thirteenth of this month": Ibid., p. 150.

58 "No coherent reply": Ibid., p. 151.

59 "Citizens!": Ibid., p. 246.

59 "whose revenue source": (*cuja fonte de receita*) Teixeira Fernandes, p. 8.

60 "the whole population": de Marchi, p. 159.

60 "disgrace": Ibid.

60 "Crusade of Regeneration": Bennett, p. 122.

7 THE HYPNOTIC CURRENT

61 "The people, who had been soaked": de Marchi, p. 141.

61 "No one can escape": Ibid.

62 "nose, eye and nasolabial fold": Dalleur, p. 18n.

62 "a remarkable spectacle in the sky": de Marchi, p. 140.

62 "people were shouting and weeping": Ibid., p. 141.

62 "a fact which destroys": Ibid., p. 142.

63 "solar prodigy": Michel de la Sainte Trinité, *The Whole Truth,* vol. 1, p. 343.

63 "whirled on itself": de Marchi, p. 137.

63 "Up to the present": Ibid., p. 136.

64 "Most observers": Meessen, p. 2.

64 "radical and Jacobinist": Jaki, p. 108.

64 "Times of great calamities": Ibid., p. 21.

64 "I looked hard": Ibid., p. 37.

64 "Mass suggestion": Ibid., p. 48.

65 "A clear-cut, sharp-edged, brilliantly shining disk ": Ibid., p. 134.

65 "coolly and calmly": Ibid., p. 137.

65 "meticulous synthesis of history": Fernandes and d'Armada, quotes from back cover and p. 240.

66 "Look at the sun!": de Marchi, p. 135.

66 "Miracle, miracle!": Jaki, p. 31.

66 "beings and manifestations": Stanford, p. 60.

67 "This isn't a game": Harrigan.

68 "wild and uninteresting": Santuária de Fátima, p. 158ff.

8 BEARER OF GOD

71 "born of a woman": Galatians 4:4. All biblical quotes are from the Douay-Rheims Version.

71 "Hail, full of grace": Luke 1:28.

72 "was minded to put her away privately": Matthew 1:19.

72 "save people from their sins": Matthew 1:21.

72 "knew her not": Matthew 1:25.

72 "How shall this be done": Luke 1:34.

72 "the Holy Ghost shall come upon thee": Luke 1:35.

72 "the handmaid of the Lord": Luke 1:38.

72 "Blessed art thou": Luke 1:42.

72 "the consolation of Israel": Luke 1:25.

73 "thy own soul a sword shall pierce": Luke 1:35.

73 "Did you not know": Luke 2:49.

73 "kept all these words in her heart": Luke 2:51.

73 "my hour has not yet come": John 2:4.

73 "the disciple . . . whom he loved": John 19:26–27.

74 "cleaned herself up from her discharges": Gathercole, p. 8.

74 "She's a young girl": Ibid., p. 10.

74 "Who has ensnared me?": Ibid., p. 13.

74 "a virgin has given birth": Ibid., p. 17.

75 "brother of the Lord": Galatians 1:19.

75 "the untarnished vessel of virginity": Rubin, p. 44.

75 "If Jesus was more than he ever claimed": Ibid., p. 13.

76 "closed gate": Ibid., p. 27.

76 "the primeval curse": Ibid., p. 38.

76 "by an entirely unique privilege": Pius XII.

77 "foolishness and games": McLure, pp. 14–15.

77 "Our Lady usually appears": "Questions and Answers," Medjugorje: Apparitions of the Virgin Mary Queen of Peace, medjugorje.com/.

77 "when it is time": Ibid.

77 "a beautiful, indestructible, permanent sign": Ibid.

78 "the mother of the very true deity God": Poole, p. 28.

78 "I will listen to their weeping": Ibid.

80 "This appears": Ibid., p. 84.

9 I AM TO SUFFER VERY MUCH

82 "displaced kidney": Santos, *Fatima,* vol. 2, p. 151.

83 "Look here": Ibid., p. 19.

84 "He was so good": de Marchi, p. 179.

84 "Are you suffering a lot": Santos, *Fatima,* vol. 1, p. 163.

84 "A smile passed over his lips": de Marchi, p. 185.

84 "This grief": Santos, *Fatima,* vol. 1, p. 166.

84 "I am to suffer very much": Barthas and Fonseca, p. 128.

84 "big dark house": Santos, *Fatima,* vol. 1, p. 60.

85 "like a skeleton": de Marchi, p. 189.

85 "I tried to comfort her": Santos, *Fatima,* vol. 1, p. 63.

85 "a heartrending farewell": Ibid.

85 "a little angel had come": de Marchi, p. 198.

86 "leaving a wound": Michel de la Sainte Trinité, *The Whole Truth,* vol. 2, p. 151.

86 "Everything was accomplished": Ibid., p. 153.

86 "When I arrived in the town": de Marchi, p. 207.

86 "came knocking on my door": Santos, *Fatima,* vol. 1, p. 109.

87 "He was the only one": Ibid., p. 110.

88 "I must put a stop to this ridiculous fairy tale": de Marchi, p. 214.

88 "The projected parade": Ibid., p. 219.

89 "set off by the pale light": Santos, *Fatima,* vol. 2, p. 187.

90 "Off you go, child": Ibid., p. 188.

90 "a mountain maid": Michel de la Saint Trinité, *The Whole Truth,* vol. 2, p. 211.

90 "I wanted seclusion": Carmel of Coimbra, p. 173.

90 "suddenly the room lit up": Ibid., p. 158.

90 "surrounded with thorns": Ibid.

90 "in a tepid and indifferent manner": Santos, *Fatima,* vol. 1, p. 196.

91 "make the consecration of Russia": Ibid., p. 198.

92 "the spiritual capital of the nation": Bennett, p. 187.

92 "They say that I am [God's] Vicar on earth": Socci, p. 182.

92 "Take it from our fragile hands": Michel de la Sainte Trinité, *The Whole Truth,* vol. 2, p. 391.

93 "Intercede for Portugal": Ibid., p. 392.

10 FATIMIZED

97 "might almost be called": "Our Lady of Fatima - Ven Bishop Fulton J Sheen," video on YouTube.

99 "This was the Peace plan from Heaven": McGrath, p. 2.

99 "fatimize your homes": Dooley, p. 8.

99 "in a spiritual sense": Ibid., p. 141.

102 "the sins which cause most souls to go to hell": de Marchi, p. 198.

102 "sins of the flesh": de Marchi, p. 198n.

11 HEAVEN'S SECRETS

106 "Oh daughter": Carmel of Coimbra., p. 200.

106 "Goodbye, until we meet in Heaven": Ibid., p. 201.

106 "such a thing was out of the question": Santos, *Fatima,* vol. 2, p. 194.

106 "this too could not be allowed": Ibid.

106 "When you see a night": Santos, *Fatima,* vol. 1, p. 124.

107 "God manifested that sign": Ibid., p. 130.

107 "Her glance is serene": Michel de la Sainte Trinité, *The Whole Truth,* vol. 2, p. 5.

108 "I feel myself in a mystery of light": Carmel of Coimbra, p. 225.

108 "I am not surprised": Ibid., p. 232.

108 "poor and humble prayers": Ibid., p. 233.

108 "I was so enraptured!": Santos, *Fatima,* vol. 1, p. 33.

109 "my mission on earth is being completed": Michel de la Sainte Trinité, *The Whole Truth,* vol. 3, p. 38.

109 "I was at peace": Carmel of Coimbra, p. 241.

109 "this order made me shudder": Ibid.

110 "Be at peace": Ibid., p. 243.

110 "Because then it will seem clearer": Michel de la Sainte Trinité, *The Whole Truth,* vol. 3, p. 474.

110 "communism will reach its maximum height": Ibid., p. 251.

111 "I asked him many times": Ibid., p. 467.

111 "Especially the Secret!": Ibid., p. 480.

111 "most clement Mother": Pius XII, "*Sacro Vergente Anno*: Consecration of Russia to the Immaculate Heart of Mary," July 7, 1951, vatican .va/.

112 "I have seen the 'miracle of the sun'": Pronechen, James, "This Marian Pope Popularized Fatima—and It's Not Who You Think," *National Catholic Register,* August 11, 2017, ncregister.com/.

112 "Secretum Sancti Officii": Michel de la Sainte Trinité, *The Whole Truth,* vol. 3, p. 485.

12 DARK, BLACK DEPTHS

114 "anguished wait of the entire Catholic universe": Michel de la Sainte Trinité, *The Whole Truth,* vol. 3, p. 634.

115 "sprang up": Tobin, p. 109.

115 "abstruse locutions": "The Third Secret Controversy—Part VI," Salve Maria Regina, salvemariaregina.info/.

115 "This makes no reference to my time": Alonso, p. 51.

115 "sealed it, and sent it": Ibid., p. 50.

115 "It is most probable": Michel de la Sainte Trinité, *The Whole Truth,* vol. 3, p. 579.

116 "to publish the 'third Secret'": Ibid., p. 822.

116 "The third part of the secret revealed at the Cova da Iria": "The Message of Fatima," Congregation for the Doctrine of the Faith, vatican.va/.

117 "the most unyielding and terrible adversary of Fatima": Michel de la Sainte Trinité, *The Whole Truth,* vol. 1, p. 389.

118 "Let us observe": Ibid., p. 402.

118 "very concerned, pale": Alonso, p. 109.

119 "storm of ridicule": Ibid., p. 111.

119 "I know nothing": Ibid., p. 112.

119 "The greatest World War will happen": Ibid., p. 115.

120 "Our Lady is not a sensationalist": Miguel, p. 162.

121 "Contrary to common newspaper usage": "Address to the Greater Houston Ministerial Association" (video), John F. Kennedy Presidential Library and Museum, jfklibrary.org/.

13 WILD HORSES OF MODERNISM

132 "wild horses of modernism": Kramer, p. 51.

132 "The perpetrators": Ibid., p. xxi.

132 "They had taken the modernist bait": Ibid.

132 "groundless hopes for peace": François de Marie des Anges, p. 63.

132 "that a special protection would be granted": Carmel of Coimbra, p. 282.

133 "make the consecration of Russia": Santos, *Fatima*, vol. 1, p. 198.

14 THE PATH OF THE BULLET

134 "reserve": Symonds, p. 361.

134 "Your Holiness": Diaz.

134 "as radical as the saints": Bertone, p. 58.

134 "Since that day": Symonds, p. 361.

135 "If there is a message": Lynch, pp. 50–51.

136 "I did it": Sterling, p. 48.

136 "I did not kill Ipekci": Ibid., p. 51.

136 "the Commander of the Crusades": Ibid., p. 19.

136 "Others have a cause": Ibid., p. 47.

136 "the last great secret of our time": Bernstein and Politi, p. 296.

137 "Our Lady of the Bright Mountain": Kengor, p. 188.

137 "malicious, lowly, perfidious, and backward toady": Weigel, p. 423.

138 "was our enemy": Bernstein and Politi, p. 274.

138 "Use all possibilities available": Kengor, p. 198.

138 "The second shot immediately followed": Dziwisz, p. 131.

138 "I soon saw": Ibid., pp. 125–126.

138 "final anointing": Ibid., p. 133.

140 "Two thirteenths of May!": Ibid., p. 135.

140 "he recognized his own destiny": Ibid., p. 136.

140 "One hand shot": Ibid.

140 "At times": Morrow.

141 "What we talked about will have to remain": Ibid.

141 "In the course of our conversation": John Paul II, p. 163.

141 "Could I forget": Ibid.

141 "That was his principal concern": Ibid.

142 "to the Madonna, my spiritual mother": "John Paul II's Assailant Wants to Be a Priest," *CathNews*, July 13, 2016, cathnews.com/.

142 "The people spoiled everything": Michel de la Sainte Trinité, *The Whole Truth,* vol. 2, p. 340.

143 "leaned over [the statue]": de Marchi, p. 168.

143 "And so I come here today": "Homily of Bl. John Paul II; May 13, 1982" ("Mary's Maternal Love"), Pierced Hearts of Jesus and Mary, piercedhearts.org/.

144 "I accuse you of destroying the Church": Miguel, pp. 80–81.

15 THE GNAWING BEAST

145 "Is it true": Carmel of Coimbra, p. 362.

146 "If it were possible": Ibid., p. 363.

146 "the Vicar of Christ on earth whom I revere": Ibid., p. 364.

146 "No": Ibid.

146 "had a sort of generic aversion": Socci, p. 199.

146 "Show us Lucia": Ibid., p. 366.

146 "Here she is!": Ibid.

147 "In truth": Fox, p. 164.

147 "I have come to understand": Tindal-Robertson, p. 11.

147 "We have to talk fast": Carmel of Coimbra, p. 376.

147 "agree that it was more prudent": Ibid.

148 "Happy are you, my daughter": Miguel, p. 88.

148 "The moment has come": Santos, *Fatima,* vol. 1, p. 198.

148 "the power of this consecration": Tindal-Robertson, p. 19.

148 "This is a gift for Our Lady": Miguel, p. 112.

149 "None of us were able to say a word": Ibid.

16 NOBODY THERE

150 "and where each stone reminded me": Carmel of Coimbra, p. 280.

151 "While kneeling down there after so many years": Ibid., p. 278.

151 "It is not that I intend to find in Carmel": Ibid., p. 295.

151 "very simple . . . a child of the mountains": McGlynn, p. 57.

151 "There seemed to be both passive and active qualities": Ibid., p. 60.

151 "Wrinkles formed on her brow": Ibid., p. 61.

152 "without anyone else knowing": Carmel of Coimbra, p. 294.

152 "Often on Sunday afternoons": Fox, p. 294.

152 "I would be happier to be buried in leprosy": Carmel of Coimbra, p. 256.

152 "The door is open": Ibid., p. 294.

153 "Our Reverend Mother Prioress": Fox, p. 313.

154 "The temptations of the devil": Santos, *"Calls" from the Message,* p. 197.

154 "consecrated souls": Ibid., p. 196.

154 "plunge themselves into His immense Being": Ibid., p. 197.

17 THE VEIL OF THE FUTURE

159 "a probable transverse myelitis": Silva, p. 212.

159 "rapid, complete, lasting": Ibid., p. 211.

159 "immense light": Homily of His Holiness Pope John Paul II: Beatification of Francisco and Jacinta Marto, Shepherds of Fatima, May 13, 2000, vatican.va/.

160 "appropriate commentary": Address of Cardinal Angelo Sodano Regarding the "Third Part" of the Secret of Fatima at the Conclusion of the Solemn Mass of John Paul II, May 13, 2000, vatican.va/.

161 "contains a prophetic vision": Ibid.

161 "will probably prove disappointing": Congregation for the Doctrine of the Faith, "The Message of Fatima," vatican.va/.

161 "Eminence, if you had to explain": Symonds, p. 379.

162 "The immediate reaction of millions of Catholics": Kramer, p. 105.

162 "a utopian world 'brotherhood'": Ibid., p. xxi.

162 "Fatima lite": Alban, p. 201.

162 "KGB operatives in the garb of priests": Ibid., p. 46.

162 "we have been sold a bill of goods": Ibid., p. 149.

163 "The image which the children saw": Congregation for the Doctrine of the Faith, vatican.va/.

163 "the Holy Father will consecrate Russia to me": Santos, *Fatima,* vol. 1, p. 179.

163 "a truly explosive little phrase": Socci, p. 67.

163 "The incomplete phrase": Kramer, p. 7.

165 "In traditionalist circles": Socci, p. 16.

165 "divine warning": Ferrara, p. 31.

165 "from somewhere or other the smoke of Satan": Ibid., p. 28.

165 "belong to the past": Congregation for the Doctrine of the Faith, vatican.va/.

165 "the 'secret' of Fatima brings": Ibid.

165 "The Secret is wider": Alban, p. 268.

166 "supposed *omissis*": Bertone, p. 27.

166 "likeable old chatterbox": Ibid., p. 61.

166 "everything has been published": Ibid., p. 55.

166 "private revelation": Congregation for the Doctrine of the Faith, vatican.va.

167 "because it could be badly interpreted": Socci, p. 123.

167 "ventriloquist's dummy of the anti-Fatima forces": Alban, p. 96.

167 "pro-Communist Vatican-Moscow *Ostpolitik*": Ibid., p. 68.

18 THE LAST SHEEP OF THE FLOCK

168 "The idea I have of my soul": Fox, pp. 172–173.

169 "We watch TV": Socci, p. 26.

169 "After that": Maria Celina de Jesus Crucificado, p. 24.

169 "the last sheep of the flock": Fox, p. 260.

170 "If they know that there is another secret": Maria Celina de Jesus Crucificado, p. 24.

171 "I long for my Homeland": Fox, p. 177.

172 "A short while ago": Ibid., p. 175.

176 "a monstrous word for a monstrous idea": Luther, "A Prelude by Martin Luther on the Babylonian Captivity of the Church," Project Wittenberg, projectwittenberg.org/.

183 "At the end": Maria Celina de Jesus Crucificado, p. 28.

184 "Our Lady said I was to remain here for a while": Ibid.

184 "the beginning of a new, painful and difficult phase": Ibid., p. 2.

184 "I come to affirm our affectionate union": Carmel of Coimbra, p. 421.

184 "as if to say: 'You take it'": Ibid., p. 420.

19 THE SANCTUARY

190 "It was night in the dingy hospital": Walsh, p. 182.

190 "a rosy flush on her cheeks": Ibid.

194 "Christ, of the Virgin Mother of God, and of the other saints": "On the Invocation, Veneration, and Relics, of Saints, and on Sacred Images," The Council of Trent Session 25, thecounciloftrent.com/.

195 "I looked at her and she looked at me": McKenna, p. 79.

197 "We will be the Blue Army of Mary and Christ": "The History of the World Apostolate of Fatima," World Apostolate of Fatima International Secretariat, worldfatima.com/.

198 "It's up to you to present this Vision truthfully and vividly": Ernster.

198 "the most moving, sincere and profound confession": Ibid.

198 "I will paint what I see": Ibid.

198 "The soul of a sinner is like a snail": Ibid.

202 "It was done!": Mahowald.

205 "[It] has accompanied me through my life": Santos, *Fatima*, vol. 2, p. 188.

205 "It reminds me": Ibid.

205 "I entrust you to Her": Ibid.

Bibliography

Alban, Francis, with Christopher A. Ferrara, Esq. *Fatima Priest*. Pound Ridge, NY: Good Counsel Publications, 2013.

Alonso, Joaquin Maria, C.M.F. *The Secret of Fatima: Fact and Legend*. Cambridge, MA: Ravengate Press, 1979.

Arnold, Catharine. *Pandemic 1918*. New York: St. Martin's Griffin, 2018.

Barry, John M. *The Great Influenza*. New York: Penguin Books, 2018.

Barthas, Chanoine C., and Père G. Da Fonseca, S.J. *Our Lady of Light*. Milwaukee: Bruce Publishing Company, 1947.

Bennett, Jeffery S. *When the Sun Danced: Myth, Miracles, and Modernity in Early Twentieth Century Portugal*. Charlottesville: University of Virginia Press, 2012.

Bernstein, Carl, and Marco Politi. *His Holiness: John Paul II and the Hidden History of Our Time*. New York: Doubleday, 1996.

Bertone, Cardinal Tarcisio. *The Last Secret of Fatima*. New York: Image, 2008.

Borelli, Antonio, and John R. Spann. *Our Lady at Fátima: Prophecies of Tragedy or Hope?* York, PA: American Society for the Defense of Tradition, Family and Property, 2002.

Brochado, Costa. *Fátima in the Light of History*. Milwaukee: Bruce Publishing Company, 1954.

Carmel of Coimbra. *A Pathway Under the Gaze of Mary: Biography of Sister*

Maria Lucia of Jesus and the Immaculate Heart. Washington, NJ: Blue Army Press, 2019.

Carroll, Michael P. *The Cult of the Virgin Mary*. Princeton: Princeton University Press, 1986.

Catechism of the Catholic Church. New Hope, KY: Urbi et Orbi Communications, 1994.

Cunneen, Sally. *In Search of Mary: The Woman and the Symbol*. New York: Ballantine, 1996.

Dalleur, Philippe. "Fatima Pictures and Testimonials: In-Depth Analysis." *Scientia et Fides* 9, no. 1, 2021.

de Marchi, John. *Fatima from the Beginning*. Still River, MA: Ravensgate Press, 11th Edition, 2000.

Diaz, Ary Waldir Ramos. "Is the Mystery over the Death of John Paul I Finally Solved?" *Aleteia*, November 6, 2017. Aleteia.org.

Dooley, Lester M., S.V.D. *Fatima and You*. Notre Dame, IN: Ave Maria Press, 1951.

Duarte, Marco Daniel. "1917—Fatima, the Global Shrine." In *The Global History of Portugal: From Pre- History to the Modern World,* edited by Carlos Fiolhais, José Eduardo Franco, and José Pedro Paiva. Brighton, Chicago, Toronto: Sussex Academic Press, 2022.

———. "Os papas peregrinos de Fátima: os discursos do 'bispo vestido de branco' sobre Fátima no contexto das peregrinações à Cova da Iria." In Duarte (ed.), *Fátima, hoje: que caminhos?* Fátima: Santuário de Fátima, 2019.

Dziwisz, Cardinal Stanislaw. *A Life with Karol: My Forty-Year Friendship with the Man Who Became Pope*. New York: Doubleday, 2008.

Ernster, Barb. "Fatima Vision of Hell Helped Salvador Dali Return to God." World Apostolate of Fatima, USA. bluearmy.com.

Fatima and the Third Secret: A Historical Examination Based on a Letter of Sister Lúcia and the Carmelite Biography. Second edition. Boonville, NY: Preserving Christian Publications, 2017.

Fernandes, Joaquim, and Fina d'Armada. *Heavenly Lights: The Apparitions of Fatima and the UFO Phenomenon*. San Antonio and New York: Anomalist Books, 2007.

Ferrara, Christopher A. *The Secret Still Hidden*. Pound Ridge, NY: Good Counsel Publications, 2008.

Fox, Father Robert J. *The Intimate Life of Sister Lucia*. Alexandria, SD: Fatima Family Apostolate, 2001.

François de Marie des Anges, Frère. *Fatima: Prophecies of Tragedy and Triumph*. Buffalo: Immaculate Heart Publications, 1994.

Frossard, André, in conversation with John Paul II. *"Be Not Afraid!"* New York: St. Martin's Press, 1984.

Gaddis, John Lewis. *The Cold War: A New History.* New York: Penguin Books, 2005.

Galamba de Oliveira, Rev. Joseph. *Jacinta: The Flower of Fatima.* Washington, NJ: AMI Press, 1972.

Gathercole, Simon. *The Apocryphal Gospels.* New York: Penguin Classics, 2022.

Haffert, John M. *Meet the Witnesses of the Miracle of the Sun.* Spring Grove, PA: American Society for the Defense of Tradition, Family and Property, 1961.

Harrigan, Stephen. "Planet X! We're Waiting for You." *Texas Monthly*, February 1976.

Hatton, Barry. *The Portuguese: A Modern History.* Northampton, MA: Interlink Books, 2017.

Heseman, Michael. *The Fatima Secret.* New York: Dell Publishing, 2000.

The Holy Bible. New Testament (Douay-Rheims Version). London: Catholic Way Publishing, 2016.

Jaki, Stanley L. *God and the Sun at Fatima.* Royal Oak, MI: Real View Books, 1999.

John Paul II. *Memory and Identity: Conversations at the Dawn of a Millennium.* New York: Rizzoli, 2005.

Kaplan, Marion. *The Portuguese: The Land and Its People.* London: Penguin Books, 1991.

Kengor, Paul. *A Pope and a President.* Wilmington, DE: ISI Books, 2017.

Kramer, Father Paul. *The Devil's Final Battle.* Terryville, CT: The Missionary Association, 2002.

Lawler, Philip F. *The Smoke of Satan.* Charlotte, NC: Tan Books, 2018.

Lynch, David J. *The Call to Total Consecration to the Immaculate Heart of Mary.* St. Albans, VT: Missions of the Sorrowful and Immaculate Heart of Mary, 1991.

Machado, José Barbosa. *The Miracle of the Sun.* Malibu, CA: Spiral of Life Publishing, 2018.

Madigan, Leo. *The Golden Book of Fatima: A Pilgrim's Companion.* Fatima: Fatima-Ophel Books, 2013.

Mahowald, Steve. "An Interview with Dr. Zugibe." Eternal World Television Network (EWTN). ewtn.com.

Maria Celina de Jesus Crucificado, Sister. *Our Memories of Sister Lucia.* Second edition. Coimbra: Carmel of Coimbra, July 2007.

Martindale, C. C., S.J. *The Message of Fatima*. London: Burns, Oates & Washbourne Ltd., 1950.

Martins, Father Antonio Maria, S.J. *Documents on Fatima and the Memoirs of Sister Lucia*. Waite Park, MN: Fatima Family Apostolate, 2002.

Maunder, Chris. *Our Lady of the Nations: Apparitions of Mary in 20th-Century Catholic Europe*. Oxford: Oxford University Press, 2016.

McGlynn, Father Thomas. *Vision of Fatima*. Manchester, NH: Sophia Institute Press, 2017.

McGrath, Rt. Rev. Wm. C., P.A. *Fatima or World Suicide*. Scarboro Bluffs, ON, CA: Scarboro Foreign Mission Society, 1950.

McKenna, Thomas J. *The Fatima Century: How the Pilgrim Virgin Is Changing Our Generation*. San Diego: Catholic Action, 2017.

McLure, Kevin. *The Evidence for Visions of the Virgin Mary*. Wellingborough, UK: Aquarian Press, 1983.

Medeiros, Humberto Sousa. *Jacinta: The Flower of Fatima*. Charlotte, NC: Tan Books, 2017.

Meessen, Auguste. "Apparitions and Miracles of the Sun." Paper presented at the International Symposium "Science, Religion, and Conscience." Centro Transdisciplinar de Estudos da Consciência, Universidade Fernando Pessoa, Porto, October 23–25, 2003.

Michel de la Sainte Trinité, Frère. *The Whole Truth About Fatima*, vol. 1: *Science and the Facts*. Buffalo: Immaculate Heart Publications, 1989.

——. *The Whole Truth About Fatima*, vol. 2: *The Secret and the Church*. Buffalo: Immaculate Heart Publications, 1989.

——. *The Whole Truth About Fatima*, vol. 3: *The Third Secret*. Buffalo: Immaculate Heart Publications, 1990.

Miguel, Aura. *El Secreto que guía al Papa: La experiencia de Fátima en el pontificado de Juan Pablo II*. Madrid: Ediciones Rialp, S.A., 2001.

Morrow, Lance. "Pope John Paul II Forgives His Would-Be Assassin." *Time*, January 19, 1984. content.time.com.

Nickell, Joe. *Looking for a Miracle: Weeping Icons, Relics, Stigmata, Visions & Healing Cures*. Amherst, NY: Prometheus Books, 1998.

Pelikan, Jaroslav. *Mary Through the Centuries*. New Haven: Yale University Press, 1996.

Pelletier, Joseph A. *The Sun Danced at Fatima*. Newly revised and expanded. New York: Image Books/Doubleday, 1983.

Pius XII. "*Munificentissimus Deus*: Defining the Dogma of the Assumption." November 1, 1950. vatican.va.

Poole, Stafford. *Our Lady of Guadalupe: The Origins and Sources of a Mexican National Symbol, 1521–1797*. Revised edition. Tucson: University of Arizona Press, 2017.

Rodrigues, Jośe A. *Our Lady of Portugal: Apparitions of the Most Blessed Virgin Mary Throughout Portugal's History*. [n.p.]: Ad Te Beate Ioseph, 2020.

Rubin, Miri. *Mother of God*. New Haven and London: Yale University Press, 2009.

Santos, Ana Rita, and Marco Daniel Duarte (eds.). *Coroa Preciosa de Nossa Senhora de Fátima*. Second edition. Fátima: Santuário de Fátima, 2023.

Santos, Lucia (Sister Lucia). *"Calls" from the Message of Fatima*. Still River, MA: Ravengate Press, 1997.

———. *Fatima in Lucia's Own Words*, vol. 1. Edited by Fr. Louis Kondor, SVD. Twenty-first edition. Fátima: Fundação Francisco e Jacinta Marto, 2017.

———. *Fatima in Lucia's Own Words*, vol. 2. Edited by Fr. Louis Kondor, SVD. Sixth edition. Fátima: Fundação Francisco e Jacinta Marto, 2017.

Santuário de Fátima. *Documentação Crítica de Fátima: Seleção de Documentos (1917–1930)*. Fátima: Santuário de Fátima, 2013.

Saraiva, José Hermano. *Portugal: A Companion History*. Manchester, UK: Carcanet Press Ltd., 1997.

Schwebel, Lisa J. *Apparitions, Healings, and Weeping Madonnas: Christianity and the Paranormal*. Mahwah, NJ: Paulist Press, 2004.

Senz, Paul. *Fatima: 100 Questions & Answers about the Marian Apparitions*. San Francisco: Ignatius Press, 2020.

Silva, M. Fernando. *The Shepherds of Fatima*. Boston: Pauline Books and Media, 2008.

Socci, Antonio. *The Fourth Secret of Fatima*. Fitzwilliam, NH: Loreto Publications, 2009.

Stanford, Ray. *Fatima Prophecy: Discover the Message and Meaning of Fatima*. Virginia Beach: Inner Vision Publishing Company, 1987.

Sterling, Claire. *The Time of the Assassins*. New York: Holt, Rinehart and Winston, 1983.

Swann, Ingo. *The Great Apparitions of Mary*. Swann-Ryder Productions, 2017.

Symonds, Kevin J. *On the Third Part of the Secret of Fatima*. St. Louis: Enroute Books and Media, 2017.

Szulc, Tad. *Pope John Paul II: The Biography*. New York: Pocket Books, 2003.

Teixeira Fernandes, António. *O confronto de ideologias na segunda década do século XX: À volta de Fátima*. Porto: Biblioteca das Ciências do Homem, Edições Afrontamento, 1999.

Tindal-Robertson, Timothy. *Fatima, Russia & Pope John Paul II*. Still River, MA: Ravengate Press, 1992.

Tobin, Greg. *The Good Pope: The Making of a Saint and the Remaking of the*

Church—The Story of John XXIII & Vatican II. New York: Harper One, 2012.

Torgal, Luís Filipe. "Manuel Nunes Formigão: The Hidden Promoter of the Work of Fatima." *Portuguese Journal of Social Science* 13, no. 3 (September 2014).

Walsh, William Thomas. *Our Lady of Fatima*. New York: Image Books, 1990.

Warner, Marina. *Alone of All Her Sex: The Myth and the Cult of the Virgin Mary*. New York: Vintage Books, 1983.

Weigel, George. *Witness to Hope: The Biography of Pope John Paul II*. New York: HarperCollins, 1999.

West, Nigel. *The Third Secret: The CIA, Solidarity, and the KGB's Plot to Kill the Pope*. London: HarperCollins, 2000.

Wheeler, Douglas L. *Republican Portugal: A Political History 1910–1926*. Madison: University of Wisconsin Press, 1978.

Zimdars-Swartz, Sandra L. *Encountering Mary: From La Salette to Medjugorje*. Princeton: Princeton University Press, 1991.

Zola, Émile. *Lourdes*. Amherst, NY: Prometheus Books, 2000.

A NOTE ABOUT THE AUTHOR

Stephen Harrigan's previous novels include the *New York Times* best-selling *The Gates of the Alamo, Remember Ben Clayton* (which, among other awards, won the James Fenimore Cooper Prize from the Society of American Historians for best historical novel), and *A Friend of Mr. Lincoln*. He has also written a number of books of nonfiction, including the recent *Big Wonderful Thing: A History of Texas* and a career-spanning collection of essays, *The Eye of the Mammoth*. He is a writer-at-large for *Texas Monthly* as well as a screenwriter who has written many movies for television.

A NOTE ON THE TYPE

This book was set in Hoefler Text, a family of fonts designed by Jonathan Hoefler, who was born in 1970. First designed in 1991, Hoefler Text was intended as an advancement on existing desktop computer typography, including as it does an exponentially larger number of glyphs than previous fonts. In form, Hoefler Text looks to the old-style fonts of the seventeenth century, but it is wholly of its time, employing a precision and sophistication only available to the late twentieth century.

Composed by North Market Street Graphics,
Lancaster, Pennsylvania

Printed and bound by Berryville Graphics,
Berryville, Virginia